BOOK FOR THE
HOUR OF RECREATION

THE
OTHER VOICE
IN
EARLY MODERN
EUROPE

A Series Edited by Margaret L. King and Albert Rabil Jr.

OTHER BOOKS IN THE SERIES

HENRICUS CORNELIUS AGRIPPA
Declamation on the Nobility and Preeminence of the Female Sex
Edited and Translated by Albert Rabil Jr.

LAURA CERETA
Collected Letters of a Renaissance Feminist
Edited and translated by Diana Robin

TULLIA D'ARAGONA
Dialogue on the Infinity of Love
Edited and translated by Rinaldina Russell and Bruce Merry

CASSANDRA FEDELE
Letters and Orations
Edited and translated by Diana Robin

CECILIA FERRAZZI
Autobiography of an Aspiring Saint
Edited and translated by Anne Jacobson Schutte

MODERATA FONTE
The Worth of Women
Edited and translated by Virginia Cox

VERONICA FRANCO
Poems and Selected Letters
Edited and translated by Ann Rosalind Jones and Margaret F. Rosenthal

MARIE LE JARS DE GOURNAY
"Apology for the Woman Writing" and Other Works
Edited and translated by Richard Hillman and Colette Quesnel

LUCREZIA MARINELLA
The Nobility and Excellence of Women, and the Defects and Vices of Men
Edited and translated by Anne Dunhill with Letizia Panizza

ANTONIA PULCI
Florentine Drama for Convent and Festival
Edited and translated by James Wyatt Cook

SISTER BARTOLOMEA RICCOBONI
Life and Death in a Venetian Convent: The Chronicle and Necrology of Corpus Domini, 1395–1436
Edited and translated by Daniel Bornstein

ANNA MARIA VAN SCHURMAN
"Whether a Christian Woman Should Be Educated" and Other Writings from Her Intellectual Circle
Edited and translated by Joyce L. Irwin

LUCREZIA TORNABUONI DE' MEDICI
Sacred Narratives
Edited and translated by Jane Tylus

JUAN LUIS VIVES
"The Education of a Christian Woman": A Sixteenth-Century Manual
Edited and translated by Charles Fantazzi

María de San José Salazar

BOOK FOR THE
HOUR OF RECREATION

ꝍ

Introduction and Notes
by Alison Weber
Translation by Amanda Powell

THE UNIVERSITY OF CHICAGO PRESS
Chicago & London

María de San José Salazar (1548–1603)

Alison Weber is associate professor of Spanish at the University of Virginia.
She is the author of *Teresa of Avila and the Rhetoric of Femininity.*
Amanda Powell is senior instructor of Spanish at the University of
Oregon. She is translator of *Untold Sisters: Hispanic Nuns in Their Own Words*
and coauthor of *A Wild Country Out in the Garden:*
The Spiritual Journals of a Colonial Mexican Nun.

The University of Chicago Press, Chicago 60637
The University of Chicago Press, Ltd., London
© 2002 by The University of Chicago
All rights reserved. Published 2002
Printed in the United States of America
11 10 09 08 07 06 05 04 03 02   1 2 3 4 5

ISBN: 0-226-73454-4 (cloth)
ISBN: 0-226-73455-2 (paper)

Library of Congress Cataloging-in-Publication Data

María de San José, 1548–1603.
   [Libro de recreaciones. English]
   Book for the hour of recreation / María de San José Salazar ; introduction
and notes by Alison Weber ; translation by Amanda Powell.
      p.   cm.—(The other voice in early modern Europe)
   Includes bibliographical references and index.
   ISBN 0-226-73454-4 (alk. paper)—ISBN 0-226-73455-2 (paper : alk. paper)
   1. Teresa, of Avila, Saint, 1515–1582.   2. Christian saints—Spain—Avila—
Biography.   I. Weber, Alison, 1947—II. Powell, Amanda.   III. Title.
IV. Series.
BX4700.T4 M313 2002
282'.092—dc21
[B]   2002017353

CONTENTS

THE OTHER VOICE IN EARLY MODERN EUROPE: INTRODUCTION TO THE SERIES

Margaret L. King and Albert Rabil Jr.

THE OLD VOICE AND THE OTHER VOICE

In western Europe and the United States women are nearing equality in the professions, in business, and in politics. Most enjoy access to education, reproductive rights, and autonomy in financial affairs. Issues vital to women are on the public agenda: equal pay, childcare, domestic abuse, breast cancer research, and curricular revision with an eye to the inclusion of women.

These recent achievements have their origins in things women (and some male supporters) said for the first time about six hundred years ago. Theirs is the "other voice," in contradistinction to the "first voice," the voice of the educated men who created Western culture. Coincident with a general reshaping of European culture in the period 1300–1700 (called the Renaissance or early modern period), questions of female equality and opportunity were raised that still resound and are still unresolved.

The other voice emerged against the backdrop of a three-thousand-year history of the derogation of women rooted in the civilizations related to Western culture: Hebrew, Greek, Roman, and Christian. Negative attitudes toward women inherited from these traditions pervaded the intellectual, medical, legal, religious, and social systems that developed during the European Middle Ages.

The following pages describe the traditional, overwhelmingly male views of women's nature inherited by early modern Europeans and the new tradition that the other voice called into being to begin to challenge reigning assumptions. This review should serve as a framework for the understanding of the texts published in the series The Other Voice in Early Modern Europe. Introductions specific to each text and author follow this essay in all the volumes of the series.

TRADITIONAL VIEWS OF WOMEN, 500 B.C.E.–1500 C.E.

Embedded in the philosophical and medical theories of the ancient Greeks were perceptions of the female as inferior to the male in both mind and body. Similarly, the structure of civil legislation inherited from the ancient Romans was biased against women, and the views on women developed by Christian thinkers out of the Hebrew Bible and the Christian New Testament were negative and disabling. Literary works composed in the vernacular language of ordinary people, and widely recited or read, conveyed these negative assumptions. The social networks within which most women lived—those of the family and the institutions of the Roman Catholic Church—were shaped by this negative tradition and sharply limited the areas in which women might act in and upon the world.

GREEK PHILOSOPHY AND FEMALE NATURE. Greek biology assumed that women were inferior to men and defined them merely as childbearers and housekeepers. This view was authoritatively expressed in the works of the philosopher Aristotle.

Aristotle thought in dualities. He considered action superior to inaction, form (the inner design or structure of any object) superior to matter, completion superior to incompletion, possession superior to deprivation. In each of these dualities, he associated the male principle with the superior quality and the female with the inferior. "The male principle in nature," he argued, "is associated with active, formative and perfected characteristics, while the female is passive, material and deprived, desiring the male in order to become complete."[1] Men are always identified with virile qualities, such as judgment, courage, and stamina, and women with their opposites—irrationality, cowardice, and weakness.

Even in the womb, the masculine principle was considered superior. The man's semen, Aristotle believed, created the form of a new human creature, while the female body contributed only matter. (The existence of the ovum, and with it the other facts of human embryology, were not established until the seventeenth century.) Although the later Greek physician Galen believed that there was a female component in generation, contributed by "female semen," the followers of both Aristotle and Galen saw the male role in human generation as more active and more important.

In the Aristotelian view, the male principle sought always to reproduce itself. The creation of a female was always a mistake, therefore, resulting

1. Aristotle, *Physics* 1.9.192a20–24, in *The Complete Works of Aristotle*, ed. Jonathan Barnes, rev. Oxford trans., 2 vols. (Princeton, N.J., 1984), 1:328.

from an imperfect act of generation. Every female born was considered a "defective" or "mutilated" male (as Aristotle's terminology has variously been translated), a "monstrosity" of nature.[2]

For Greek theorists, the biology of males and females was the key to their psychology. The female was softer and more docile, more apt to be despondent, querulous, and deceitful. Being incomplete, moreover, she craved sexual fulfillment in intercourse with a male. The male was intellectual, active, and in control of his passions.

These psychological polarities derived from the theory that the universe consisted of four elements (air, earth, fire, and water), expressed in human bodies as four "humors" (black bile, yellow bile, blood, and phlegm) considered respectively dry, hot, damp, and cold and corresponding to mental states ("melancholic," "choleric," "sanguine," "phlegmatic"). In this schematization, the male, sharing the principles of earth and fire, was dry and hot; the female, sharing the principles of air and water, was cold and damp.

Female psychology was further affected by her dominant organ, the uterus (womb), *hystera* in Greek. The passions generated by the womb made women lustful, deceitful, talkative, irrational, indeed—when these affects were in excess—"hysterical."

Aristotle's biology also had social and political consequences. If the male principle was superior and the female inferior, then in the household, as in the state, men should rule and women must be subordinate. That hierarchy does not rule out the companionship of husband and wife, whose cooperation was necessary for the welfare of children and the preservation of property. Such mutuality supported male preeminence.

Aristotle's teacher Plato suggested a different possibility: that men and women might possess the same virtues. The setting for this proposal is the imaginary and ideal Republic that Plato sketches in a dialogue of that name. Here, for a privileged elite capable of leading wisely, all distinctions of class and wealth dissolve, as do, consequently, those of gender. Without households or property, as Plato constructs his ideal society, there is no need for the subordination of women. Women may, therefore, be educated to the same level as men to assume leadership responsibilities. Plato's Republic remained imaginary, however. In real societies, the subordination of women remained the norm and the prescription.

The views of women inherited from the Greek philosophical tradition became the basis for medieval thought. In the thirteenth century, the supreme scholastic philosopher Thomas Aquinas, among others, still echoed

---

2. Aristotle, *Generation of Animals* 2.3.737a27–28, in *The Complete Works*, 1:1144.

Aristotle's views of human reproduction, of male and female personalities, and of the preeminent male role in the social hierarchy.

ROMAN LAW AND THE FEMALE CONDITION. Roman law, like Greek philosophy, underlay medieval thought and shaped medieval society. The ancient belief that adult, property-owning men should administer households and make decisions affecting the community at large is the very fulcrum of Roman law.

Around 450 B.C.E., during Rome's republican era, the community's customary law was recorded (legendarily) on twelve tablets erected in the city's central forum. It was later elaborated by professional jurists whose activity increased in the imperial era, when much new legislation, especially on issues affecting family and inheritance, was passed. This growing, changing body of laws was eventually codified in the *Corpus of Civil Law* under the direction of the Emperor Justinian, generations after the empire ceased to be ruled from Rome. That *Corpus*, read and commented on by medieval scholars from the eleventh century on, inspired the legal systems of most of the cities and kingdoms of Europe.

Laws regarding dowries, divorce, and inheritance pertain primarily to women. Since those laws aimed to maintain and preserve property, the women concerned were those from the property-owning minority. Their subordination to male family members points to the even greater subordination of lower-class and slave women, about whom the laws speak little.

In the early republic, the *paterfamilias*, or "father of the family," possessed *patria potestas*, "paternal power." The term *pater*, "father," in both these cases does not necessarily mean biological father but, rather, head of household. The father was the person who owned the household's property and, indeed, its human members. The *paterfamilias* had absolute power—including the power, rarely exercised, of life or death—over his wife, his children, and his slaves, as much as his cattle.

Children could be "emancipated," an act that granted legal autonomy and the right to own property. Male children over fourteen could be emancipated by a special grant from the father or, automatically, by their father's death. But females could never be emancipated; instead, they passed from the authority of their father to a husband or, if widowed or orphaned while still unmarried, to a guardian or tutor.

Marriage under its traditional form placed the woman under her husband's authority, or *manus*. He could divorce her on grounds of adultery, drinking wine, or stealing from the household, but she could not divorce him. She could neither possess property in her own right nor bequeath any to her children upon her death. When her husband died, the household property passed not to her but to his male heirs. And when her father died, she had no claim to any family inheritance, which was directed to her brothers or more remote male relatives. The effect of these laws was to exclude women from civil society, itself based on property ownership.

In the later republican and imperial periods, these rules were significantly modified. Women rarely married according to the traditional form but according to the form of "free" marriage. That practice allowed a woman to remain under her father's authority, to possess property given her by her father (most frequently the "dowry," recoverable from the husband's household in the event of his death), and to inherit from her father. She could also bequeath property to her own children and divorce her husband, just as he could divorce her.

Despite this greater freedom, women still suffered enormous disability under Roman law. Heirs could belong only to the father's side, never the mother's. Moreover, although she could bequeath her property to her children, she could not establish a line of succession in doing so. A woman was "the beginning and end of her own family," said the jurist Ulpian. Moreover, women could play no public role. They could not hold public office, represent anyone in a legal case, or even witness a will. Women had only a private existence and no public personality.

The dowry system, the guardian, women's limited ability to transmit wealth, and total political disability are all features of Roman law adopted, although modified according to local customary laws, by the medieval communities of western Europe.

CHRISTIAN DOCTRINE AND WOMEN'S PLACE. The Hebrew Bible and the Christian New Testament authorized later writers to limit women to the realm of the family and to burden them with the guilt of original sin. The passages most fruitful for this purpose were the creation narratives in Genesis and sentences from the Epistles defining women's role within the Christian family and community.

Each of the first two chapters of Genesis contains a creation narrative. In the first "God created man in his own image, in the image of God he created him; male and female he created them" (New Revised Standard Version, Gen. 1:27). In the second, God created Eve from Adam's rib (2:21–23). Christian theologians relied principally on Genesis 2 for their understanding of the relation between man and woman, interpreting the creation of Eve from Adam as proof of her subordination to him.

The creation story in Genesis 2 leads to that of the temptations in Genesis 3: of Eve by the wily serpent and of Adam by Eve. As read by Christian theologians from Tertullian to Thomas Aquinas, the narrative made Eve responsible for the Fall and its consequences. She instigated the act; she deceived her husband; she suffered the greater punishment. Her disobedience made it necessary for Jesus to be incarnated and to die on the cross. From the pulpit, moralists and preachers for centuries conveyed to women the guilt that they bore for original sin.

The Epistles offered advice to early Christians on building communities of the faithful. Among the matters to be regulated was the place of women. Paul offered views favorable to women in Galatians 3:28: "There is neither Jew nor Greek, there is neither slave nor free, there is neither male nor female; for you are all one in Christ Jesus." Paul also referred to women as his coworkers and placed them on a par with himself and his male coworkers (Phil. 4:2–3; Rom. 16:1–3; I Cor. 16:19). Elsewhere, Paul limited women's possibilities: "But I want you to understand that the head of every man is Christ, the head of a woman is her husband, and the head of Christ is God" (I Cor. 11:3).

Biblical passages by later writers (though attributed to Paul) enjoined women to forgo jewels, expensive clothes, and elaborate coiffures; and they forbade women to "teach or have authority over men," telling them to "learn in silence with all submissiveness," as is proper for one responsible for sin, consoling them, however, with the thought that they will be saved through childbearing (I Tim. 2:9–15). Other texts among the later Epistles defined women as the weaker sex and emphasized their subordination to their husbands (I Pet. 3:7; Col. 3:18; Eph. 5:22–23).

These passages from the New Testament became the arsenal employed by theologians of the early church to transmit negative attitudes toward women to medieval Christian culture—above all, Tertullian ("On the Apparel of Women"), Jerome (*Against Jovinian*), and Augustine (*The Literal Meaning of Genesis*).

THE IMAGE OF WOMEN IN MEDIEVAL LITERATURE. The philosophical, legal, and religious traditions born in antiquity formed the basis of the medieval intellectual synthesis wrought by trained thinkers, mostly clerics, writing in Latin and based largely in universities. The vernacular literary tradition that developed alongside the learned tradition also spoke about female nature and women's roles. Medieval stories, poems, and epics also portrayed women negatively—as lustful and deceitful—while praising good housekeepers and loyal wives as replicas of the Virgin Mary or the female saints and martyrs.

There is an exception in the movement of "courtly love" that evolved in southern France from the twelfth century. Courtly love was the erotic love between a nobleman and noblewoman, the latter usually superior in social rank. It was always adulterous. From the conventions of courtly love derive modern Western notions of romantic love. The phenomenon has had an impact disproportionate to its size, for it affected only a tiny elite, and very few women. The exaltation of the female lover probably does not reflect a higher evaluation of women or a step toward their sexual liberation. More likely it gives expression to the social and sexual tensions besetting the knightly class at a specific historic juncture.

The literary fashion of courtly love was on the wane by the thirteenth century, when the widely read *Romance of the Rose* was composed in French by two authors of significantly different dispositions. Guillaume de Lorris composed the initial four thousand verses around 1235, and Jean de Meun added about seventeen thousand verses—more than four times the original—around 1265.

The fragment composed by Guillaume de Lorris stands squarely in the courtly love tradition. Here the poet, in a dream, is admitted into a walled garden where he finds a magic fountain in which a rosebush is reflected. He longs to pick one rose, but the thorns around it prevent his doing so, even as he is wounded by arrows from the God of Love, whose commands he agrees to obey. The remainder of this part of the poem recounts the poet's unsuccessful efforts to pluck the rose.

The longer part of the *Romance* by Jean de Meun also describes a dream. But here allegorical characters give long didactic speeches, providing a social satire on a variety of themes, including those pertaining to women. Love is an anxious and tormented state, the poem explains, women are greedy and manipulative, marriage is miserable, beautiful women are lustful, ugly ones cease to please, and a chaste woman, as rare as a black swan, can scarcely be found.

Shortly after Jean de Meun completed *The Romance of the Rose*, Mathéolus penned his *Lamentations*, a long Latin diatribe against marriage translated into French about a century later. The *Lamentations* sum up medieval attitudes toward women and provoked the important response by Christine de Pizan in her *Book of the City of Ladies*.

In 1355, Giovanni Boccaccio wrote *Il Corbaccio*, another antifeminist manifesto, though ironically by an author whose other works pioneered new directions in Renaissance thought. The former husband of his lover appears to Boccaccio, condemning his unmoderated lust and detailing the defects of women. Boccaccio concedes at the end "how much men naturally surpass women in nobility" and is cured of his desires.[3]

---

3. Giovanni Boccaccio, *The Corbaccio; or, The Labyrinth of Love*, trans. and ed. Anthony K. Cassell, rev. ed. (Binghamton, N.Y., 1993), 71.

WOMEN'S ROLES: THE FAMILY. The negative perceptions of women expressed in the intellectual tradition are also implicit in the actual roles that women played in European society. Assigned to subordinate positions in the household and the church, they were barred from significant participation in public life.

Medieval European households, like those in antiquity and in non-Western civilizations, were headed by males. It was the male serf (or peasant), feudal lord, town merchant, or citizen who was polled or taxed or succeeded to an inheritance or had any acknowledged public role, although their wives or widows could stand on a temporary basis as surrogates for them. From about 1100, the position of property-holding males was enhanced further: inheritance was confined to the male, or agnate, line—with depressing consequences for women.

A wife never fully belonged to her husband's family, nor was she a daughter to her father's family. She left her father's house young to marry whomever her parents chose. Her dowry was managed by her husband and normally passed to her children by him at her death.

A married woman's life was occupied nearly constantly with cycles of pregnancy, childbearing, and lactation. Women bore children through all the years of their fertility, and many died in childbirth before the end of that term. They also bore responsibility for raising young children up to six or seven. That responsibility was shared in the propertied classes, since it was common for a wet-nurse to take over the job of breast-feeding, and servants took over other chores.

Women trained their daughters in the household responsibilities appropriate to their status, nearly always in tasks associated with textiles: spinning, weaving, sewing, embroidering. Their sons were sent out of the house as apprentices or students, or their training was assumed by fathers in later childhood and adolescence. On the death of her husband, a woman's children became the responsibility of his family. She generally did not take "his" children with her to a new marriage or back to her father's house, except sometimes in artisan classes.

Women also worked. Rural peasants performed farm chores, merchant wives often practiced their husband's trade, the unmarried daughters of the urban poor worked as servants or prostitutes. All wives produced or embellished textiles and did the housekeeping, while wealthy ones managed servants. These labors were unpaid or poorly paid but often contributed substantially to family wealth.

WOMEN'S ROLES: THE CHURCH. Membership in a household, whether a father's or a husband's, meant for women a lifelong subordination to others.

In western Europe, the Roman Catholic church offered an alternative to the career of wife and mother. A woman could enter a convent, parallel in function to the monasteries for men that evolved in the early Christian centuries.

In the convent, a woman pledged herself to a celibate life, lived according to strict community rules, and worshipped daily. Often the convent offered training in Latin, allowing some women to become considerable scholars and authors, as well as scribes, artists, and musicians. For women who chose the conventual life, the benefits could be enormous, but for numerous others placed in convents by paternal choice, the life could be restrictive and burdensome.

The conventual life declined as an alternative for women as the modern age approached. Reformed monastic institutions resisted responsibility for related female orders. The church increasingly restricted female institutional life by insisting on closer male supervision.

Women often sought other options. Some joined the communities of laywomen that sprang up spontaneously in the thirteenth century in the urban zones of western Europe, especially in Flanders and Italy. Some joined the heretical movements that flourished in late medieval Christendom, whose anticlerical and often antifamily positions particularly appealed to women. In these communities, some women were acclaimed as "holy women" or "saints," while others often were condemned as frauds or heretics.

In all, though the options offered to women by the church were sometimes less than satisfactory, sometimes they were richly rewarding. After 1520, the convent remained an option only in Roman Catholic territories. Protestantism engendered an ideal of marriage as a heroic endeavor and appeared to place husband and wife on a more equal footing. Sermons and treatises, however, still called for female subordination and obedience.

THE OTHER VOICE, 1300–1700

When the modern era opened, European culture was so firmly structured by a framework of negative attitudes toward women that to dismantle it was a monumental labor. The process began as part of a larger cultural movement that entailed the critical reexamination of ideas inherited from the ancient and medieval past. The humanists launched that critical reexamination.

THE HUMANIST FOUNDATION. Originating in Italy in the fourteenth century, humanism quickly became the dominant intellectual movement in Europe. Spreading in the sixteenth century from Italy to the rest of Europe, it fueled the literary, scientific, and philosophical movements of the era and laid the basis for the eighteenth-century Enlightenment.

Humanists regarded the scholastic philosophy of medieval universities as out of touch with the realities of urban life. They found in the rhetorical discourse of classical Rome a language adapted to civic life and public speech. They learned to read, speak, and write classical Latin and, eventually, classical Greek. They founded schools to teach others to do so, establishing the pattern for elementary and secondary education for the next three hundred years.

In the service of complex government bureaucracies, humanists employed their skills to write eloquent letters, deliver public orations, and formulate public policy. They developed new scripts for copying manuscripts and used the new printing press for the dissemination of texts, for which they created methods of critical editing.

Humanism was a movement led by males who accepted the evaluation of women in ancient texts and generally shared the misogynist perceptions of their culture. (Female humanists, as will be seen, did not.) Yet humanism also opened the door to a reevaluation of the nature and capacity of women. By calling authors, texts, and ideas into question, it made possible the fundamental rereading of the whole intellectual tradition that was required in order to free women from cultural prejudice and social subordination.

A DIFFERENT CITY.   The other voice first appeared when, after so many centuries, the accumulation of misogynist concepts evoked a response from a capable woman female defender: Christine de Pizan (1365–1431). Introducing her *Book of the City of Ladies* (1405), she described how she was affected by reading Mathéolus's *Lamentations:* "Just the sight of this book . . . made me wonder how it happened that so many different men . . . are so inclined to express both in speaking and in their treatises and writings so many wicked insults about women and their behavior. . . . These statements impelled her to detest herself "and the entire feminine sex, as though we were monstrosities in nature."[4]

The remainder of the *Book of the City of Ladies* presents a justification of the female sex and a vision of an ideal community of women. A pioneer, she has not simply received the message of female inferiority but, rather, she rejects it. From the fourteenth to the seventeenth century, a huge body of literature accumulated that responded to the dominant tradition.

The result was a literary explosion consisting of works by both men and women, in Latin and in the vernaculars: works enumerating the achieve-

---

4. Christine de Pizan, *The Book of the City of Ladies*, trans. Earl Jeffrey Richards, foreword by Marina Warner (New York, 1982), 1.1.1 (pp. 3–4), 1.1.1–2 (p. 5).

ments of notable women; works rebutting the main accusations made against women; works arguing for the equal education of men and women; works defining and redefining women's proper role in the family, at court, in public, describing women's lives and experiences. Recent monographs and articles have begun to hint at the great range of this phenomenon, involving probably several thousand titles. The protofeminism of these "other voices" constitutes a significant fraction of the literary product of the early modern era.

THE CATALOGS. Around 1365, the same Boccaccio whose *Corbaccio* rehearses the usual charges against female nature wrote another work, *Concerning Famous Women*. A humanist treatise drawing on classical texts, it praised 106 notable women, ninety-eight of them from pagan Greek and Roman antiquity, one (Eve) from the Bible, and seven from the medieval religious and cultural tradition; his book helped make all readers aware of a sex normally condemned or forgotten. Boccaccio's outlook, nevertheless, is unfriendly to women, for it singled out for praise those women who possessed the traditional virtues of chastity, silence, and obedience. Women who were active in the public realm, for example, rulers and warriors, were depicted as usually lascivious and as suffering terrible punishments for entering into the masculine sphere. Women were his subject, but Boccaccio's standard remained male.

Christine de Pizan's *Book of the City of Ladies* contains a second catalog, one responding specifically to Boccaccio's. Where Boccaccio portrays female virtue as exceptional, she depicts it as universal. Many women in history were leaders, or remained chaste despite the lascivious approaches of men, or were visionaries and brave martyrs.

The work of Boccaccio inspired a series of catalogs of illustrious women of the biblical, classical, Christian, and local past, among them Filippo da Bergamo's *Of Illustrious Women*, Pierre de Brantôme's *Lives of Illustrious Women*, Pierre Le Moyne's *Gallerie of Heroic Women*, and Pietro Paolo de Ribera's *Immortal Triumphs and Heroic Enterprises of 845 Women*. Whatever their embedded prejudices, these catalogs of illustrious women drove home to the public the possibility of female excellence.

THE DEBATE. At the same time, many questions remained: Could a woman be virtuous? Could she perform noteworthy deeds? Was she even, strictly speaking, of the same human species as men? These questions were debated over four centuries, in French, German, Italian, Spanish, and English, by authors male and female, among Catholics, Protestants, and Jews, in ponderous volumes and breezy pamphlets. The whole literary phenomenon has been called the *querelle des femmes*, the "woman question."

The opening volley of this battle occurred in the first years of the fifteenth century, in a literary debate sparked by Christine de Pizan. She exchanged letters critical of Jean de Meun's contribution to the *Romance of the Rose* with two French royal secretaries, Jean de Montreuil and Gontier Col. When the matter became public, Jean Gerson, one of Europe's leading theologians, supported de Pizan's arguments against de Meun, for the moment silencing the opposition.

The debate resurfaced repeatedly over the next two hundred years. *The Triumph of Women* (1438) by Juan Rodríguez de la Camara (or Juan Rodríguez del Padron) struck a new note by presenting arguments for the superiority of women to men. *The Champion of Women* (1440–42) by Martin Le Franc addresses once again the negative views of women presented in *The Romance of the Rose* and offers counterevidence of female virtue and achievement.

A cameo of the debate on women is included in the *Courtier,* one of the most read books of the era, published by the Italian Baldassare Castiglione in 1528 and immediately translated into other European vernaculars. The *Courtier* depicts a series of evenings at the court of the duke of Urbino in which many men and some women of the highest social stratum amuse themselves by discussing a range of literary and social issues. The "woman question" is a pervasive theme throughout, and the third of its four books is devoted entirely to that issue.

In a verbal duel, Gasparo Pallavicino and Giuliano de' Medici present the main claims of the two traditions. Gasparo argues the innate inferiority of women and their inclination to vice. Only in bearing children do they profit the world. Giuliano counters that women share the same spiritual and mental capacities as men and may excel in wisdom and action. Men and women are of the same essence: just as no stone can be more perfectly a stone than another, so no human being can be more perfectly human than others, whether male or female. It was an astonishing assertion, boldly made to an audience as large as all Europe.

THE TREATISES. Humanism provided the materials for a positive counterconcept to the misogyny embedded in scholastic philosophy and law and inherited from the Greek, Roman, and Christian pasts. A series of humanist treatises on marriage and family, on education and deportment, and on the nature of women helped construct these new perspectives.

The works by Francesco Barbaro and Leon Battista Alberti—*On Marriage* (1415) and *On the Family* (1434–37), respectively—far from defending female equality, reasserted women's responsibilities for rearing children and managing the housekeeping while being obedient, chaste, and silent. Nevertheless, they served the cause of reexamining the issue of women's nature by placing domestic issues at the center of scholarly concern and reopening the pertinent classical texts. In addition, Barbaro emphasized the companionate nature of marriage and the importance of a wife's spiritual and mental qualities for the well-being of the family.

These themes reappear in later humanist works on marriage and the education of women by Juan Luis Vives and Erasmus. Both were moderately sympathetic to the condition of women, without reaching beyond the usual masculine prescriptions for female behavior.

An outlook more favorable to women characterizes the nearly unknown work *In Praise of Women* (ca. 1487) by the Italian humanist Bartolommeo Goggio. In addition to providing a catalog of illustrious women, Goggio argued that male and female are the same in essence, but that women (reworking from quite a new angle the Adam and Eve narrative) are actually superior. In the same vein, the Italian humanist Maria Equicola asserted the spiritual equality of men and women in *On Women* (1501). In 1525, Galeazzo Flavio Capra (or Capella) published his work *On the Excellence and Dignity of Women.* This humanist tradition of treatises defending the worthiness of women culminates in the work of Henricus Cornelius Agrippa *On the Nobility and Preeminence of the Female Sex.* No work by a male humanist more succinctly or explicitly presents the case for female dignity.

THE WITCH BOOKS. While humanists grappled with the issues pertaining to women and family, other learned men turned their attention to what they perceived as a very great problem: witches. Witch-hunting manuals, explorations of the witch phenomenon, and even defenses of witches are not at first glance pertinent to the tradition of the other voice. But they do relate in this way: most accused witches were women. The hostility aroused by supposed witch activity is comparable to the hostility aroused by women. The evil deeds the victims of the hunt were charged with were exaggerations of the vices to which, many believed, all women were prone.

The connection between the witch accusation and the hatred of women is explicit in the notorious witch-hunting manual, *The Hammer of Witches* (1486), by two Dominican inquisitors, Heinrich Krämer and Jacob Sprenger. Here the inconstancy, deceitfulness, and lustfulness traditionally associated with women are depicted in exaggerated form as the core features of witch behavior. These traits inclined women to make a bargain with the devil—sealed by sexual intercourse—by which they acquired unholy powers. Such bizarre claims, far from being rejected by rational men, were broadcast by intellectuals. The German Ulrich Molitur, the Frenchman Nicolas Rémy, and the Italian Stefano Guazzo all coolly informed the public of sinister orgies and midnight pacts with the devil. The celebrated French jurist, historian, and political philosopher Jean Bodin argued that because women were especially prone to diabolism, regular legal procedures could properly be suspended in order to try those accused of this "exceptional crime."

A few experts raised their voices in protest, such as the physician Johann Weyer, a student of Agrippa's. In 1563, he explained the witch phenomenon thus, without discarding belief in diabolism: the devil deluded foolish old women afflicted by melancholia, causing them to believe that they had magical powers. Weyer's rational skepticism, which had good credibility in the community of the learned, worked to revise the conventional views of women and witchcraft.

WOMEN'S WORKS. To the many categories of works produced on the question of women's worth must be added nearly all works written by women. A woman writing was in herself a statement of women's claim to dignity.

Only a few women wrote anything prior to the dawn of the modern era, for three reasons. First, they rarely received the education that would enable them to write. Second, they were not admitted to the public roles—as administrator, bureaucrat, lawyer or notary, or university professor—in which they might gain knowledge of the kinds of things the literate public thought worth writing about. Third, the culture imposed silence upon women and considered speaking out a form of unchastity. Given these conditions, it is remarkable that any women wrote. Those who did before the fourteenth century were almost always nuns or religious women whose isolation made their pronouncements more acceptable.

From the fourteenth century on, the volume of women's writings crescendoed. Women continued to write devotional literature, although not always as cloistered nuns. They also wrote diaries, often intended as keepsakes for their children; books of advice to their sons and daughters; letters to family members and friends; and family memoirs, in a few cases elaborate enough to be considered histories.

A few women wrote works directly concerning the "woman question," and some of these, such as the humanists Isotta Nogarola, Cassandra Fedele, Laura Cereta, and Olympia Morata, were highly trained. A few were professional writers, living by the income of their pen—the very first among them being Christine de Pizan, noteworthy in this context as in so many others. In addition to *The Book of the City of Ladies* and her critiques of *The Romance of the*

Rose, she wrote *The Treasure of the City of Ladies* (a guide to social decorum for women), an advice book for her son, much courtly verse, and a full-scale history of the reign of King Charles V of France.

WOMEN PATRONS. Women who did not themselves write, but encouraged others to do so, boosted the development of an alternative tradition. Highly placed women patrons supported authors, artists, musicians, poets, and learned men. Such patrons, drawn mostly from the Italian elites and the courts of northern Europe, figure disproportionately as the dedicatees of the important works of early feminism.

For a start, it might be noted that the catalogs of Boccaccio and Alvaro de Luna were dedicated to the Florentine noblewoman Andrea Acciaiuoli and Doña María, first wife of King Juan II of Castile, while the French translation of Boccaccio's work was commissioned by Anne of Brittany, wife of King Charles VIII of France. The humanist treatises of Goggio, Equicola, Vives, and Agrippa were dedicated, respectively, to Eleanora of Aragon, wife of Ercole I d'Este, Duke of Ferrara; to Margherita Cantelma of Mantua; to Catherine of Aragon, wife of King Henry VIII of England; and to Margaret, Duchess of Austria and Regent of the Netherlands. As late as 1696, Mary Astell's *Serious Proposal to the Ladies, for the Advancement of Their True and Greatest Interest* was dedicated to Princess Ann of Denmark.

These authors presumed that their efforts would be welcome to female patrons, or they may have written at the bidding of those patrons. Silent themselves, perhaps even unresponsive, these loftily placed women helped shape the tradition of the other voice.

THE ISSUES. The literary forms and patterns in which the tradition of the other voice presented itself have now been sketched. It remains to highlight the major issues around which this tradition crystallizes. In brief, there are four problems to which our authors return again and again, in plays and catalogs, in verse and in letters, in treatises and dialogues, in every language: the problem of chastity; the problem of power; the problem of speech; and the problem of knowledge. Of these the greatest, preconditioning the others, is the problem of chastity.

THE PROBLEM OF CHASTITY. In traditional European culture, as in those of antiquity and others around the globe, chastity was perceived as woman's quintessential virtue—in contrast to courage, or generosity, or leadership, or rationality, seen as virtues characteristic of men. Opponents of women charged them with insatiable lust. Women themselves and their defenders—without disputing the validity of the standard—responded that women were capable of chastity.

The requirement of chastity kept women at home, silenced them, isolated them, left them in ignorance. It was the source of all other impediments. Why was it so important to the society of men, of whom chastity was not required, and who, more often than not, considered it their right to violate the chastity of any woman they encountered?

Female chastity ensured the continuity of the male-headed household. If a man's wife was not chaste, he could not be sure of the legitimacy of his offspring. If they were not his, and they acquired his property, it was not his household, but some other man's, that had endured. If his daughter was not chaste, she could not be transferred to another man's household as his wife, and he was dishonored.

The whole system of the integrity of the household and the transmission of property was bound up in female chastity. Such a requirement only had an impact on property-owning classes, of course. Poor women could not expect to maintain their chastity, least of all if they were in contact with high-status men to whom all women but those of their own household were prey.

In Catholic Europe, the requirement of chastity was further buttressed by moral and religious imperatives. Original sin was inextricably linked with the sexual act. Virginity was seen as heroic virtue, far more impressive than, say, the avoidance of idleness or greed. Monasticism, the cultural institution that dominated medieval Europe for centuries, was grounded in the renunciation of the flesh. The Catholic reform of the eleventh century imposed a similar standard on all the clergy and a heightened awareness of sexual requirements on all the laity. Although men were asked to be chaste, female unchastity was much worse: it led to the devil, as Eve had led mankind to sin.

To such requirements, women and their defenders protested their innocence. Furthermore, following the example of holy women who had escaped the requirements of family and sought the religious life, some women began to conceive of female communities as alternatives both to family and to the cloister. Christine de Pizan's city of ladies was such a community. Moderata Fonte and Mary Astell envisioned others. The luxurious salons of the French *précieuses* of the seventeenth century, or the comfortable English drawing rooms of the next, may have been born of the same impulse. Here women might not only escape, if briefly, the subordinate position that life in the family entailed, but they might make claims to power, exercise their capacity for speech, and display their knowledge.

THE PROBLEM OF POWER. Women were excluded from power: the whole cultural tradition insisted on it. Only men were citizens, only men bore arms, only men could be chiefs or lords or kings. There were exceptions, which did not disprove the rule, when wives or widows or mothers took the place of men, awaiting their return or the maturation of a male heir. A woman who attempted to rule in her own right was perceived as an anomaly, a monster, at once a deformed woman and an insufficient male, sexually confused and, consequently, unsafe.

The association of such images with women who held or sought power explains some otherwise odd features of early modern culture. Queen Elizabeth I of England, one of the few women to hold full regal authority in European history, played with such male/female images—positive ones, of course—in representing herself to her subjects. She was a prince, and manly, even though she was female. She was also (she claimed) virginal, a condition absolutely essential if she was to avoid the attacks of her opponents. Catherine de' Medici, who ruled France as widow and regent for her sons, also adopted such imagery in defining her position. She chose as one symbol the figure of Artemisia, an androgynous ancient warrior-heroine, who combined a female persona with masculine powers.

Power in a woman, without such sexual imagery, seems to have been indigestible by the culture. A rare note was struck by the Englishman Sir Thomas Elyot in his *Defence of Good Women* (1540), justifying both women's participation in civic life and prowess in arms. The old tune was sung by the Scots reformer John Knox in his *First Blast of the Trumpet against the Monstrous Regiment of Women* (1558), for whom rule by women, defects in nature, was a hideous contradiction in terms.

The confused sexuality of the imagery of female potency was not reserved for rulers. Any woman who excelled was likely to be called an Amazon, recalling the self-mutilated warrior women of antiquity who repudiated all men, gave up their sons, and raised only their daughters. She was often said to have "exceeded her sex" or to have possessed "masculine virtue"—as the very fact of conspicuous excellence conferred masculinity, even on the female subject. The catalogs of notable women often showed those female heroes dressed in armor, armed to the teeth, like men. Amazonian heroines romp through the epics of the age—Ariosto's *Orlando Furioso* (1532) and Spenser's *Faerie Queene* (1590–1609). Excellence in a woman was perceived as a claim for power, and power was reserved for the masculine realm. A woman who possessed either was masculinized and lost title to her own female identity.

THE PROBLEM OF SPEECH. Just as power had a sexual dimension when it was claimed by women, so did speech. A good woman spoke little. Excessive speech was an indication of unchastity. By speech, women seduced men. Eve had lured Adam into sin by her speech. Accused witches were commonly accused of having spoken abusively, or irrationally, or simply too much. As enlightened a figure as Francesco Barbaro insisted on silence in a woman, which he linked to her perfect unanimity with her husband's will and her unblemished virtue (i.e., her chastity). Another Italian humanist, Leonardo Bruni, in advising a noblewoman on her studies, barred her not from speech but from public speaking. That was reserved for men.

Related to the problem of speech was that of costume—another, if silent, form of self-expression. Assigned the task of pleasing men as their primary occupation, elite women often tended toward elaborate costume, hairdressing, and the use of cosmetics. Clergy and secular moralists alike condemned these practices. The appropriate function of costume and adornment was to announce the status of a woman's husband or father. Any further indulgence in adornment was akin to unchastity.

THE PROBLEM OF KNOWLEDGE. When the Italian noblewoman Isotta Nogarola had begun to attain a reputation as a humanist, she was accused of incest—a telling instance of the association of learning in women with unchastity. That chilling association inclined any woman who was educated to deny that she was or to make exaggerated claims of heroic chastity.

If educated women were pursued with suspicions of sexual misconduct, women seeking an education faced an even more daunting obstacle: the assumption that women were by nature incapable of learning, that reason was a particularly masculine ability. Just as they proclaimed their chastity, women and their defenders insisted on their capacity for learning. The major work by a male writer on female education—that by Juan Luis Vives, *On the Education of a Christian Woman* (1523)—granted female capacity for intellection but still argued that a woman's whole education was to be shaped around the requirement of chastity and a future within the household. Female writers of the next generations—Marie de Gournay in France, Anna Maria van Schurman in Holland, Mary Astell in England—began to envision other possibilities.

The pioneers of female education were the Italian women humanists who managed to attain a Latin literacy and knowledge of classic and Christian literature equivalent to that of prominent men. Their works implicitly and explicitly raise questions about women's social roles, defining problems that beset women attempting to break out of the cultural limits that had bound them. Like Christine de Pizan, who achieved an advanced education through her father's tutoring and her own devices, their bold questioning makes clear the importance of training. Only when women were educated to the same standard as male leaders would they be able to raise that other voice and insist on their dignity as human beings morally, intellectually, and legally equal to men.

THE OTHER VOICE. The other voice, a voice of protest, was mostly female, but it was also male. It spoke in the vernaculars and in Latin, in treatises and dialogues, in plays and poetry, in letters and diaries, and in pamphlets. It battered at the wall of prejudice that encircled women and raised a banner announcing its claims. The female was equal to (or even superior to) the male in essential nature—moral, spiritual, intellectual. Women were capable of higher education, of holding positions of power and influence in the public realm, and of speaking and writing persuasively. The last bastion of masculine supremacy, centered on the notions of a woman's primary domestic responsibility and the requirement of female chastity, was not as yet assaulted—although visions of productive female communities as alternatives to the family indicated an awareness of the problem.

During the period 1300–1700, the other voice remained only a voice, and one only dimly heard. It did not result—yet—in an alteration of social patterns. Indeed, to this day, they have not entirely been altered. Yet the call for justice issued as long as six centuries ago by those writing in the tradition of the other voice must be recognized as the source and origin of the mature feminist tradition and of the realignment of social institutions accomplished in the modern age.

We would like to thank the volume editors in this series, who responded with many suggestions to an earlier draft of this introduction, making it a collaborative enterprise. Many of their suggestions and criticisms have resulted in revisions of this introduction, though we remain responsible for the final product.

PROJECTED TITLES IN THE SERIES

Isabella Andreini, *Mirtilla*, edited and translated by Laura Stortoni

Tullia d'Aragona, *Complete Poems and Letters*, edited and translated by Julia Hairston

Tullia d'Aragona, *The Wretch, Otherwise Known as Guerrino*, edited and translated by Julia Hairston and John McLucas

Giuseppa Eleonora Barbapiccola and Diamante Medaglia Faini, *The Education of Women*, edited and translated by Rebecca Messbarger

CHRONOLOGY OF THE LIFE
OF MARÍA DE SAN JOSÉ SALAZAR

1548   María is born in Toledo. Spends her childhood in the palace of Doña Luisa de la Cerda.

1562   From January to June, Teresa de Jesús resides in Doña Luisa's palace in Toledo.

1567   María composes *Ansias de Amor,* a free paraphrase of the Song of Songs.

1570   María takes the habit in the Discalced Carmelite convent of Malagón. Doña Luisa provides her dowry.

1571   María completes her novitiate and takes formal vows as a nun.

1572   María is elected prioress of the Malagón convent.

1575   Teresa chooses María to accompany her in establishing new convents in Beas, Caravaca, and Seville. On May 29, the convent in Seville is founded and María is elected prioress. In December, a novice denounces Teresa to the Inquisition, but the Inquisition declines to bring formal charges against her.

1576   The Calced (unreformed) Carmelite friars intensify their opposition to the Discalced reform. Teresa is ordered into reclusion in Toledo.

1577   John of the Cross is kidnaped by the Calced Carmelites and imprisoned at Medina del Campo.

1578   Conflicts with the confessor of the Seville convent result in María's loss of office and imprisonment. María and Jerónimo Gracián de la Madre de Dios are denounced to the Inquisition for immoral behavior. Gracián is imprisoned by the Calced Carmelites.

1579   Carmelite Vicar General Angel de Salazar restores María's privilege to participate in convent governance.

1580   Gracián is freed. Papal brief of Gregory XIII of separation, *Pía consideratione,* establishes the Discalced Carmelites as a separate Carmelite province.

1581   Constitutions for Discalced convents, revised under Teresa's supervision, are approved at the Alcalá chapter. Gracián is elected first provincial of the independent province.

1582   Teresa dies in Alba de Tormes on October 4 (October 15, according to the Gregorian reformed calendar).

1584   In December, María departs from Seville to make a foundation in Lisbon.

1585   Nicolás de Jesús María Doria is elected second Discalced provincial and soon after initiates plans to modify the constitutions governing Discalced convents. Probable year of composition of *Book for the Hour of Recreation.*

1588   The stigmata of María de la Visitación disappear when her hands are washed with soap. María de San José writes letters in defense of Gracián, who has been charged with moral laxity. Doria forbids her to speak or write to him.

1590   Discalced nuns, led by María de San José and Ana de Jesús, appeal to Pope Sixtus V to preserve the integrity of the 1581 constitutions. Sixtus V accedes to their request; the brief *Salvatoris* confirms the constitutions and requires papal approval for any modifications.

1591   Papal brief *Quoniam non ignoramus* of Gregory XIV revokes the provisions of *Salvatoris* and sanctions amendments proposed by Doria. Juan de la Cruz (John of the Cross) is deprived of his offices as definitor and *consilario;* he is exiled to the monastery of La Peñuela.

1592   Gracián is expelled from the Discalced Congregation.

1593   María is imprisoned incommunicado for nine months.

1594   Doria dies on May 6.

1603   The third Discalced Carmelite vicar general, Francisco de la Madre de Dios, orders María's transfer to the isolated convent in Cuerva. Shortly after her arrival, she dies on October 19.

1991   The Discalced Carmelite nuns of Andalusia propose the cause for the beatification of Ana de Jesús and María de San José.

1999   The general definitory of the Discalced Carmelites officially revokes Gracián's expulsion from the order and expresses grave regret for the severe punishment imposed on Ana de Jesús and María de San José.

INTRODUCTION TO
MARÍA DE SAN JOSÉ SALAZAR
(1 5 4 8 – 1 6 0 3)

THE OTHER VOICE

The proposal to include in this series a text by an obscure follower of Saint Teresa of Avila who was neither a mystic nor a famous reformer will perhaps seem puzzling. What "voice" can we expect to hear from a woman who dedicated most of her adult life to solitude and silence, a woman who, moreover, was for several years quite literally imprisoned and silenced by her male superiors? María de San José never contemplated, as far as we know, the question of women's political and economic inequality, never protested the inheritance laws, marriage politics, and educational practices that limited her own opportunities and those of other women for self-actualization. Rather, *Book for the Hour of Recreation* voices the concerns of a woman who was content—or perhaps resigned—to work within the parameters of what she understood to be the nonnegotiable limitations on women's roles during the Catholic Reformation. But within these parameters, María defended women's right to define their spiritual experience and asserted women's ability to teach, inspire, and lead other women in the reformation of their church. In seeking to accomplish these goals she found some men to be sympathetic collaborators and others to be harsh opponents. Although she undoubtedly knew there was little chance that her manuscript would circulate among readers beyond the walls of her own convent, her writing is imbued with a remarkable conviction that what she had to say *mattered*, and that she and her sisters had a vital role to play at a crucial moment in the history of

Much of the work for this study was made possible by a research associateship in the Women's Studies in Religion program at Harvard Divinity School during the academic year 1998–99. I am especially grateful for the encouragement I received from the director of the program, Ann Braude. I would also like to express my appreciation to Dianne Dugaw, Anne Schutte, Kathleen Myers and Jodi Bilinkoff for their comments and suggestions on this introduction. Amanda Powell has been an invaluable reader and guide throughout our collaboration on this project.

Christianity. In short, María was neither an anomalous Renaissance feminist nor the paradigmatic "interpellated" subject of patriarchy. Her writing points to an alternative to the antitheses of rebellion and acquiescence and asks us to consider that women's experience of power in the early modern period may have been more complex and ambiguous than we have previously imagined.

THE LIFE AND CAREER OF MARÍA DE SAN JOSÉ

Early Life

María Salazar was born in 1548 in the Castilian city of Toledo. Her parents, according to a seventeenth-century Portuguese chronicler, were nobles distantly related to the duke of Medinaceli. Curiously, archival investigation has failed to uncover any trace of these noble progenitors. We do know that María was raised in the palace of Doña Luisa de la Cerda, the daughter of the second duke of Medinaceli and wife of Arias Pardo de Saavedra, one of the wealthiest men in Castile. In the Pardo palace María received an extraordinary education for a woman of her day—she learned to read and write in Spanish, and could additionally read French and Latin. Her poetry, composed both before and after her entrance into the convent, demonstrates that she had mastered a wide variety of metrical forms, from the Italianate sonnet to the folkloric Castilian *villancico*. The absence of genealogical records for her family, her unusual education, and a certain high-handedness in her dealings with others all suggest that she may have been not a distant relative but an illegitimate child of a highly placed member of Doña Luisa's household.[1]

In 1562 Doña Luisa, disconsolate over the recent death of her husband, asked the Carmelite provincial of Castile to allow Teresa de Jesús, a Carmelite nun from Avila with a growing renown for saintliness, to stay with her in Toledo. Though Teresa was reluctant to leave her convent, she complied with her superior's orders to comfort the grieving noblewoman. María, who was thirteen at the time, relates that she and her companions were fascinated by the nun and more than once spied on her through cracks in the door as she prayed in ecstasy. As María recounts in *Book for the Hour of Recreation,* despite

---

1. The Portuguese Carmelite Belchior de Santa Anna provides the earliest sources for biographical information on María de San José in *Chronica de Carmelitas Descalços, particular do Reyno de Portugal e provincia de San Felippe,* 3 vols. (Lisbon, 1657). María Pilar Manero Sorolla offers the plausible theory of a close relationship to a member of Doña Luisa's household in "On the Margins of the Mendoza: Luisa de la Cerda and María de San José (Salazar)," in *The Women of the Mendoza Family in the Spanish Renaissance,* ed. Helen Nader (unpublished manuscript).

her admiration for Teresa she was not immediately drawn to a religious vocation and for years continued to be attached to the refinements of palace society. In 1570, however, with a dowry supplied by Doña Luisa, María took the Carmelite habit. Two years later she was elected prioress of the convent endowed by her patroness on the latter's family fief in Malagón. Soon after, she departed for Andalusia in order to participate in founding a series of reformed convents.

The Discalced Carmelite Reform

The reformers, led by the future Saint Teresa of Avila, were known as the Discalced or barefoot nuns. Though they in fact wore hemp sandals, their chosen name reflected their desire to return to a life of austerity based on the original or primitive Carmelite rule, one that had been mitigated over the centuries through a series of papal decrees. This reform was characterized, paradoxically, by monastic women's determination to serve, from within the confines of strict enclosure, a church in crisis. Teresa and her followers believed that through a life of intense prayer (requiring practices that could only be carried out through withdrawal from the world), women religious could contribute to the defense of Roman Catholicism, imperiled by war and schism. Forbidden to preach or travel as missionaries, they channeled their apostolic desires into praying for the defenders of the church: priests, preachers, and missionaries. They also believed that by embracing the poverty, solitude, and egalitarianism of their order's original rule, they might inspire the spiritual transformation of a larger Christian community.[2] Although the Discalced Carmelites' commitment to austerity and strict enclosure anticipated the recommendations for female monastics proposed by the Council of Trent, other aspects of their reform disrupted traditional economic relationships, dynastic alliances, and ecclesiastical hierarchies. Furthermore, a movement led by a woman, one that additionally gave women broad pedagogical, economic, and administrative authority, represented a challenge to a church that was in the process of reaffirming the exclusive apostolic privilege of its male clergy. Consequently, the Discalced nuns (and later friars) frequently were drawn into bitter struggles with civic officials, patrons, and ecclesiastical authorities.

Such was María's experience in Seville, a foundation beset with conflict

---

2. For a concise history of this movement, see Jodi Bilinkoff, "Teresa of Jesus and Carmelite Reform," in *Religious Orders of the Catholic Reformation: Essays in Honor of John C. Olin on His Seventy-fifth Birthday,* ed. Richard L. DeMolen (New York: Fordham University Press, 1994), 165–86.

from the start. The reformers found themselves in the middle of a jurisdictional dispute between Teresa's immediate superior, the apostolic visitator in Andalusia, Jerónimo Gracián, who had ordered Teresa to make the foundation, and Juan Bautista Rubeo, the prior general, who had forbidden the Discalced Carmelites to expand into Andalusia. To make matters worse, local officials were opposed to a religious house founded without an endowment, one that would therefore depend on the city's charitable resources. The nuns suffered initially from scarce food, decrepit housing, and the relentless heat of the Andalusian summer. At the end of the first year, an unhappy novice denounced Teresa and her nuns to the Inquisition for alleged heretical practices. The denunciations played on ecclesiastical fears of Illuminism, a diffuse sixteenth-century movement that laid claim to unmediated personal experience of the divine through passive divine "enlightenment."[3] After lengthy investigation, the community was absolved of all charges. By 1576 the Calced friars (those who continued to follow the mitigated rule), enraged by Gracián's efforts to discipline their monasteries, made every effort to halt the Discalced reform in Andalusia. General Rubeo, who had initially given Teresa permission to make more foundations, turned against the Discalced Carmelites and ordered Teresa to return to Castile. The leadership of the community in Seville fell into the hands of the twenty-seven-year-old María, who had recently been elected prioress.

The tranquility of the convent was again disrupted in 1578 when two nuns began to report prophetic visions and revelations. Their confessor soon subjected them to "general confessions" that lasted for days. María, alarmed at this disruption in convent routine and worried that the nuns' written accounts of their supernatural experiences would again attract the attention of the Inquisition, dismissed the confessor. He in turn appealed to the Calced friars, who seized the opportunity to spread salacious rumors about their enemies, alleging that Gracián kissed and embraced the nuns and danced naked before them, that he spent the night in the convent, and that he was involved in illicit relationships with María and Teresa. The Calced provincial, Diego Cárdenas, removed María from office, deprived her of voice and vote (that is, she lost all right to participate in convent governance), and confined her to

---

3. At this time a group of Illuminists (*alumbrados* in Spanish) in western Spain were suspected of engaging in sexual fondling as part of their religious practices. See Alastair Hamilton, *Heresy and Mysticism in Sixteenth-Century Spain* (Toronto: University of Toronto Press, 1992); and Alison Weber, "Demonizing Ecstasy: Alonso de la Fuente and the *Alumbrados* of Extremadura," in *The Mystical Gesture: Essays on Medieval and Early Modern Spiritual Culture in Honor of Mary E. Giles*, ed. Robert Boenig (Aldershot, U.K.: Ashgate Press, 2000), 147–65.

her cell for six months. To further her humiliation, she was replaced as prioress with Beatriz de la Madre de Dios, her principal accuser.

Not satisfied with this coup, the dismissed confessor and the two nuns he had singled out for attention then sent reports to the Inquisition denouncing María and Teresa as procuresses for a house of prostitution. As María describes these terrible days: "This was the first time, in a visitation by the Inquisition, that we saw excommunications, oaths before Christ, and threats in our house, and thus foolishly all the nuns helped the Inquisitors and said what the latter needed in order to give credit to the lies that had already been spread."[4] One of the nuns also alleged that María had interfered with the sacrament of confession: "I said that sometimes our mother prioress would sit on the stairs and say to the nuns who were about to confess, and to me in particular: 'What do you have to confess now? Go on, don't stay more time than it takes me to say the creed. If you stay longer, you can't take Communion.'"[5] This statement, though later retracted, suggests what was at the heart of the conflict in Seville: a power struggle between prioress and confessor over who would direct the spiritual life of the nuns. Again, the Inquisition decided not to pursue the case further. In June 1579, a new Carmelite general restored María's voice and vote in the community, and she was soon after reelected prioress.

A Problematic Friendship

After Teresa returned to Castile in 1576, she would never see María again. María did, however, maintain a warm but sometimes contentious correspondence with the foundress. Since María's letters to Teresa have not survived, we must attempt to reconstruct the tenor of their relationship through the sixty-four extant letters Teresa wrote to María between 1576 and 1582 (the year Teresa died). These letters reveal affection as well as admiration for the intelligence and wit of the recipient: "Oh, how vain you must be to know that you are a 'semiprovincial.' And how amused I was by your offhand remark, 'The sisters send you the enclosed couplets' when I know you yourself are behind it all."[6] Teresa inquires solicitously after María's health and prescribes favorite remedies: "Until I hear that your fever is gone, I will continue

---

4. "Ninth Recreation," 155.

5. The text of the inquisitorial denunciations has not survived; however, their substance can be surmised from the nuns' subsequent retractions. This quotation is from the retraction made by Beatriz de la Madre de Dios, María's principal accuser. See Enrique Llamas Martínez, *Santa Teresa de Jesús y la Inquisición Española* (Madrid: CSIC, 1972), 206.

6. Teresa of Avila, letter of January 9, 1577, in *Obras completas de Santa Teresa*, ed. Efrén de la Madre

to worry. Perhaps it's an eye ailment of the kind caused by weak blood. I have had it often, though I don't know why. The remedy was to inhale steam from a mixture of sulphurwort, coriander, eggshells, a little oil, a very little rosemary, and a little lavender, taken while in bed. I assure you that it cured me."[7] When María suffers from a urinary tract infection, Teresa writes: "For the love of God, please take care of yourself. They say that this is a good remedy for bladder problems: gather some ripe rose hips, dry them, and grind them into powder; and take a pinch the size of a half *real* in the morning. Ask a doctor about this. And please don't go so long without writing me again."[8] As the financial situation of the Seville convent improved, María began to send Teresa presents—orange blossom water, lemons, quince jelly, a tuna, a coconut—for which Teresa graciously thanked her. And when María invented an especially efficient stove, Teresa praised her ingenuity and sent her own brother to copy its design for other convents.

The relationship was nevertheless repeatedly strained by María's independence and aristocratic self-assurance, traits that exasperated Teresa, who for her part frequently found it difficult to relinquish decision making to the prioresses of the new foundations. When María, believing the house in Seville to be unhealthy, made arrangements to move the convent without securing Teresa's approval, she received a harsh rebuke. As Teresa wrote to Gracián in 1579, "I am extremely sorry about the foolish behavior of the Seville prioress: she has gone down a long way in my opinion. I see a certain mischief in that house that I can't stand, for the prioress is shrewder than befits her vocation. . . . To keep telling the poor nuns that their house is bad for them is enough to make them ill from believing it. I have written her some terrible letters, but it's like talking to a brick wall."[9]

Another serious disagreement occurred over María's delay in repaying a loan from Teresa's brother Lorenzo. Although the financial status of the Seville convent had improved since its foundation, María ignored Teresa's repeated requests for the funds she needed to finance a memorial chapel for Lorenzo, who had recently died. Still, the elder nun continued to express affection for María, even while chastising her: "Your Reverence must pardon

---

de Dios y Otger Steggink (Madrid: Católica, 1962), 811 (hereafter *OCST*). Translations from Saint Teresa's letters are my own. Provincials were friars who oversaw convents and monasteries in a particular region. Teresa coins the term "semiprovincial" to tease María about her new authority as prioress.

7. Teresa of Avila, letter of December 13, 1979, in *OCST,* 796.

8. Teresa of Avila, letter of July 4, 1980, in *OCST,* 974–75.

9. Teresa of Avila, letter of October 4, 1579, in *OCST,* 938–39.

me. I am intolerable to those I love, for I would not want them to go astray in any way.[10] I really do love you more than you think—and tenderly—and that's why I want you to make the right decision, especially in such an important matter."[11] In a poignant letter written shortly before her death, Teresa expressed her desire to see María as her successor:

> It amuses me to know how proud you are of your new belfry, and if it is as fine as you say, you have reason to be proud. I hope in God that all may be well in your house, because you have suffered greatly.
>
> Your Reverence puts everything so well, that if my opinion were sought, after my death they would elect you foundress, and even while I am alive I would gladly see them do so, for you know so much more and are better than I. It is true that I have the advantage of a little more experience, but I am not worth much notice anymore. You would be shocked to see how old and useless I am.[12]

María's Life after the Death of Teresa

María did not become Teresa's successor; instead, she found herself on the losing side of the internecine struggle over Teresa's legacy. In 1584, two years after Teresa's death, María, along with a small group of nuns, friars, and pious laymen, left Seville to make a foundation in Lisbon. The following year María was elected prioress of the new convent of San Alberto, and the Discalced nuns and friars were granted complete independence from the Calced Carmelites. Independence brought only further political strife, however, this time between Jerónimo Gracián, the first Discalced provincial, and his Italian successor, Nicolás Doria, the son of a wealthy banker. Gracián was affable and gregarious; he would have led the Discalced Carmelites in the direction of preaching and missionizing. Doria, a severe ascetic who embraced the ancient eremitical tradition of the order, feared that an active apostolate would lead to laxity. He also expected the worst from contact between nuns and friars. Appalled by the amount of time Gracián spent with María and the nuns of the newly founded Lisbon convent, Doria publicly rebuked him and threatened him with expulsion. Rumors of an illicit relationship between Gracián and María that had figured in the Seville denunciations surfaced again. Gracián was accused of spending too much time in convents, accept-

---

10. Teresa of Avila, letter of December 21, 1579, in *OCST,* 946.
11. Teresa of Avila, letter of February 8, 1580, in *OCST,* 958.
12. Teresa of Avila, letter of March 17, 1582, in *OCST,* 1052.

ing linen shirts from nuns, and letting them do his laundry and prepare special meals for him. Throughout this period, María wrote impassioned letters in Gracián's defense. Incensed, Doria removed her from office and ordered her imprisoned in her cell, forbidden to communicate with her nuns or outsiders.

The personal animosity of these protagonists made manifest a profound disagreement over essential issues, especially women's role in monastic governance and the appropriate relationship between monastic men and women. Gracián believed that monastic enclosure was not incompatible with a relaxed familiarity between nuns and their prelates. Doria insisted that contact should be brief, infrequent, and formal. Doria also sought to standardize and centralize convent administration. According to the model of governance established by Teresa, prioresses enjoyed a remarkable degree of autonomy from their male superiors. They had the authority to select and change confessors and preachers for the convent without securing the permission of the provincial; along with the novice mistresses, they played important roles in directing the spiritual lives of the sisters; and they enjoyed considerable discretionary powers in areas of financial administration, the selection of novices, and convent discipline. Many prioresses developed influential friendships with high-ranking ecclesiastics and nobles. When Doria took over the leadership of the Discalced Carmelites in 1585, he initiated efforts to centralize authority, curb the nuns' extramural contacts, reinforce austerity, limit the prioresses' role in spiritual direction, and, in general, place the nuns more securely under masculine control.

In 1590, María and Ana de Jesús, the prioress of Madrid, led what is known as "the nuns' revolt," appealing directly to Rome for protection from Doria's proposed changes in governance. They were initially successful; Pope Sixtus V issued a papal brief confirming the authority of the Teresian constitutions and forbidding the friars to make further changes without papal approval. Sixtus V's brief, however, was overturned the following year by his successor, Gregory XIV. Doria retaliated against the leaders of the revolt and their sympathizers: John of the Cross, who had supported the rebel nuns, was stripped of office; Ana de Jesús was sentenced to three years in a locked cell; and María de San José was punished by loss of voice and vote for two years and confinement incommunicado for one year. Gracián was expelled from the Discalced congregation for "excesses in his conduct with nuns as well as excessive familiarity with one of them [i.e., María]."

A period of tranquility for María followed Doria's death in 1594, but she once again fell into disfavor when Francisco de la Madre de Dios assumed the office of prior general in 1600. For reasons that remain obscure, in 1603 María was ordered to abandon Lisbon for an isolated convent in Cuerva, six leagues from Toledo. There, nine days after making the arduous journey, she died on October 19. In the first decades after her death, a few friars and nuns attributed miraculous properties to her tunic. Although a seventeenth-century Portuguese historian of the order records that her disinterred body was incorrupt, her cult did not thrive. Today, the site of her grave is unknown.[13]

CONVENT CULTURE

Women's Education

In Spain as in the rest of Europe, Renaissance humanists advocated an education for women yet limited it to training considered appropriate to their sex. As Luis Vives wrote: "A woman's only care is chastity; therefore when this has been thoroughly elucidated, she may be considered to have received sufficient instruction."[14] In the first decades of the sixteenth century, Cardinal Ximénez Cisneros (d. 1517) promoted the publication of religious works in the vernacular, precisely to make them accessible to women. Girls from prosperous urban families sometimes benefited from lessons given by their brothers' tutors, but it is probable that most learned to read and write from their mothers. Still others received lessons from nuns while residing as boarders in convents. Nevertheless, almost all other formal instruction and all university training strictly excluded women. Even this limited enthusiasm for female education diminished, however, as Spain prepared to meet the threat of the Protestant reformation. The prominent role of women as teachers in Protestant and Erasmian sects heightened the suspicion of women who were more than marginally literate. Despite the example set by Queen Isabel, whose four daughters were accomplished Latinists, very few families thought it desirable to teach their daughters the language of intellectual debate and theol-

---

13. Belchior de Santa Anna incorporates extensive translations from her works in his history and describes her disinterred body as incorrupt. Belchior's Spanish counterpart, Francisco de Santa María, however, gives her scant attention. Francisco de Santa María notes María's close friendship with Teresa but omits mention of her role as prioress in Seville and Lisbon or her opposition to Dorian reforms. María is treated more kindly in the major twentieth-century history of the order by Silverio de Santa Teresa, *Historia del Carmen Descalzo*, 15 vols. (Burgos: El Monte Carmelo, 1935–), 8:435–72. Two contemporary Carmelite historians have attempted to vindicate Gracián and reassess the significance of the nuns' rebellion. See Ildefonso Moriones de la Visitación, *Ana de Jesús y la herencia teresiana* (Rome: Edizioni del Teresianum, 1968); and Anselmo Donázar Zamora, *Principio y fin de una Reforma: Una revolución religiosa en tiempos de Felipe II* (Bogotá: Guadalupe, 1968).

14. Juan Luis Vives, *The Education of a Christian Woman*, ed. and trans. C. Fantazzi (Chicago: University of Chicago Press, 2000), par. 3, p. 47.

ogy. Some aristocrats deemed even basic literacy superfluous. One of Teresa's noble patrons, Teresa de Laíz, was unable to sign her name on the deed endowing a convent.

It would be a mistake, however, to assume that female literacy was exceptional in early modern Spain. The availability of inexpensive printed books and pamphlets in a variety of genres from devotional readings to secular entertainment, the Counter Reformation initiative to teach basic prayers and doctrine to all parishioners, and possibly even improvements in the postal system enhanced the motivation and opportunities for some women —especially daughters of merchants and the urban gentry—to learn to read and write. We should also remember that literacy comprises various skills and levels of proficiency—the ability to decipher words, the ability to read silently, the ability to write—that are not mastered simultaneously. The experience of the Discalced nun Ana de San Bartolomé illustrates how the acquisition of literacy, as we understand it today, sometimes extended over decades in early modern Europe. Ana, who was from a prosperous peasant family, had somehow learned to read as a child (she mentions that her parents hired tutors for her brothers). She did not learn to write, however, until the age of thirty-three. At this time, Teresa, who had recently broken her arm, encouraged Ana to learn to write so that she could help her with her correspondence. Ana went on to pen—though in a hand that is scarcely legible—chronicles of her order, two versions of her life story, and numerous devotional works.[15]

The opportunities for a woman to become literate could be augmented by a religious vocation. Reading undoubtedly constituted an important part of Discalced Carmelite life. Novices who aspired to be choir nuns (with responsibilities that included liturgical reading and chanting) were expected to be minimally literate when they joined the order, and during their novitiate they received additional lessons from the novice mistress and other professed nuns. Solitary and group reading formed a part of every monastic day: nuns read to each other during meals and during recreation hours, and they were expected to read alone in their cells (or pray) for an hour after matins. Reading from spiritual books was considered an important preparation for the practice of mental prayer. Teresa and her prioresses were also prolific letter writers. The Discalced Carmelites, who wrote the histories of their foundations, biographies of exemplary sisters, ballads, and other forms of devotional poetry, circulated their manuscripts among convents. Unless or-

15. See Ana de San Bartolomé, *Obras completas*, ed. Julián Urkiza, 2 vols. (Rome: Teresianum, 1981, 1985).

dered to do so by their confessors, however, they were discouraged from writing about visions and revelations, topics that could bring them under inquisitorial scrutiny.

María's educational attainments as evidenced by her ability to read and write in three languages, her familiarity with a broad range of religious texts, and her mastery of rhetorical tropes and metrical forms was nevertheless extraordinary. We can only speculate as to why or how María acquired these skills. She had the advantage of being raised in an aristocratic family with a long tradition of literary achievement. Doña Luisa may have indulged her talented young protégée by providing her with books or even a tutor. And as we have seen, María chose to join an order that encouraged solitary and communal reading and offered access to manuscripts as well as printed books.

María's detailed familiarity with biblical literature is as surprising as her knowledge of Latin and French. There are references in her writings to twenty books of the Old Testament (citations from the Psalms, Proverbs, and Song of Songs predominate) and to the Gospels as well as the Pauline Epistles of the New Testament. A principal debate of the Counter Reformation disputed the extent to which the laity (as well as women religious) should be allowed to read the Bible. Although the Council of Trent did not issue any concrete prohibitions on the matter, Spain acted on its own to restrict access to Scripture. The Indexes of Prohibited Books issued by the Spanish Inquisition in 1551, 1554, and 1559 all forbade the publication and reading of Scripture in the vernacular, although citations were permitted in books of spiritual content. Religious writers made ample use of this exemption, so that it would have been possible to reassemble from scattered passages something close to the entire Bible in Spanish. María may also have had access to the Vulgate Bible. Additional sources available to her were psalters, books of hours, and possibly Spanish editions of the New Testament published prior to the Indexes. Her access to scriptural sources was undoubtedly facilitated by her friendship with Gracián, son of a humanist scholar, brother to the king's secretary, graduate in theology from the University of Alcalá de Henares, and a prolific writer himself.[16] Whatever the basis for her knowledge, it is evident that María's use of Scripture was not simply ornamental or rhetorical; indeed, the dialogue of *Book for the Hour of Recreation* offers daring acts of exegesis.

---

16. On María's knowledge of Scripture, see María Pilar Manero Sorolla, "La Biblia en el carmelo femenino: La obra de María de San José (Salazar)," *Actas del XII Congreso de la Asociación Internacional de Hispanistas, 21–26 de agosto de 1995, Birmingham,* ed. Jules Whicker (Birmingham, England: University of Birmingham, 1998), 3:52–58.

Daily Life and Recreation

For some early modern women, monastic life offered opportunities for intellectual and artistic self-expression that would have been difficult to achieve outside the convent walls. Nuns wrote poetry, staged plays, painted, embroidered, and commissioned works of art. However, it is important to recognize that the time and material resources available for these activities varied enormously according to the religious order. Discalced Carmelite nuns had chosen a life of poverty and solitude; opportunities for creative expression were limited by a demanding schedule of work and prayer. Nuns could expect to spend approximately twelve of the eighteen hours that constituted the monastic day in solitary activities: in prayer, devotional readings, and manual labor. The sisters normally arose at 5:00 A.M. (the day began an hour later in winter) and spent the first hour of the day in silent prayer, then recited the rosary collectively. They came together again at eight o'clock for lauds, the first of four daily sessions of liturgical prayer, and then attended Mass. After this, they retired to their individual cells for work, principally spinning and sewing, but excluding elaborate needlework that required careful attention, for they were required to keep their minds free to pray. Shortly before eleven o'clock, they gathered for the "examination of conscience," in which they confessed to their sisters infractions in their observance of the rule.[17] They then took their main meal, after which the rule of silence was rescinded for an hour of conversation. They recited vespers at two o'clock, following with an hour of spiritual reading or silent prayer alone in their cells. Books recommended by the constitutions for such purposes included *The Life of Christ* by Ludolf of Saxony, *The Imitation of Christ* (attributed to Thomas à Kempis), and the *Flos Sanctorum* (a collection of the lives of saints). The rest of the afternoon was dedicated to work. All participated in menial tasks, as the constitutions prescribed, with the prioress the first to take up the broom. When not occupied with other responsibilities, nuns were encouraged to retire to hermitages (huts) in the convent garden to pray. Compline was said at six o'clock, followed by supper and another period of conversation. From eight o'clock to nine, nuns dedicated themselves to a second hour of silent prayer. The day ended with the recitation of matins at nine o'clock and a second examination of conscience; on specified days, they would exercise self-flagellation before retiring.

17. The nuns' daily confessions of faults among each other should not be confused with sacramental confession to a priest followed by Communion, sacraments that the Discalced Carmelites observed on a weekly schedule.

Food and dress were austere. The nuns abstained from meat, except during illness; they wore a habit of coarse cloth or rough wool, hemp sandals, and stockings made of tow (a coarse fabric of woven flax). Although dedication to poverty and solitude marked every aspect of their life, the Discalced Carmelites also believed that a life of unremitting austerity would be intolerable and pernicious to their health. Under the strict rules of enclosure adopted by the reform, nuns were prohibited from leaving the convent, but they could receive family and friends in the locutory, a special parlor in which a screen separated the veiled nun from her visitor. Frivolous conversations, however, were discouraged, for the locutory was intended as a place where mutually beneficial spiritual friendships might flourish.

The constitutions also provided two hours of recreation each day following meals: "When they are through with the meal, the Mother prioress may dispense from the silence so that all may converse together on whatever topic pleases them most as long as it is not one that is inappropriate for a good religious. And they should all have their distaffs with them there. Games should in no way be permitted, for the Lord will give them the grace to entertain the others. . . . They should strive not to be offensive to one another, but their words and jests must be discreet."[18] We know that during the hours of recreation the nuns sang, played the guitar and tambourine, and composed ballads and couplets. During Advent and on the occasion of a novice's profession, they also staged *fiestas*, short theatrical pieces in verse.[19]

Discalced Spirituality

The spirituality that motivated the reformers was the result of the confluence of diverse currents of religiosity, some with roots in the Middle Ages and others that emerged during the ferment of the Catholic prereform and

18. *Constitutions*, in *The Collected Works of St. Teresa of Avila*, trans. Kieran Kavanaugh and Otilio Rodríguez, 3 vols. (Washington, D.C.: Institute of Carmelite Studies, 1976–85), 3:327–28.

19. Stacey Schlau has edited a bilingual edition of works by another Discalced Carmelite nun, including two such dramatic pieces: *Viva al siglo, muerta al mundo: Selected Works/Obras Escogidas de/by María de San Alberto (1568–1640)* (New Orleans: University Press of the South, 1998). Belchior de Santa Anna also describes plays depicting the lives of famous martyrs that María wrote and performed with her sisters in Lisbon. Victor García de la Concha and Ana María Alvarez Pellitero have published a collection of ballads composed by Discalced Carmelite nuns during this period: *Libro de romances y coplas del Carmelo de Valladolid*, 2 vols. (Salamanca: Consejo de Castilla y León, 1982). For convent drama in the Trinitarian order, see *Literatura conventual femenina: Sor Marcela de San Felix, hija de Lope de Vega: Obra Completa*, ed. Electa Arenal and Georgina Sabat-Rivers (Madrid: PPU, 1988).

Counter Reformation. An emphasis on inward devotion and reading Scripture drew upon the fourteenth-century practice of the *devotio moderna* as well as Erasmian influences from the early sixteenth century.[20] Teresa's belief that intimate knowledge of God was accessible to the "unlettered" (those unable to read Latin) was undoubtedly nourished by the long tradition of medieval women's spirituality, but the spread of literacy and the publication of spiritual books in the vernacular also contributed to the Discalced openness to the democratization of spirituality. The desire to recapture the eremitical simplicity of the primitive Carmelites was reinforced by a disdain for notions of honor, status, and "blood purity" that obsessed sixteenth-century Spanish society. The Discalced attitude toward the body reflects a similar synthesis of old and new: accepting the need to discipline the body with fasting and self-flagellation, they moderated their penitential practices due to their conviction (shared, notably, by the Jesuits) that both mental and physical health were necessary for a rigorous life of apostolic service.

The spirituality that Teresa promoted in the Discalced convents was based primarily on a dedication to mental prayer, a method that encompassed various stages of devotion. Active preparation through thanksgiving and repentance, silent reading, and directed meditation on Christ's life could in time lead to the "infused" or divinely granted experience of "recollection," in which all faculties of sense and thought are quieted and become centered in God. The Discalced day devoted at least two hours to mental prayer, and it was expected that nuns would continue to pray as they performed their daily tasks. In contrast to the ritual chanted prayers that were offered as petitions for specific individuals (whether for the living or for departed souls in purgatory), mental prayer held as its object the spiritual transformation of the individual through "conversation with God." It emphasized supplication for the larger Christian community over specific petitions for patrons or kin, and receptivity to God's will over intellectual effort. Teresa was motivated to initiate her reform in large part to provide nuns with the solitude and structure necessary to practice mental prayer, not only so that they could pursue their individual spiritual goals, but also in order to fulfill an ecclesial mission.

---

20. Erasmus's *Enchiridion*, published in Spanish in 1526, was enormously popular. By the 1530s Erasmianism was suspect in the eyes of the Inquisition. The Index of 1551 included Erasmus's *Colloquies*, and the Index of 1559 listed fourteen works of his in Spanish, including the *Enchiridion*. Nevertheless, some of his works continued to be available in Spain throughout the sixteenth century. Furthermore, aspects of Erasmianism were disseminated by such figures as San Juan de Avila and Luis de Granada, who succeeded (though not without difficulty) in affirming their orthodoxy. See Henry Kamen, *The Spanish Inquisition: A Historical Revision* (New Haven, Conn.: Yale University Press, 1997), 83–91, 105, 109–10.

Finally, in prayer they sought the strength and determination to engage in the arduous struggle to extend the reform and found new monasteries.[21]

Mental prayer, especially when practiced by women, was not without its critics. Some theologians feared that it could lead to a disdain for or a neglect of vocal prayer. Others thought it presumptuous for women to aspire to an advanced form of devotion, one difficult for priests to monitor or direct. Another point of contention was the nature and purpose of supernatural sensations that sometimes resulted in the course of mental prayer: visions, locutions (hearing God speak), or raptures. Some critics believed that impressionable women might imagine divine messages or, worse, be deceived by the devil "disguised as an angel of light" (2 Corinthians 11:13–14). Teresa argued throughout her life that the fears of demonic deception in prayer were greatly exaggerated. At the same time, she diminished the significance of the supernatural effects of prayer. Such "favors," even moments of supreme ecstasy, she believed, were never proof of sanctity; rather, they were intended to strengthen the soul in its determination to do works. In *Book for the Hour of Recreation*, as we shall see, María promoted this shift in emphasis from ecstatic absorption and charismatic gifts to the extended effects of prayer as spiritual renewal.

This is not to imply that Discalced spirituality rejected all forms of intercessory or charismatic religiosity. The Discalced Carmelites saw ample evidence of God's miraculous intervention in their mission. They believed that their reform was part of God's providential plan, that he communicated with them through supernatural visions and locutions, and that when necessary he consoled them with the ecstatic assurance of his presence. They also feared that the devil worked tirelessly to thwart their efforts, although they trusted in God's superior power to protect them. After Teresa's death, her devotees worked to achieve her canonization as a miracle worker. In contrast, we find in Teresa's and María's writings a notion of female sanctity that differs from, though it draws upon, the medieval tradition of the female charismatic. For them, the saintly woman is not an exceptional vessel for divine power, but someone who, empowered by God's love, is able to inspire the members of her community. Perhaps to an even greater degree than Teresa, María considered charismata incidental to the spiritual life.

Another important Discalced contribution to spirituality, whose novelty may be difficult for the modern reader to appreciate, is *suavedad*, or gentle-

---

21. On Teresa's concept of mental prayer as an ecclesial mission, see Jodi Bilinkoff, "Woman with a Mission: Teresa of Avila and the Apostolic Model," in *Modelli di santità e modelli di comportamento,* ed. Giulia Barone et al. (Turin: Rosenberg and Sellier, 1994), 295–305.

ness. Broadly speaking, *suavedad* refers to the belief that a life of piety need not be mournful: that it can encompass delight in one's relationship with God and be expressed in gentleness toward oneself and joy in the company of others. A deep appreciation for humor expresses yet another aspect of *suavedad*. As we shall see, María frequently recalls Teresa's wit, cheerfulness, and capacity to find amusement in the grimmest of circumstances. The Discalced Carmelites' commitment to *suavedad* had important implications for their disciplinary, medical, and recreational practices, which were less severe than those of other reformed orders. Although it is important not to overestimate the modernity of their practices (which included self-mortification, austerity in diet and dress, and on occasion corporal punishment), Discalced *suavedad* constituted a significant shift in monastic attitudes toward the body—a rejection of the idea that piety required extreme self-imposed suffering.[22]

MARÍA DE SAN JOSÉ'S BOOK FOR THE HOUR OF RECREATION

Around 1585, María learned of Doria's intention to curtail or abolish the hours of recreation as part of his effort to reverse what he saw as the Discalced Carmelites' slide toward laxity. In response she wrote a dialogue representing conversations between fictional nuns during the course of several hours of recreation. Though she does not address Doria's threat specifically, the work implicitly defends and illustrates the idea that recreation, as a manifestation of *suavedad*, is spiritually beneficial.

María's text defies clear-cut generic definition. María's principal formal model was the Renaissance dialogue, a genre adapted by her day to a broad range of subjects. It had become a popular didactic forum, in which an authority figure (a teacher or priest) expounded the author's doctrine for one or more speaker-pupils, who in turn held naive or erroneous opinions. Since the dialogue was the genre considered suitable for debate or instruction, it is not surprising that it was cultivated by few women. In fact, of the hundreds of dialogues written in Spain in the sixteenth century, we can point to only two by

---

22. In some poems María does express her ascetic fervor to suffer for Christ. And like John of the Cross and Teresa, she describes ecstasy in terms of pleasurable pain. See, for example, María's poems "Ansias de padecer" [Longings to suffer] and "Heridas de amor místico" [Wounds of mystical love], in *Escritos espirituales*, ed. Simeón de la Sagrada Familia (Rome: Postulación General O.C.D., 1979), 485, 487.

women: Luisa Sigea's Latin *Duarum virginum colloquium* and María's own *Book for the Hour of Recreation*. Thus María's is—as far as we know—the first female-authored dialogue in the Spanish vernacular.[23]

In the prologue, María addresses her audience, the sisters of the convent of San Alberto, explaining her purpose in writing: first, to relate the life of their foundress, Teresa, and second, to portray the nuns' "trato y vida," their day-to-day dealings with each other, something that will require a "living representation," or dialogue. María's expressed desire to depict relationships leads us to speculate that the dialogue was read aloud by one or more readers, precisely during the hours of recreation. The playful representation of day-to-day friction between different personalities suggests that, like other forms of convent drama, this dialogue may have served as a necessary escape valve for the inevitable tensions of communal life.[24] The first chapter presents, in a second fictional prologue, the principal characters and dramatic situation of the dialogue. Two nuns converse in the garden during the hour of recreation. The younger, Gracia, laments to her sister Justa that her confessor has ordered her to record her spiritual life. Although Gracia desires to comply with her confessor's command, she is beset by fears of her own inadequacy and worries that she may be deceived about the nature of delights she has experienced in prayer: "I do not know if this inability be caused by the devil, or by the fear to which we women are so given." Justa proposes the following solution to Gracia's dilemma: instead of telling the story of her own life, she can relate the biography of their founding mother, Angela (Teresa's pseudonym in the dialogue). Gracia gratefully accepts Justa's suggestion, and soon they are joined by other nuns who, while listening and adding comments, will take turns writing down Gracia's recollections.

Book for the Hour of Recreation thus constitutes, in an important sense, a parody of the most common (and at times the only possible) genre available to monastic women in Counter-Reformation Spain—the *vida por mandato*, or "autobiography by mandate." María's audience would immediately have understood the nature of Gracia's anxious response to her confessor's request for an

---

23. Erasmus's colloquies are representative of another class of Renaissance dialogue that employs a dialectical approach to moral issues. Instead of being presented with an authoritative mouthpiece for the author, the reader of the Erasmian dialogue is challenged to arrive at a moral position after considering the divergent points of view of the various interlocutors. Erasmus's colloquies were placed on the Spanish Index of Prohibited Books of 1551. It is improbable, therefore, although not impossible, that María was familiar with them.

24. On convent drama's function in relieving tensions in monastic life, see Elissa B. Weaver, "Spiritual Fun: A Study of Sixteenth-Century Tuscan Convent Theater," in *Women in the Middle Ages and the Renaissance*, ed. Mary Beth Rose (Syracuse, 1986), 173–206.

account of her spiritual life. Such confessional narratives were part of the process by which the confessor judged the orthodoxy of the nun's practice of prayer and the authenticity of any spiritual experiences derived from it. In complying with this mandate, nuns risked exposing themselves to charges of presumption, delusion, or possession. Indeed, the confessors who first ordered Teresa to write her *vida* had at one time concluded that her visions were demonic in origin.

But María's depiction of the monastic woman's "anxiety of authorship" is ironic. In the first place, Gracia's apprehension is humorous, since the "mandating" confessor, "Elias," is none other than their congenial prelate and cofounder, Jerómino de Gracián. Second, the nuns show no compunction about ignoring the confessor's command and transforming the "vida por mandato" into a collaborative, recreational activity: recalling the life of the beloved "Angela." Nor do they feel compelled to stick to their principal subject. In fact, as one nun remarks, they will create an *olla podrida*, or hodgepodge stew, made up of humble ingredients. María thus humorously subverts the restrictions of the autobiography by mandate, according to which the confessor commands, defines, and ultimately judges the life writing of his penitential daughter. Instead, her fictional persona transforms the mandate and takes advantage of the informal, collective nature of her redefined task to range freely on issues of vital concern to her monastic community. By transgressing the boundaries of the traditional "nun's genre" and inventing a multigeneric, dialogic text, María multiplies her addressees as well as the uses of the text: she offers it—to her sisters and her sympathetic confessor— as entertainment, as edification, and as inspiration. Perhaps chiefly, *Book for the Hour of Recreation* aims to impart information about the exemplary life of María's mentor, Saint Teresa of Avila; to justify and defend the work of Teresa's reform movement; and to offer detailed guidance in the Teresian method of mental prayer.

Although Gracia is readily identifiable as María's persona, *Book for the Hour of Recreation* is never monological in its pedagogical impulse. No single voice of authority predominates; rather, the two principal interlocutors, Gracia and Justa, represent divergent attitudes, each in need of the corrective or moderating influence of the other. The names are suggestively multivalent. Justa, "the just one," is a punctilious defender of the letter of the law. But *justo/a* as an adjective implies "just enough" or "barely sufficient." Her self-righteousness calls out for Gracia's ironic humor as a complement. Gracia, of course, indicates the theological gift of grace, as well as human charm, hu-

---

25. It is possible that María chose this as her nom de plume in homage to her confessor and intellectual mentor, Gracián.

mor, and wit.[25] But Gracia's wit can be bitter and sarcastic; she relies on Justa to temper her defiance and remind her of the Carmelite virtue of humility. The voices of the other nuns provide additional perspectives. No single nun "teaches" the others; rather, they collectively encourage, supplement, correct, chide, and tease each other, and throughout, as María says in the prologue, "show that they have learned."

In the second chapter, Gracia responds to Justa's questions about her experience of mental prayer. Gracia loses no time in addressing its principal danger: the possibility that its ecstatic pleasures and visions might be the effect of the devil. Although Gracia does not deny that the devil does indeed counterfeit the "pleasures and caresses" of prayer, she expresses confidence in her own capacity to distinguish true from demonic sensations. Like Teresa, she is relatively skeptical regarding the extent of the devil's powers over practitioners of mental prayer and rejects the notion that they must inevitably suffer demonic temptations.[26] She is equally cautious about attributing miracles or revelations to prayer, and when Justa presses her to reveal more about her experiences, she discreetly declines. Gracia's insistence that ecstatic prayer is an intimate, private experience represents a rejection of an alternative, but highly problematic, model of female sanctity, the public healer and prophetess. This alternate model was, perhaps, the dominant one in late-sixteenth-century Lisbon. A contemporary of María, the Dominican María de la Visitación, had attracted devotees from all of Europe with her stigmata and visions, and at the time María was writing *Book for the Hour of Recreation*, was predicting the victory of the Spanish Armada over England. Whether motivated by skepticism or pragmatism, María distanced herself from the visionary politics of the Dominican nun.[27]

In the subsequent four chapters, Gracia and an older nun, Atanasia, recount the history of the Order of Carmel. They are interrupted from time to time by Justa, who alternately amazed and shocked by Gracia's liberal citations from Scripture. María's typological history traces the fabled origins of the order to the Old Testament prophets Elijah and Elisha (in fact, it was founded by twelfth-century hermits in Palestine) and celebrates its recent renewal under female leadership in Spain. María's emphasis on the Carmelites' Judaic origins suggests that she was aware that Teresa herself was a *conversa*, a

---

26. On Teresa's attitude toward the devil, see Alison Weber, "Saint Teresa, Demonologist," in *Culture and Control in Counter-Reformation Spain*, ed. Anne J. Cruz and Mary Elizabeth Perry (Minneapolis: University of Minnesota Press, 1992), 171–95.

27. María de la Visitación was denounced and exposed as a fraud in 1588 after being implicated in Portuguese separatist politics. Although María de San José had close ties with the Portuguese nobility and although the Discalced Carmelites also had enjoyed the hospitality of the Dominicans on their arrival in Lisbon, they were careful not to dispute Philip's annexation of Portugal.

descendant of converted Jews. Whatever María's covert intentions may have been, this chapter expresses pride in the Carmelites' role as transmitters of a continuous Judeo-Christian tradition.[28]

The history of Carmel is followed by a long (and for modern readers, somewhat tedious) catalog of the qualities of the precious stones found on Mount Carmel. We learn, for example, that carbuncle inspires confidence, jacinth defends against wrath, topaz engenders charity, coral protects against epilepsy, chrysolite defends against madness and delusions, and so on. Although it at first appears that the meaning of the stones is allegorical— that these are the virtues nourished by Carmelite tradition—we note that specific medical qualities are ascribed to some of the minerals. It is unlikely that María included this lapidary chapter for practical reasons; the Discalced Carmelites were too poor to afford such expensive remedies for their ailments. Perhaps she was motivated by a desire to entertain—or even dazzle —her sisters with her exotic knowledge. These chapters also evince a certain air of reckless defiance, as María quotes Scripture, interprets its typology, and then ventures into the arcane subject matter of the Renaissance lapidary, a genre that had recently come under inquisitorial scrutiny.

Chapter 7 opens with Justa's confession that she dreads the obligatory hours of mental prayer, which give her only headaches. Here María treats the restrictions on women's participation in theological discourse with subversive irony. When Atanasia expresses reluctance to give advice on mental prayer, Justa impatiently concedes that although it is not permitted for women to write about "important and essential matters," they should be able to offer advice on "tiny and tangential little things." Furthermore, she argues, just as a woman may be better than a wise doctor at curing "female indispositions," women may be better than learned men in discerning their sisters' *spiritual* ailments. Reassured by these arguments, Atanasia and Gracia proceed to offer practical suggestions on contemplation: Justa should be sure to start her prayer with a clear conscience, she should not hold her breath, and she should not expect or strive to achieve ecstasy. María thus protectively defines her discourse on prayer as incidental and minor, a separate and inferior pedagogy by and for women. We should not, however, let María's irony obscure her argument for a feminine pedagogy. The conversation among the three women (none of whom has the last word) demonstrates that women can be competent spiritual teachers to each other. Indeed, María implies, their

28. Teresa's grandfather, Juan Sánchez, accused of practicing Judaism in secret, was reconciled to the church in an auto da fe held in Toledo in 1485. As mentioned above, María's own racial heritage is mysterious. It should be noted that aristocratic families were known to have intermarried with *conversos* during the fifteenth century.

shared experience, intimate knowledge of each other's character, and egalitarian relationship may allow them to succeed as spiritual guides where men might fail.

In chapter 8, María offers one of the very first biographical accounts of Teresa. Although she writes that Teresa came from "an illustrious lineage," she differs from other contemporary sources in making no claim for her "great nobility" and "Old Christian" blood, a further indication that María knew of Teresa's *converso* origins. In the middle section, the narrator's voice yields to Teresa's as she quotes lengthy passages from Teresa's *vida*. Gracia explains that she will use the saint's own words to give her sisters "greater pleasure," while taking the liberty of omitting Teresa's many digressions and exclamations of her wretchedness and clarifying the order of events. It is interesting that María's text, though claiming to quote Teresa, in fact considerably revises her colloquial syntax so that it conforms more closely to contemporary norms for written discourse. One example will have to suffice. Teresa writes in chapter 27 of *The Book of Her Life*: "When I was in prayer once, on glorious Saint Peter's day, I saw next to me or I felt next to me, to put it better, because with the body's eyes and the soul's I saw nothing, but it seemed to me that Christ was next to me and I saw that it was He who was speaking to me, as it seemed to me. Since I was very ignorant of what such a vision could be, I was very much afraid at first and did nothing but cry, although when He said just one single word to reassure me, I remained as before, still and with a pleasurable feeling and without any fear. It seemed to me that Jesus Christ was by my side always, but since it was not an imaginary vision, I did not see in what form; but I felt Him always on my right side very clearly and felt that He was a witness of everything that I did, and I never withdrew into recollection or was free from distractions so little that I couldn't feel Him next to me."[29] María's abbreviated and "writerly" version is as follows: "Once in prayer on the feast of the glorious Saint Peter, I felt Christ our Lord beside me, and I felt it was He who was speaking to me. He was always on my right side, and He was the witness of what I said, and whenever I recollected, I found Him near me; I knew this through an intellectual vision."[30] The chapter ends with a remarkably detailed description of Teresa's appearance: "She was more robust than thin and well proportioned in all ways; she had very lovely hands, though they were small. On the left side of her face, she had

29. *OCST*, 106. Translation by Alison P. Weber. Readers may consult the complete text of *The Book of Her Life* in vol. 1 of *The Collected Works of St. Teresa of Avila*.

30. *Book for the Hour of Recreation* standardizes Teresa's "rustic" lexicon: "siguridad," for example, becomes "seguridad." We cannot say for certain whether these corrections were made by María or by a later copyist.

Ch. 8

three moles raised like little warts, all in a straight line, beginning with the largest one below her mouth, and the next between her mouth and nose, and the last on her nose, closer to the bottom than the top of it." The portrait, affectionate but ungilded, seems emblematic of María's attitude toward Teresa as literary and spiritual foremother.

María's voice, having merged with Teresa's in chapter 8, supplements and diverges from hers in chapter 9, as Gracia/María recounts, from her perspective, the story of the troubled Seville foundation recorded in Teresa's own *Book of Foundations*.[31] The hardships of the journey—filthy lodgings, oppressive heat, dangerous river crossings, brawling crowds at inns—are vividly detailed. María also pays homage to Teresa's wit and ability to extract humor from the recollection of past tribulations. With a comic timing worthy of Teresa's best pages, María tells how the neighbors, who had so inadequately furnished their lodgings in Seville, begin to show up and, one by one, reclaim their possessions: "Just when we had begun to think that these made up at least the beginnings of a house, along with a few jugs and plates and things of that sort that we found, then the neighbors—who had lent these things for that day—began sending, this one for the frying pan, another for the oil lamp, and another for the ladle and the table, so that finally not one thing was left to us, not a frying pan or a mortar or even the rope to the well."[32]

There is also more bitterness in María's history than in Teresa's, a lingering resentment over the humiliations she suffered at the hands of the "melancholy" confessor and "simple-minded nuns" who denounced her to the Inquisition. Where Teresa is apt to see conflict as the result of the devil's opposition to the reform, María is more inclined to see human stupidity and egotism. And while Teresa tends to gloss over the more troublesome episodes of each foundation and focus on the happy outcome, María records with psychological immediacy the violence, loneliness, and despair of these turbulent days.

MARÍA'S LITERARY LEGACY

María's literary legacy is unfortunately fragmentary; most of her letters, her convent plays, and many of her poems have been lost. *Book for the Hour of Recreation* itself is a fragment: the only known manuscript is a seventeenth-century

31. Teresa's *Book of Her Life* was published in 1588. However, *The Book of Foundations* did not appear in print until 1610. It is obvious that María was familiar with manuscript copies of Teresa's writings.

32. "Ninth Recreation, 144."

copy that ends three quarters of the way down a page, as Gracia prepares to tell the story of the Lisbon foundation. It is unclear whether María abandoned her project, the original manuscript was intentionally mutilated, or it was accidentally destroyed.[33] Other surviving writings (which remained unpublished until the beginning of this century) include two autobiographical letters, three treatises on convent governance, twenty-three religious poems, and testimony given in the beatification proceedings of Teresa de Jesús.[34] Although a seventeenth-century Portuguese history treats María with great reverence, her role in the reform was largely ignored by early Spanish historians of the order.[35] Two developments have stimulated renewed interest in this nearly forgotten figure: the reforms of the Second Vatican Council (which urged women's religious orders to reexamine the history of their constitutions) and the rise of feminist studies. In 1991 the order initiated causes for the beatification of María, Ana de Jesús, and Gracián, and in 1999 revoked Gracián's expulsion while expressing regret for the harshness with which all three figures had been treated. In 1989, Electa Arenal and Stacey Schlau published selections from María's works, with English translations by Amanda Powell, in *Untold Sisters: Hispanic Nuns in Their Own Works*, a landmark anthology that has stimulated scholarship on women's monastic literature in Spanish.

MARÍA DE SAN JOSÉ AND THE FEMINIST TRADITION

Gerda Lerner has described "feminist consciousness" in terms of four stages of development: "(1) the awareness that women belong to a subordinate group and that, as members of such a group, they have suffered wrongs; (2) the recognition that their condition of subordination is not natural, but societally determined; (3) the development of a sense of sisterhood; (4) the articulation of specific goals and strategies for changing their condition."[36] Such

---

33. In her prologue María announces that her work will be divided into five parts. The extant manuscript covers the material described in the first four parts. However, the manuscript is divided not into parts but into nine chapters, or "recreations." We cannot be sure if this discrepancy reflects a modification in María's original plan or a change introduced by the copyist.

34. These works were published for the first time in 1913 and reedited by Simeón de la Sagrada Familia under the title *Escritos espirituales* (Rome: Postulación General O.C.D., 1979). For our translation we have consulted this edition as well as the manuscript of *Libro de recreaciones*, now held in the Biblioteca Nacional de Madrid. Fragments of a copy of *Libro de recreaciones* are also held in archives of the Discalced Carmelites of Seville. See our bibliography for full references.

35. See n. 13 above.

36. Gerda Lerner, *The Creation of Feminist Consciousness from the Middle Ages to Eighteen-seventy* (New York: Oxford University Press, 1993), 274.

a definition of feminist consciousness is inevitably shaped by a historical tra-
jectory that has evolved toward modern notions of secular rights and capa-
bilities. Nevertheless, Lerner's stages afford a useful framework for analysis,
provided we bear in mind that María's consciousness of gender was realized
within and was circumscribed by her monastic vocation.

María was not a feminist foremother in the school of the medieval mystics. That is, she did not claim her authority on the basis of private communication with God or supernatural signs of His favor.[37] Although she was the
disciple of a great mystic, she emulated Teresa's apostolic convictions more
than her mystical path to self-realization. María's was instead an ecclesial
feminism; it derived from her conviction, based on her own scriptural readings and experience as disciple of a reformer, that women had a legitimate
role in serving the Christian community, and that this role was under attack.
She keenly felt that women belonged to a subordinate group *within the church*
and that they suffered wrongs as members of that church. Further modifying
Lerner's framework, we can recognize that María manifests an awareness that
women's *apostolic* subordination is not natural, but societally determined. Let
us consider how she challenges the interpretation of I Corinthians 14:34—
"Let your women keep silent in the churches: for it is not permitted unto
them to speak"—the proof text wielded in some sectors of Counter Reformation Spain not simply to exclude women from preaching but also to restrict their spiritual lives to the most routine forms of religious devotion. At
the beginning of the first recreation, Gracia explains her anxiety over taking
up the pen to write the "mandated autobiography" in the following terms:
"What most daunts me is being a woman, who by the law that custom has
created seems to have been forbidden to write; and with good reason, for it is
women's proper task to spin and sew, since having no learning, they tread
perilously close to error in whatever they might say." Here, María ironically
echoes those voices in the Counter Reformation church that urged women
to abstain all forms of interior devotion and "stick to their distaffs and
rosaries." Although she appears to be intimidated by those who interpreted
Saint Paul's injunction as a total prohibition against women's religious writing, at the same time she undermines the major premise with carefully chosen qualifications. Gracia affirms that the strictures that *seem* to prohibit
women from writing are products of *custom*; it is women's lack of letters (that
is, knowledge of Latin) that exposes them to the *risk* of error. In short, she ex-

---

37. For the mystics as feminist foremothers, see Lerner, *The Creation of Feminist Consciousness*,
chaps. 4 and 5.

poses the Pauline silence imposed on women as custom masquerading as divine law.

It is not difficult to see how Lerner's third stage—the development of a sense of sisterhood—was facilitated by, indeed central to, monastic life. In addition, in María's writings, sisterhood acquires a historical dimension. Like Teresa and other women religious before her, María found authorization for her apostolic desires in the example of the New Testament women.[38] In the following passage, she cautiously wends her way through a semantic mine-field in order to include women within the mandate of propagating the Christian message:

> Our sweet Master acted in favor of women with that kindness He showed them when He did not disdain to hold a long and lofty conversation with the Samaritan woman . . . teaching her and making her the one to divulge His holy word. We also know that He first revealed the most high mystery of His Resurrection to Mary Magdalene and the other Marys and commanded them to announce it to their brothers. So there is no reason for us to be excluded from speaking and communicating with God, nor should we be kept from telling of His greatness or from wanting to know of the teachings; and in this lies what should serve as a bridle to curb bold women. I say we should speak and know of the teachings, not that we should teach. I believe the Lord Himself showed Mary Magdalene this point when, after having revealed to her a mystery so high and so necessary to our faith, and having commanded her to be the messenger of this good news to the grieving apostles, He did not allow her to come to Him, saying, "Touch me not."[39]

Here, María reminds her readers not only that Christ spoke at length with women, but that they were in fact among the first messengers of his word. María thus offers a remarkable counterproof text to I Corinthians 14:34, "Let your women keep silent in the churches." If in the passage cited earlier she had suggested that the Pauline injunction to silence had been misconstrued and sanctioned by custom rather than divine law, here she alludes to John 20:17:

38. On the significance of the Samaritan woman and Mary Magdalene in the development of Teresa's Christian feminism, see Carole Slade, "Teresa's Feminist Figural Readings of Scripture," chap. 2 of *Teresa of Avila, Author of a Heroic Life* (Berkeley: University of California Press, 1995), 39–64; and Alison Weber, "The Fortunes of Ecstasy: Teresa of Avila and the Carmelite Reform," *Harvard Divinity Bulletin* 28, no. 4 (1999): 11–15. As Lerner notes, women have, over the centuries, independently rediscovered and reinterpreted these New Testament women as authorizing figures. See chap. 7 of *The Creation of Feminist Consciousness*, "One Thousand Years of Feminist Bible Criticism," especially 145–46.

39. "Eighth Recreation, 101–2."

"Touch me not; for I am not yet ascended to my Father: but go to my brethren, and say unto them, I ascend unto my Father, and your Father; and to my God, and your God." María accepts Christ's warning to Mary Magdalene, "touch me not," as defining the limits of women's apostolic authority. María stops short of claiming an equal exegetical role for women: speculative theology ("scrutinizing mysteries") is out of bounds. Nonetheless, between these two proof texts— *taceant mulieres* and *noli me tangere*—María negotiates the space for women to *denunciar* (announce), that is, to be the messengers of the Good News.

The "goals and strategies" for change indicated in Lerner's fourth stage of feminist consciousness must be evaluated, once again, from within an ecclesial framework. María's insistence that women be counted among Christ's disciples represents an appeal for greater apostolic authority for women, as well as a new model for female sanctity, one that moved beyond (without repudiating) the late medieval model that confined women, as petitioners for souls in purgatory, to an "apostolate for the dead." At the same time, María participated in an experiment that sought to change the nature of women's religious leadership. As a prioress of the Discalced reform, her authority derived not from the power to advance dynastic interests or control significant resources, but from her influence over nuns, friars, laymen, and laywomen who sought her spiritual counsel.[40] As we have seen, this vision of women's authority radiating from a physically enclosed but spiritually permeable convent was rejected by those who controlled the reform after Teresa's death. It would be years before the church was willing to accommodate monastic women's desire for an active apostolate in the world.[41]

Given the limited scope of her sense of solidarity, her accommodation to the patriarchal authority of the church, and the demise of the nuns' rebellion, we could read María's story as the history of a failed feminist consciousness. Alternatively, and more instructively I believe, we can listen to her as an "other voice" of the early modern period, as a woman who attempted to negotiate the terms of women's participation within an institution that inspired and constrained her.

40. Belchior records that "great crowds" of the nobility sought María's advice in the locutory and cites this as one of the reasons why she was expelled from Lisbon.

41. On the Counter Reformation controversy over an active apostolate for women, see Ruth Liebowitz, "Virgins in the Service of Christ," in *Women of Spirit: Female Leadership in the Jewish and Christian Traditions,* ed. Rosemary Ruether and Eleanor McLaughlin (New York: Simon and Schuster, 1979), 132–52. For a description of the more traditional monastic model, according to which monastic women's authority derived from their role in fortifying dynastic networks, see Angela Muñoz Fernández, *Acciones e intenciones de mujeres: Vida religiosa de las madrileñas (ss. XV–XVI)* (Madrid: Editorial Horas, 1995); and for a French example, Joanne Baker, "Female Monasticism and Family Strategy: The Guises and Saint Pierre de Reims," *Sixteenth Century Journal* 28 (1997): 1091–1108.

A NOTE
ON THE TRANSLATION

Any literary translation of even a moderately complex text interprets a world and a culture for readers who are located in another linguistic, geographical, social, or historical context. The translator undertakes an especially active interpretive role when assumptions, customs, and styles of living and of making literature vary widely between the worlds of author and reader. María de San José Salazar inhabited a historical period and a religious milieu about which many informed twenty-first-century readers of the English-speaking world may "know" a great deal that is untrue or incomplete. Her writings display a degree of learning and wit at odds with our period's notions about women, especially nuns, in that early modern period. Another element that may surprise us is the tempered yet trenchant humor with which she describes problematic male clerics. At the same time, she expresses a strong sense of fruitful collaboration with certain friars, bishops and nuns in positions both of power over and subordination to her. Her intellectual as well as devotional inquiry into religious matters, and the scope she found within the cloister for a vital and demanding activist commitment, diverge from generally held notions about women of the period, especially in Spain and its colonies.

The translation that follows attempts above all to make readable the purposes and priorities of a book that declares at the outset its many intended functions. This cross-genred text means to be used for entertainment, for ed-

Significant work for this translation was made possible by a research grant from the Center for the Study of Women in Society at the University of Oregon in spring 1999. Mary E. Giles gave keen assistance with the terminology and spirit of early modern Carmelite prayer and mysticism. The Sisters of Carmel of Maria Regina, Eugene, Oregon, graciously provided citations from their library on specific points in Carmelite history. I also thank Dianne Dugaw and Kathleen A. Myers for their comments and encouragement.

ification, and for inspiration. Perhaps chiefly, *Book for the Hour of Recreation* aims to impart information about the exemplary life of María's mentor, Saint Teresa of Avila; to justify and defend the work of Teresa's reform movement; and to offer detailed guidance in the Teresian method of mental prayer. While readers today will approach María's text with different preparation and expectations than those of the Discalced Carmelite nuns of the sixteenth century, we hope the book remains user friendly by contextualizing and clarifying its explicit themes, its underlying preoccupations, and its manners of expression.

The chief balance our translation attempts lies between clarity of content and fidelity to style. Any text is permeated by its cultural context in ways that come into sharp focus at the moment of translation. María Salazar's text is, naturally, steeped in the religious culture of the convent generally, and specifically in the hotly contested issues at stake in the Discalced Carmelite reform just after Teresa's death. María meant *Book for the Hour of Recreation* to be accessible to other members of her Carmelite world, but even in her time outsiders to the new and embattled Discalced order, however literate or sympathetic, would find a great many in-jokes and oblique references. While not a cryptically encoded work, the book does assume a familiarity with general and specific matters, from the goals of contemplative life to the identities of Carmelite figures, that may in part have been a means to keep the text relevant to and approachable by only its intended audience. Needless to say, many such specific allusions elude almost any reader today. In this sense, the introductory study and the annotations given here form an integral part of the translation, that is, the contextualized "carrying over" of María's words. At times, however, we embed in the translated text itself allusions that can be concisely conveyed. For example, the character Gracia speaks of her joy on leaving "the world" for the convent in terms that allude to the Hebrew exodus from slavery. The original says only "The Lord took me out of Egypt" [el Señor me sacó de Egipto];[1] we amplify this, for readers less immediately familiar with María's references, as "the Lord took me out of bondage in Egypt."

María shows in this and other works that she was an elegant stylist in the ornate articulations of her time. An Englishing that adheres too closely to stylistic and structural qualities of sixteenth-century Castilian prose will fail to be true to the book's everyday and heuristic function. We have hoped to give a translation that richly and fairly emphasizes distinctive matters of dic-

---

1. "Libro de recreaciones," in *Escritos espirituales*, ed. Simeón de la Sagrada Familia (Rome: Postulación General O.C.D., 1979), 69 (hereafter *Escritos espirituales*).

tion (e.g., colorfully colloquial or archaic locutions) and of style (e.g., syntactic structures that are highly complex) without slighting the functions of the text. This means rendering stylistic as well as linguistic conventions of her early modern period and its Spanish language into those of our milieu. Overall, when considered within the terms common to literary practices of her day, María's style is readable and consistently lively. Yet her long sentences and complicated syntactical structures, which were typical then, would seem tedious and misleadingly idiosyncratic if replicated now. At the same time, we hope to keep some flavor of the original by the occasional use of structures and word choices that stretch what is current in American English written style. Some examples follow.

It is María's learned yet graphic and often colloquial style that we attempt to convey in bringing *Book for the Hour of Recreation* to English readers. María was well read not only in sacred but in secular literature. She demonstrates familiarity with and often playful enjoyment of such generic conventions of the period as the dialogic form, and she gives shape and emphasis to her sentences with rhetorical devices practiced by orators and authors. As an emphatic flourish, for instance, she uses polyptoton, the repetition of a word having the same root but different endings:

> For this reason, as [the nuns'] simple and unshowy words in fact show that they do know Scripture, I tried showing that mute tongues beget clear understanding such as all the Sisters possess, as they are greatly instructed in the things of God.[2]

The example, from María's introduction, employs her word play with forms of "show" ("unshowy"/"show"/"showing") [*mostrar*, in the original as *sin muestra/ se muestra/mostrar*]. "Show" [*mostrar*] is not a neutral verb in this text, and cultural context, where women's ability to know and to demonstrate what they know is deeply contested. María's redundancy draws our attention to the verb; we seek to replicate her emphasis in translation. Another feature of María's writing visible in this passage is her use of, and crafted variations on, popular *refranes* or proverbial expressions. The phrase "mute tongues beget clear understanding" [lenguas mudas engendran entendimientos claros] may be an invented "saying," but when it crops up in the dialogue between nuns whose conversation constitutes María's book, it has the generalizing, authoritative ring of proverbial speech (as in "Still waters run deep"; "A word to the wise is sufficient"). The synecdoche by which "mute tongues *beget* [lenguas

2. Por esta razón, viendo que se muestra en sus palabras simples y sin muestras que saben de la Escritura, quise con esto mostrar que las lenguas mudas engendran entendimientos claros, como todas las tienen, y tan enseñadas a las cosas de Dios (*Escritos espirituales*, 48).

... engendran] understanding" serves to emphasize the difference between the *act* of speech (frequently denied women, as is at issue in this book) and the *capacity* for intelligent speech. This seemingly commonplace, popular saying is in fact a pointed utterance chosen from the repertoire of Spanish oral tradition and then crafted by María in advocacy for the intelligence and capacities of silenced women. As in this instance, our translation seeks to preserve María's resonant uses of different registers, from colloquial to highly literary, as well as her playful and conceptually important uses of figurative language.

At times, María's writing varies from her usual complex, articulate style to become unwieldy in syntactical structure. Actual fragmentary or outright ungrammatical sentences are mentioned in the notes (and may result from a copyist's lapses). Otherwise, we attempt to replicate rather than to smooth over moments of awkward structure. Another example, following directly from the passage quoted above, shows the occurrence of anacoluthon, in which a sentence makes an abrupt internal shift to a second grammatical construction different from the first:

> With good reason are many learned men amazed at the wealth of these treasures, which I wanted to report not so that others might think I am one of the nuns who know something; rather, although I have achieved little, being the dullest and most ignorant of all, I confess that whatever I do know, I learned from these nuns.[3]

While at times indicative of an inattentive writer or speaker, or a faulty manuscript copyist, anacoluthon is at others a device consciously used for rhetorical effect, as we consider to be the case here. In this passage and elsewhere we see María carrying out the difficult, highly gendered feat of showing (to mistrustful male clerics) while sharing (with nuns as vulnerably positioned as she) what she knows, without claiming "unwomanly" authority for speaking, let alone teaching. The awkward structure here shifts the subject grammatically from the third-person "many learned men" [muchos doctos], to first person, to the neutral "others might think" [entienda], and again to first person. This approach perhaps deliberately draws attention to the "treasures" admired by "learned men," while downplaying syntactically as well as explicitly the author's own "report" (that is, the book that follows) and the nature and authenticity of "whatever [she does] know." We have opted to leave

3. Y con razón muchos doctos se admiran de la riqueza de estos tesoros, de los cuales quise hacer reseña, no porque entienda ser yo de las que algo saben, mas, aunque como la más ruda e ignorante he alcanzado poco, mas confieso que tal cual es lo aprendí de ellas (*Escritos espirituales*, 48)

some such moments of opacity. They indicate the challenge María faced and strategies she formed in writing under order of obedience. Like other writing nuns, she was commanded, paradoxically, to maintain a womanly silence and yet to speak; spiritually, she sought to maintain a fitting humility, and yet to make proud claim to her personal and empowering knowledge of and friendship with a saint.

An artful indirectness sometimes characterizes María's statements about delicate subjects. A passage from the second recreation has the autobiographical character Gracia speak of the discomfort she felt while being persecuted by her confessor, her prelate, numerous superiors from her own and other Carmelite communities, and finally nuns that she herself had trained as novices—all this while under threat of investigation by the Inquisition:

> For see here, there was a great deal to regret when they considered me lacking in faith and brought proceedings and witnesses before that very severe tribunal—as just and holy as it is—along with a thousand other things you all know about already, in which the Lord gave me the courage and happiness that I showed in outer ways, with no pretense at all. But given that I did not regret that, does it not seem to you, Sister, that it would be a very great affliction to see the entire Order and my Father Eliseus suffering, and the more so because it was on my account?[4]

The structure of Gracia's utterance deflects her interlocutors' attention away from her own difficulties toward the sufferings of "the entire Order and my Father Eliseus." First and last, however, she intimates strongly the causes she herself had for feeling "affliction," chief among which is (with lovely circularity) her own responsibility for the order's and Eliseus's sufferings. While we have tried to make the translation "functionally" clear in the ways described earlier, we hope that it captures significant moments of deliberate indirection, rather than smoothing or clarifying these.

A note on biblical references: Passages from the Bible are cited from the Old and New Testament of the Douay-Rheims version, which were translated into English in 1609 and 1582, respectively, from the Latin Vulgate that was known to María. We have used this version because it offers an English-

---

4. Pues de sentir mucho era tenerme por falta en la fe, y presentar procesos y testigos en tribunal tan riguroso, aunque justísimo y santísimo, con otras mil cosas que todas sabéis, en las cuales me daba el Señor el ánimo y alegría que en lo de fuera mostraba, sin fingir nada. Pero ya que esto no sintiese, ¿no te parece, hermana, que era harta aflicción ver padecer a toda la Religión y a mi Padre Eliseo, y más por mi causa? (*Escritos espirituales*, 79).

language rendering, contemporary to María, of the Latin she read and heard in the divine offices and other observations and celebrations of her convent life. Certain proper names, however, are given in the form that would be familiar to readers of other biblical translations, where the Douay form might make these unrecognizable. This is especially the case with places (e.g., Mount Lebanon for Mount Libanus). Where the Douay form varies only slightly from the more familiar, we leave it (Isaias for Isaiah).

BOOK FOR THE
HOUR OF RECREATION

INTRODUCTION

I have wished, my Sisters, that all persons might know of this angelic Life, I would not be so bold as to write these dialogues, but [I have done so][1] to satisfy in some measure the great desire that is mine, and because I believe my writing may work to some good effect. For indeed, even if my knowledge and ability were greater, it would be difficult to make known, to those who have not enjoyed them, the favors of heaven that are found in these divine gardens where the celestial Bridegroom takes His recreation.

I believe I must explain two things. First: why, given my intention of telling the Life of our holy Mother and the greatness of Carmel, should this subject be mixed in with such a variety of matters? For many things that I include here seem irrelevant and serve only to make the work long winded, such as the quarrels between the nuns and other extraneous conversations that are mixed in beside the point. In this regard I declare that my chief intent is to portray the nuns' friendly conversation and way of life—their humility and simplicity and mortification, their continual practices of prayer, their contempt for fine dress and their selflessness, along with their happy and holy diversions. It did not seem to me that this could be indicated by words alone, however earnestly I might speak them, but rather that I would have to create some sort of living representation, though at the same time as if it were all painted.

The second is a point I must not only explain but for which I must apologize, as I have done at the end, because of the offense I commit against the humble way these Daughters of the Most Blessed Virgin speak among themselves, for I have dared to bring in a great many passages from Holy Scrip-

---

1. This addition and other bracketed words and phrases are, unless otherwise indicated, by the editor of María Salazar's works, Simeón de la Sagrada Familia.

ture. This practice is quite foreign to my Sisters and was indeed censured by our holy Mother [Teresa], as you shall see further on. For this reason, as their simple and unshowy words in fact show that they do know Scripture, I tried showing that mute tongues beget clear understanding[2] such as all the Sisters possess, as they are greatly instructed in the things of God. With good reason are many learned men amazed at the wealth of these treasures, which I wanted to report not so that others might think I am one of the nuns who know something; rather, although I have achieved little, being the dullest and most ignorant of all, I confess that whatever I do know, I learned from these nuns.

Dearest Sisters, it now lies with you to make mighty efforts to follow our Captain, eschewing any womanish spirit. You must give a thousand lives so that not one jot may be lost of what was renewed by dint of such labor. In times like these there is great need for us all to renew both interior and exterior penance and austerity, so as to oppose two very wicked heretics.[3] Then be grateful to that sovereign Lord, for He chose you so that it might be said, as it was in the time of the valiant Deborah: "The Lord chose new wars."[4] May His Majesty, who brought you to this apostolic life, give you His divine grace and remove from you those nuns who did not come to religion with this true spirit. Amen.

This work has five parts.

1   The first fulfills an order of obedience that obligates me to tell some things about my life; this may be endured, as it goes under an assumed name.

2   The second tells how ancient and great is the Carmelite Order.

3   The third relates the life and death of our holy Mother Teresa of Jesus, under the name of Angela.

4   The fourth tells of the monasteries she founded, and where, and the qualities that each one possesses.

5   The last part is a brief summation of the effects created by the love of God in those souls where it is found, together with some octaves in thanksgiving for their principal benefits—creation, redemption, preservation—which, as this is titled *Book for the Hour of Recreation*, does not stray from its purpose.

---

2. Mute tongues beget clear understanding [lenguas mudas engendran entendimientos claros]: María may be playing on a *refrán* or proverbial expression here.

3. Two very wicked heretics: Luther and Calvin.

4. Judges 5:8; see n. 14, below.

FIRST RECREATION

In the year of Our Lord fifteen hundred and eighty-three, on the feast of our seraphic Father Saint Francis, when one year to the day had passed since the flower of Carmel withered away,[5] I invoked both weeping and mourning, as the Order was thus left bereft of its gentle Mother, Teresa of Jesus, of whom two of her Daughters were speaking as they stood in the shade of a lovely poplar grove, calling her by the name of Angela. And although it was not fine weather for seeking the fresh green leaves and fields, which in spring can be so delightful, yet the talk between them was aided by solitude and the sound of the wind that moved all things to feel their sorrow; with tears in their eyes, they recalled death's thievery in leaving them without their Mother, their shepherdess, and their consolation. And having wept awhile, with their eyes cast down to earth, they lifted them at last to heaven and thus tempered their grief, considering that there, safe and secure, was their treasure. So, taking pleasure in the pleasure that was hers, they fell silent for some time.

Gracia, for that was the name of the one who appeared the younger, now changing the subject of their talk, said to Justa: "Dearest Sister, many days ago Father Eliseus[6] ordered me to write an account of my life, in which I should tell him about my way of [mental] prayer and the favors that God has thus granted me. I could not venture to tell you why he wants it; but you know his zeal and how he turns everything to advantage, so that from the venom of my vices he draws the honey of doctrine for all his Daughters. But this aside—for it is an offense to such brilliance of mind and virtue to set my dull tongue to speak his praise—I shall tell you why I began this story for you. I am greatly distressed since he ordered me to write, because from the moment I attempted to begin my mind has been so dull that I have been unable to write a word, and all that I have said until now of prayer seems to me a lie and a whim. What most clearly appear before me are my sins, of which I could write at great length; but I have no heart to write of them. It is bad indeed to be so backward that I am ashamed to tell my Prelate what I ought to reveal to him with the best of wills, and not to tell him of my delight in

---

5. Saint Teresa had died on the night of October 4, 1582, the feast of Saint Francis of Assisi.

6. Father Eliseus: Jerónimo Gracián de la Madre de Dios, María's confessor and collaborator during the Lisbon foundation. During the period in which the Discalced Carmelites were under attack by nonreformed members of their order, in her correspondence Teresa often referred to Gracián by the cryptonym Eliseo. Eliseus (alternate spelling Elisha) was a Hebrew prophet of the ninth century, a successor of Elijah, and according to legend one of the founders of the Carmelite order. María follows Teresa's practice in using cryptonyms and also pays homage to Gracián as Teresa's successor.

prayer. Yet I cannot speak of such delight with the same certainty as I can of my sins, knowing I have committed so many; I do not know if this inability be caused by the Devil, or by the fear to which we women are so given. But I console myself that whatever I may say is destined for the hands of one who even a hundred leagues off would understand what it is. I ask you, my Sister, to commend me heartily to God, that I may fulfill this order of obedience."

And Justa, who had listened to her most attentively, then said: "I am greatly surprised, my dear Sister Gracia, to see that you should find distasteful a single thing that you know would please our Father, for besides the fact that he is our Prelate, who must serve as a model of Christ to us, many considerations oblige you to hide from him nothing that is in your heart."

"May God forbid," answered Gracia hastily, "that I should fall into such vice, or hide from him a single thing that is in my soul; because, besides proving me ungrateful to one whom I love so dearly and owe so much, it would only do me harm, for we know how much is gained by speaking clearly with those whom the Lord has set in His place. And believe me when I say that the Devil has never tempted me to such a thing; rather, my very soul seemed to foretell, from the first day I saw him, when he was not yet my Prelate, all the good I would receive from him. Indeed, all the good that I asked of our Lady the Virgin, I asked in the name of Father, and it seemed that what I asked in his name was later granted me; and thus what grieves me now is that I do not know what to say of myself. This is why I have told you, so that you may give me your advice and help me with your prayers."

"What you can do, Sister," said Justa, "as God called you and brought you to the religious life[7] through our heroic and admirable Mother Angela, is to begin with her and tell all the things you saw her do from the time you first knew her; and in speaking of such a sweet Mother, you will forget about yourself, and you will fulfill the order of obedience and will please Father Eliseus even more, for on hearing the name of his Angela, he will lend its grace to whatever you might say gracelessly."

"May Our Lord God reward you, Sister," said Gracia, prostrating herself on the ground, "and may He be blessed, for He so quickly shows us how good it is to humble ourselves and seek advice; and since God has illumined you that you might give me this plan, tell me how I should start, and don't leave me alone but stay and help me. And I will say what I know; give me your

7. The religious life [religión]: The word *religión* is used variously in religious discourse of this period. Among the Discalced Carmelites, it frequently means "the order" or "the Teresian rule." It may also have the sense of "religious life" or "devotion." We have translated it throughout this work as befits the subject under discussion in a particular context.

command so that I may write in accordance with it. For your name is 'Justice,' which gives each thing its due: Glory to God for all things; and to our holy Mother, eternal remembrance for the part she played that I and many other nuns might come to the Order; and to me, shame, for how little I have taken to advantage the very riches of the Indies that are here."

"Begin at once," said Justa, "for it gives me great pleasure to hear about our Angela."

"Oh, Sister Justa! How gladly would I undertake this theme," said Gracia, "because for many days I have been wanting to make a report of some of the things I saw and heard from our good Mother; but it seems to me impossible to carry it out—first because of my dullness, which will not know what to say, and in the second place what most daunts me is being a woman, who by the law that custom has created seems to have been forbidden to write; and with good reason, for it is women's proper task to spin and sew, since having no learning, they tread perilously close to error in whatever they might say."

"I admit," answered Justa, "that it would be a very great error to write about or meddle in Scripture, or in learned things; I mean, for those women who know no more than women, for there have been many who have been equal and even superior in learning to a great many men. But let us leave that aside; what harm can there be if women write of household things? For they also have the duty, as do men, of recording the virtues and good works of their mothers and teachers, concerning things that only those women who tell of them could know, that are perforce hidden from the men; besides which, it may be that such writings, though written in ignorance and without style, will be better suited to the women in days to come, than if they were written by men, because when it comes to writing and speaking of the courage and virtue of women, we usually consider them to be somewhat doubtful, and at times they may do us harm, because it is impossible that the heroic virtues of so many weak women should not cause them embarrassment, as we see, by God's mercy, in these flowering times of renewal."

"You speak truly, Sister," said Gracia, "when you say that it would be an embarrassment, if men were to believe what women write. But do you not see that they have gloried in holding women to be weak, inconstant, imperfect, and indeed useless and unworthy of any noble undertaking! And in this regard, I shall tell you a story that will certainly amuse you. You know, dearest, that when our Mother Angela went to Seville to found a convent, many servants of God came to confess us, among whom one stayed on longer than the others—a very good priest, though given to the disposition of those we have described; and he grew very angry when he saw us crossing ourselves in

[handwritten marginal notes:] ironía— thay're debating intellectual things —a woman is writing this— a dialogue forma literaria protagiosa

Latin[8] as if we were uttering heresies. And quite deliberately he set about reproving us, and told us that women should on no account meddle in all sorts of presumptuous babble and deep waters."

"Without a doubt, that servant of God must have been a bit simple," said Justa, "for he was not aware that it pleases our Holy Church to have us nuns recite the divine office and help with the holy offices and the Sacrifice of the Mass."

"Simple, Sister!" said Gracia. "He didn't act as a simpleton, for he was very far indeed from any such thing; but there are people who are shocked by a puff of wind, and if I were to relate to you all the trials and persecutions we underwent in that foundation, with those sorts of dispositions, I would never finish telling them all.[9] And because we nuns were discussing Our Lord and matters of the faith that every Christian is obliged to know, such as the articles of the faith and so forth, they so frightened the frailer among us that it caused great suffering, making them think that they were heretics. I consider it a great folly to create obstacles where there are none, giving these poor women to think that everything is a heresy; but that is a long story, so let us leave it. It may be that one day the Lord will order it to be written elsewhere, that our Sisters may know how many trials and afflictions our holy Mother was obliged to undergo in order to found the convents, so that they may gather strength to undergo the same thing, feeling envy for the nuns who enjoyed those festive days.

"And returning to what I had begun, I say, Sister, that whatever we might say has little strength and is scarcely to be given credence, just because we are women."

"What does that matter to us?" said Justa. "Those for whom this is written will believe it; and how much more so, for whatever it may say of our great Angela! The Lord has shown Himself to work such wonders through her life and death that all the world knows of it. And so begin, Sister, and remember that you are telling it to the Sisters in their recreations; and if you should make any foolish remarks, which I cannot say you won't, you know

---

8. He saw us crossing ourselves in Latin [de vernos persignar en latín]: The Spanish verb *persignar* comes from the Latin *per signum crucis*, "by the sign of the cross": that is, the nuns repeat the Latin phrase while making the sign of the cross. In Counter-Reformation Spain, women were discouraged (though not prohibited) from studying Latin lest they read heretical works or engage in theological discourse. This confessor's reaction is, nevertheless, extreme, for as Justa goes on to note, the nuns were expected to recite the divine office in Latin.

9. If I were to relate . . . I would never finish telling them all: As Gracia will later recount, in 1575 the nuns of the Seville convent were accused of being *alumbradas*, or Illuminist heretics. The identity of the confessor is unclear.

how receptive they are at such times, and willing to praise, so you may have no fear that the Sisters would not forgive you a single one of them."

"May it please God, dearest Sister," said Gracia, "that it might serve as recreation to these angels, because there is nothing I enjoy more than to see them happy with one another, and my soul is gladdened, for there one sees the love and sisterhood and great contentment they possess, as well as the mortification[10] of each one, not showing any sort of hurt, though their foolishness might be laughed at; for that was the aim of our Mother Angela in desiring that, after the midday meal and after collation,[11] they should gather together with their needlework to take pleasure in the Lord [with many others],[12] for it is well known that one must needs relieve the spirit from fasting, prayer, and continual silence."

"It is very important," said Justa, "that all of this proceed with the same perfection that our Mother intended. And now tell me of her."

"Do not think," answered Gracia, "that because I linger on certain topics, I am deliberately leaving the matter at hand, for <u>everything we know that is good or useful is due to her</u>. The fruit redounds to the praise of the tree that produced it, and so anything I may say of the virtues and graces of the Sisters must be understood to have been achieved through her clear intellect and heroic virtue. But tell, for mercy's sake: how can you ask me to tell of the greatness of that admirable woman, knowing as you do my dull-wittedness?"

"To be sure, Sister," said Justa, "I do not think Our Lord holds the story of His servant in such low account that He would submit it to the hands of such a wretched chronicler.[13] Indeed, one would need more wit than yours or mine to tell of such feats as those which God, by means of this brave woman, has wrought in our own time. For not only has she roused weak women to

10. "Mortification" is used here in the sense of a process of purification (purging of material desires) through which the individual seeks spiritual perfection.

11. Collation: The *comida* is the main midday meal, first of the day, taken after Communion. The collation [*colación*] is the light refreshment between the main meal and supper (see "Constitutions," in *The Collected Works of St. Teresa of Avila,* trans. Kieran Kavanaugh and Otilio Rodríguez, 3 vols. [Washington, D.C.: ICS Publications, 1985], chap. 6, no. 8).

12. With many others [con otros muchos]: The meaning of this phrase in the original is not clear; the switch to the masculine plural *otros* is puzzling. María may have wished to indicate that the Discalced friars also permitted themselves hours of recreation.

13. Such a wretched chronicler [tan ruin cronista]: Among the Carmelites, *ruin* (translated here as "wretched") is a frequent expression of humility with a broad semantic range, from "vile," "base," or "despicable" to "insignificant" and "humble." Carol Slade notes Teresa's use of *ruin* at the opening of her *Book of Her Life* as a "weak epithet . . . which refers generally to the fallen condition of humanity" (*St. Teresa of Avila: Author of a Heroic Life* [Berkeley: University of California Press, 1995], xi).

take up Christ's cross, but she has shamed the men, and dragged them out to the field of battle; and when they had turned their backs on discipline and primitive virtue, made them follow the banner of their woman Captain, so that they might face their enemies who had risen to become so lordly. She began like another Deborah[14] to inspire the army of God, promising victory to their side and never staying behind in the tent, but exposing herself to the greatest dangers and affronts. Nor did she rest in times of peace, but, with the greatest hardships and the sweat of her brow, went about planting and transplanting this holy garden of Carmel that was so abandoned and destroyed and had lost its rightful beauty—that beauty which God placed in her own soul and body, showing full well the purpose for which He had raised her, endowing her with so many gifts and graces and such beauty, with a perfect countenance, as further on you will have to say, though in everything you will fall short. For how could one describe how witty and tactful she was, and how loving and gentle in manner; how prudent and wise, with the caution and simplicity of a dove; how describe her faith and hope and spirit of prophecy, the grace given her of bringing souls to God, her marvelous gift of counsel?—for, indeed, many of the nobles of Spain took her advice in the gravest matters. And thus, Sister, things like these are not for such as you or me—I mean, for you alone to tell. Well then, from among all these, see that you create some girlish trifle[15] to console our Sisters, until such time as someone who knows better how to do it shall write it for us. And you must say what you heard and saw her do, for you were with her in the founding of some of the convents, although what you say may not seem like much to you; for it seems to me that you have scarcely yet begun."

On hearing this, Gracia started to prostrate herself upon the ground, knowing that Justa spoke the truth; the latter stopped her, and said:

"Begin now, Sister, for indeed, it is high time."

"I told you at the very start," said Gracia, "that you must help me, and as you command me to write it for the recreations, tell me what form it should take, or what name we should give it."

"Let us call Sister Josefa and Sister Dorotea," answered Justa, "for in matters concerning our recreations their judgment is very sound."

With this Gracia arose and went to call them, and when, with permis-

---

14. Judges 4–5. Deborah is a revered judge and a mighty warrior.

15. Girlish trifle [alguna niñería]: an excellent example of the "rhetoric of feminity" that is also found in Teresa's writing. María minimizes the significance of her "feminine" chronicle in order to forestall accusations of presumption.

sion, they had come, Justa said to them: *"Deo gratias,*[16] Sisters—was it any trouble to you that they should summon you from the hermitages?"[17]

Dorotea straightway said: "Well then, dearest Sister, and is that the way among the Discalced nuns, to be troubled by whatever obedience commands? No indeed, nor do I think Sister Josefa came unwillingly."

And Josefa then said, "For my part, I can say that I was well pleased, because I wanted to ask permission to come and hear something about Our Lord, but I remembered that I still had to do one of the mortifications that I have been commanded to perform each day, and so I put aside my wish; and the Lord granted that I should be ordered to come. May His name be praised! For nothing goes unrewarded that is done in His name."

"Come then, Sisters!" said Gracia. "Let us fulfill our obedience and see what name should be given to what our Sister Justa here is making me write."

"We must see it first," said Josefa, "to give our opinion."

"A fine idea," said Gracia, "but I am sure that whatever name might be bestowed on it by Your Charity[18] will not promote vainglory among us."

"You speak truly, Sister," replied Josefa, "for from what little I have heard, it is beginning to resemble a real hodgepodge,[19] which is made up of many things."

"Salad might be a truer name," said Dorotea, "or those eggs they give us in the refectory, with a lot of bread crumbs, which the Cellaress tells us is a whole egg, and I will wager cannot be more than one-fourth for each nun."

Gracia and Josefa, hearing this, prostrated themselves on the ground, and Justa asked, "Why do you prostrate yourselves, Sisters?"

One of them answered, "Because our Sister speaks of food, which is against the Constitutions."

Dorotea replied, "I did not say it was well or poorly cooked, which is what the Constitutions forbid. But it is permissible to observe that there is little of it,[20] especially when the stomach is faint with hunger, as it is even

16. *Deo gratias:* "Thanks be to God." The Latin phrase was a form of greeting in the convent.

17. Hermitages: huts in the garden where the nuns could withdraw in solitude to engage in prayer.

18. Your Charity: The author here plays on *vuestra caridad* (literally, "your charity") as a form of address used by nuns (much like "Your Reverence") and as the virtue of selflessness.

19. Hodgepodge: This is a sixteenth-century English term for *olla podrida*, literally, "rotten [that is, slowly simmered] pot"; a meat and vegetable stew.

20. But it is . . . little of it: Actually, Dorotea's remark is incorrect. The constitutions state, "Let no Sister comment on whether the food given to eat is much or little, well or poorly seasoned" ("Constitutions," in *The Collected Works of St. Teresa of Avila,* 3:22).

permissible to keep hold of the plate when Sister Inocencia, because she is nearsighted, thinks that it is all finished and snatches it away."

Delighting in Dorotea's words and remembering those critical moments in which the same thing had happened to each of them, they all decided, with one opinion, that the book should be called *For the Hour of Recreation;* for that could not stray from its subject, mixed as it was with diverse things related to the nuns' pastimes, all of which, composed of many different matters, have as a common goal the praise of God.

With this, Josefa, who was the one who most extolled this name and the story, said to Gracia: "Begin, Sister, and I will go to fetch the hat, for I suspect that you will certainly need it."

"The Lord be praised!" said Gracia. "For now I see the works of my own hand shown to good effect, because they give some recreation to my Sisters! But as we are in a hurry and there will not be time to applaud each little foolishness with formal ceremony, by putting the hat on me,[21] do Sister bring the book of chronicles where such things are usually written, and set down whatever I may say."

At once Josefa, with great promptness, said: "Of such work Your Charity deprives us, for it will write these things with its own hand."

Justa, who thought Josefa's witty response quite amusing, after having solemnly set it down with the others, ordered Gracia to begin; and the other Sisters left, as the bell for prayers had rung.

SECOND RECREATION

In which, as Justa and Gracia continue, the latter recounts what she saw
of Mother Angela and how long she has known her

Gracia, raising her eyes to heaven, began by asking the Lord to move her tongue, and said: "You must know, dearest Sister, that I have known Mother

---

21. The ceremony of the hat (*sombrero*) may be a parody of academic ritual; it does not seem to recall Teresian anecdotes, and we have found no other direct reference. The nuns did wear wide-brimmed straw hats when working in the convent gardens and, presumably, during periods of recreation outdoors. The following indicate possible allusions here (although we tend to suspect a more straightforward joke, known to the nuns but obscure to us): (1) It was customary to show respect for such documents as papal bulls, ecclesiastical briefs, and royal edicts by placing them on one's head; hence, the expression "to place (something) on one's head" came to signify holding it in great esteem (*Diccionario de la Real Academia Española*). (2) *Sombrero* was a term given to the covering or "roof" placed above the pulpit in period churches to direct the sound of the priest's voice (also known as a *torna grito* or "shout deflector"; *Diccionario de Autoridades*). It is possible that Josefa is teasing Gracia, implying that she is "climbing into a pulpit" and will need a *torna grito* or *sombrero* to magnify her voice.

Angela for twenty years and more, since before she founded the first convent
of Discalced nuns, when she was a nun in the Convent of the Incarnation,
where she was widely held to be saintly. And a certain lady,[22] the daughter of
a grandee of this kingdom, upon hearing of her, asked that Angela be
brought for her consolation. For this lady was recently widowed and sore afflicted and therefore everyone sought to bring her all the godly people there
were, as she was a most Christian woman and only this could give her any
comfort; and so they brought before her the priest Fray Pedro de Alcántara,
whom our holy Mother remembers in her books. And so too the saint[23] went
to her, through obedience to her superiors, which could still be done in those
days, as this was before the holy Council of Trent was published.[24] Indeed,
this was done, as I later understood, by God's own commandment, in order to
finish arranging the revenues for her first convent, which was founded not
long after. I was then thirteen or fourteen years old; she was in the house, on
that occasion, about six months or so.

"Now, Sister, I wish I had another tongue than my own to tell of the
transformation wrought in us all by her holy conversation and her practice of
prayer and mortification. The entire household began to confess with the
Society of Jesus, for until then, there was no regular practice of sacraments
and almsgiving. And so that we may fulfill what holy obedience demands
(though I confess my fault in saying that I do this with great reluctance, because it seems to me a case of mixing shadows with the light), I shall speak of
my own life, which is all darkness where it concerns myself."

"It matters little," said Justa, "that you speak of yourself, for though you
have been most ungrateful and haughty and slothful, your wicked life will
not dim the light God shone in His holy one. Rather, it is well to show such
a torch upon your own steps, so that you may the better see what you have

22. A certain lady: Doña Luisa de la Cerda, in whose palace in Toledo, Spain, María Salazar
lived from girlhood.

23. Our holy Mother . . . the saint [nuestra santa Madre . . . la santa]: In early modern Spanish,
as in other romance languages, *santo/a* as a noun or adjective (a derivate from the Latin *sanctus*)
referred both to deceased persons officially canonized by the Catholic Church and to those esteemed as holy. María frequently refers to Teresa as *la santa* or *la santa Madre*, although Teresa was
not canonized at the time that María was composing her text (she was beatified in 1614 and canonized in 1624). Given the Discalced community's expectation that Teresa would be canonized,
we have opted to render the noun as "the saint," while we give the adjective as "holy," as in "our
holy Mother."

24. This was . . . Trent was published: In December 1563 the Council of Trent issued a decree
requiring the enclosure of nuns. However, this ruling was not enforced in Spain until 1566.
Teresa resided in Doña Luisa's palace in the spring of 1562. María evidently felt it important to
emphasize that Teresa's absence from her convent was legitimate.

been and how you have neither resembled nor kept to the measure of such holy precepts."

"Oh, Sister, if you only knew," said Gracia, "how true the words you speak are, and how much I have resisted God, and what great good I have lost by my fault! And I shall not deny that whatever good I have gained has been through our angelic Mother, because at the time of which I spoke, the Lord called me with special favors and love to solitude and exercises in prayer, in which His Majesty conveyed to me certain feelings while in prayer and particular things that I did not then understand. I made a general confession, and I began as much as possible to change my devotional practices, as much as I could, given the life that is usually lived at court, but in such a way that no one could understand my aims; and not even in my thoughts did I hide this out of humility, but because I thought myself fickle, and I wanted to leave the door open—I don't know to what, except to the Devil so that he could come in and tempt me, as indeed he did many times, taking me away from virtuous exercises and from many hours of prayer to many vanities, scandalizing those around me and thus giving me occasion to offend God. That loving Lord Who poured out His blood for our health soon remedied this, because, whenever I would most fervently give myself over to occasions of sin, He would take away my health. This would happen to me every time I drew away from Him, which was frequently; and by means of this remedy I soon returned to the hands of the merciful Shepherd, who then dealt with my frailty by carrying me with so many caresses that at times I went about as if outside my senses. All the joys of this world seemed but rubbish to me in comparison to a bit of solitude, so that I defied all delights and abhorred all that I formerly loved, such as music, conversation, and finery. I went on in this way until the triumph of that mighty arm, which was fighting for me against myself, bore me to the paradise of delights, to the house of God and gateway to heaven.

"And to go back to our Mother and to the great good she worked for each and all in that house, where she was held in great esteem[25]—thus, eager to see something of what we understood God would do with her, we watched her a few times from behind the door of her cell, and we saw her seized by ecstasy, and with my own eyes I saw her several times, and how she would leave the cell with a great deal of dissembling. For you know full well, Sister, how circumspect she was at all times and with what prudence she hid the magnificent things the Lord imparted to her. And at that time we women, who had

---

25. And to go back . . . in great esteem: This phrase is grammatically incomplete in the manuscript copy.

heard so much about her great humility, all understood that she disguised her spirit with a most excellent grace and discretion, as she had a particular gift for such dissembling. And thus it was necessary, so that people might understand how God was working in her and so that His Majesty should mortify her, to seize her up in rapture in public, as I witnessed twice in that same house, although that was after she founded the convents of Avila and Medina del Campo, upon her return to found the one in Malagón.[26]

"At that time the Lord called me to the religious life, as I was seeing and speaking with our Mother and her companions, who would move the very stones with their admirable lives and conversation. And what made me follow them was the gentleness and prudence of our good Mother. In truth I believe that if those whose work it is to bring souls to God were to use the same schemes and skill that were used by this saint, many more women would come to religious life than are coming now; for, since our nature is inclined to seek gladness and to flee travail, then to depict virtue and service to God as harsh and difficult frightens away those frail men and women who have not tasted how sweet it is to suffer for Christ."

"It seems to me, Sister Gracia," said Justa, "that you are meddling in what has not been asked of you, nor is it yours to do."

"In what?" said Gracia.

"In writing doctrine," Justa replied to this, "and teaching others how they should bring souls to God. Leave that to them, for if it is their office and God has given it to them, He will teach them what they must do; do not think that all must go by your road."

"May God forbid," Gracia replied to this, "that I should speak thus of the Lord's ministers or of those whom the Church, our Mother, has assigned to teach us, for whom I feel and shall always feel great reverence. When I hear the word of God from whoever may be in the pulpit, or when anyone speaks to me in the confessional, through God's grace I am filled with love, which I feel in my soul with great reverence, and I consider it a favor that God has granted me and indeed one of the favors I value most highly. And so, leaving aside those men whose office it is to teach, I speak of you, and me, and all the rest of us whose obligation it is to bring souls to God by our good example and who pride ourselves on being of Christ's own flock and of those who communicate most closely with Him: we should not go about all scowling and sad, lest we misrepresent our conversation with God to those who have not experienced it, giving them to understand that the practice of prayer, silence, and spiritual exercises is a melancholy and desperate thing. For, as is

---

26. To found the one in Malagón: At the end of March 1568.

the way in this world, nothing more will be needed to make them flee from God than our telling them they must go through life being sad. And I believe this is not a bad way, for as you know, our Life invites us, 'O taste, and see that the Lord is sweet.'[27] I tell you, Sister, that the greatest impulses I have felt in this life have been to go through the streets to undeceive those who think it is a hardship to serve God. And believe me that a great many are ignorant in this, for there are many who praise the virtues to the skies, as they certainly deserve, but in such a way that they make it seem impossible for weaker souls to achieve them, as if truly there were no weak soul who might reach virtue with the help of divine grace. But because, as you said, it is not my place to write doctrine, I shall leave this matter to return to our purpose.[28]

"I already told how, on her way to found the monastery in Malagón, our Mother returned to the house of that lady where I had been raised, and at that time when I was twenty years old the Lord called me to follow the life of those holy women, whose company and conversation I enjoyed whenever I could, although no sooner had I discovered my desires than the Holy Spirit who gave them to me must have revealed them to His servant Angela. Because she spoke to all the other women as was her custom, guiding them so that they could live a worldly life without offending God, and instructing them that if their parents ordered them to dance and adorn themselves, they should do so with the intention of obeying and being perfect according to their stations. I was the only one she rebuked every time she saw me because I went about dressed in finery. And she told me that the exercises I was doing were not fitting for a nun, which astonished me as I had not told her or a single soul what I wanted to be, because the Devil must have tied my tongue, and the Lord meant to untie it by means of His servant, as He did.

"And at last I spoke to her of my vocation, encouraged by my knowledge that it was in the Constitutions of those nuns to have mental prayer, of which I had already grown very fond without knowing what it was. In addition, I felt such strength to vanquish my inclinations when I was in prayer that I was convinced that with it I could endure the austerity of religious life, which in my opinion was unbearable, and only by means of prayer could I imagine enduring it as gently and joyfully as it was endured by those holy nuns. If, as I say, I had seen them sad and severe, believe me, my fear would have grown

27. Psalms 33:9.

28. We should not . . . of divine grace: Here, María defends two crucial features of Discalced spirituality: gentleness (spiritual joyfulness) and the "universality of perfection," the belief that individuals who were not completely free of vice could nevertheless aspire to contemplative prayer. On the Discalced concept of "gentleness" see introduction, 15–16.

and I would have lost all hope of succeeding. For my wanting to be a nun was not because I abhorred the things of the world, which seemed good to me as I had not yet tasted its trials and miseries; I wanted to renounce the world, convinced by my reason which showed the danger my soul was in if I stayed in it.

"I spent many days in this battle, because I felt two conflicting things in myself, which I later understood as what Saint Paul said, of *the law he had in his members, fighting against the law of his spirit.*[29] The Devil sought in this way to bring me down. This turned out to be a great mercy of God; because I didn't speak of it to anyone, and the Devil, as if with an ignorant soul, made me believe that mine was not a true vocation since I did not abhor the things of this world, so that I suffered a great deal, until one day when I was at Mass. They were chanting the gospel: *If any man will come after me, let him deny himself, and take up his cross, and follow me.*[30] Then His Majesty gave an extraordinary light to my understanding, and I understood what the Lord wanted from me and what those words meant, which I had not understood until then. From that moment I remained calm and began with great determination to declare my desires."

"You were wrong not to reveal your spirit to our Mother," said Justa, "for you could easily have done so and trusted in her opinion, especially because of her knowing all about it before you did and being ahead of you as she was."

"That, Sister, was my own ignorance," said Gracia, "and the Devil's snare to rob me of such good. If I had said that I wanted to be a nun not by my own will, but obliged by my reason—although at that time I did not even know what caused me to desire it or to spurn it—she would be bound to think that it was not a true vocation, and she wouldn't have wanted to receive me. From this, I was able to understand how strong and steadfast my desire was, for I fled anything I thought might hinder it. And as our Lord saw that my not communicating this was because I thought that silence would achieve my goal, He brought forth good from what could have done me harm. And thus I spent two years in terrible straits without speaking of this to anyone, not even my confessor, although he was from the Society of Jesus. My only relief was in shutting my eyes to the arguments the Devil placed before me, some of which bore many appearances of truth, so that my soul lost a great deal and was made to turn back to the ways of vanity. For whenever I remember the dangers to which, in the end, I exposed myself, which certainly deserved

29. Romans 7:23 (we have here modified the Douay version to fit María's quotation of this passage in Spanish).
30. Matthew 16:24.

the Lord's withdrawing His grace from me, I would like to be dissolved in praise to Him for the supreme mercy He showed me. For though I had gone back to my wicked life, my determination to be a nun was not one jot lessened. With all the effort with which I went through those travails, I many times repeated: *In te, Domine, speravi.*[31] At times with these words I would feel that my soul was strengthened so that I could trust in God, since I was not moved by any goal other than His honor and glory and wanting to please Him. And though it is a consolation to me to recall how much I owe our Lord, yet at the same time I see how poorly I have repaid Him for so many blessings, so that I cannot imagine when I could ever finish with this topic— and thus let us go back to our Angela.

"At this time a maid who served that lady, who suffered greatly with her wisdom teeth and earache and was afflicted with great pain, went and asked her [Angela] to make the sign of the cross over her, for she had great confidence that this would take it away. When our Mother saw the sick woman come to her as to a saint expecting to be healed by the touch of her hand, with her holy dissembling she jestingly pushed her away, and pretending to be angry she told her: 'Get away from there, don't be foolish; you must cross yourself, for the virtue of the Holy Cross is not in my hand.' And the very moment she touched her, the woman felt well, and for the entire time I knew her after that, I saw her free of that suffering, though she had been, as I say, very sick."[32]

"What you have just said has given me a rare joy," said Justa, "because it has reminded me of how cleverly she used that very gesture when we went to ask her the same thing. And I recall even now, as you must, how Sister Valeria had a sudden illness, so that one night we thought she was going to die, and just as soon as our Mother put her hand on her she was well. She made use of a trick that came from her great humility, which was to order that some remedies should be given to the sick nuns just when she was to get there, so that it would be thought that health came from the medicines and not from her."

"I remember this very well," said Gracia, "because similar things happened to me. And though I have many things to say about that time, they will have to wait for their place, which will be when we discuss her life with deliberation; and what is here will serve so that this bit of ground may not be

31. *In te, Domine, speravi:* In thee, O Lord, have I hoped (Psalms 30:2).
32. On Teresa's reluctance to display the thaumaturgical powers attributed to holy women at this time, see Alison Weber, "Saint Teresa's Problematic Patrons," *Journal of Medieval and Early Modern Studies* 29 (1999): 359–79.

left without a few flowers for the recreation of anyone who may pass this way, against the tedium such a person must feel on reading of my life, though what I say here is the best my life holds. My works are thorns among the flowers of this sacred garden.

"When that happy day arrived for me in which the Lord took me out of bondage in Egypt and brought me to religious life, when I was nearly twenty-two, on the Feast of the glorious Saint Gregory of Nazianzus—whom since that day I consider my Father and refuge—in the year 1570, on the ninth of May; I cannot express, dearest Sister, the contentment the Lord gave me from that moment. And to this very day not the slightest stirring has occurred in my thoughts to make me regret or feel discontent, but rather, the happiness I felt in my soul was so great that many times I could not contain my laughter."

"In that, Sister," said Justa, "you are not alone among the Discalced nuns, for as was once said by one great servant of God, the spirit that Eliseus called for was redoubled;[33] for in our sacred Order there is the penance, recollection, and prayer, the poverty and austerity that are shared among all the Orders, and moreover a redoubled spirit of happiness in all the monks and nuns."

"I did not only mean to say that I am happy," replied Gracia, "for I see happiness in all my Sisters, but that not even for a short time have I been tempted in my vocation, nor have I noticed to this day that the Devil has brought me any temptation that has not been aimed at taking me from prayer; and in prayer, apart from the mercies that God has granted me there, I have come to understand that it is His will that I practice it. Woe is me, how many more times have I obeyed the Devil in prayer than Christ! And I have more to say about this, but as I am so proud, I will be better able to portray anything that might look like my own good than to convey my sins, which are beyond counting."

"What, you've committed that many sins?" said Justa.

Gracia answered, with a great sigh: "I think I possess as many sins as the Devil and all men ever given to vice have ever invented."

"I do not think," said Justa, "that humility based on a lie like that is good humility, since we can be more or less certain that you have never stolen your

---

33. The Carmelites considered that the Old Testament prophets Elijah and Eliseus were the ancient fathers of their order. Elijah was thought to be the first holy hermit and Eliseus his ecstatic disciple. María here uses the prophets to justify her arguments that austerity is not incompatible with *suavedad*, gentleness or spiritual joyfulness. The "great servant of God" to whom María refers is probably Gracián, who shared María's views on this issue, and whom she calls "Father Eliseus" as noted above.

neighbor's wealth, or struck men dead, or done other wicked deeds that may be done."

"Oh, Justa!" said Gracia, "how deep was I in that ignorance you have just shown yourself to possess! And I would almost grow angry when I heard the Sisters say that they were worse than thieves and wicked women, and I would be astonished that they could believe such a thing. For the fervor and spirit with which a nun said it would show clearly how deeply she believed this truth, which is a great one, as our holy Mother says in one of her books.[34] Because I know the Lord has not kept you from this knowledge, I'd not venture to prove to you how very true it is."

"Rather, it will give me great happiness to hear you affirm what you doubted before," said Justa. "Because I remembered how difficult you used to find that humility of the Sisters, I wanted to contradict you. I shall be very happy now to know how you are undeceived."

"I already said that I did not want to say this," answered Gracia, "and I say now that all I know is that most truly I am worse than all other creatures on this earth. For as our glorious Saint Francis used to say, if they had been given the light that has been given to me, they would have made much better use of it. And I know of myself that I would fall with less occasion than another person, and with more help I cannot manage to get up, and whatever is in me I use entirely to bad purpose. And this truth is so firmly impressed in my soul by my experience of all my falls, that if the whole world gathered to tell me otherwise, I would not believe it. And that sufficed.[35] So much so, Sister, that the thefts I have made in the house of God are beyond numbering, when I have attributed the honor and glory that are due to His Majesty alone, to that monstrous beast[36] which has been the cause of so many spiritual deaths. How many times have I committed adultery by failing to keep, with the purity I should, what I promised at my profession to my Bridegroom. Alas, Sister, how little attention we pay to things that we consider small and the Lord considers important, because He is very jealous! And thus I say of the evils I have not committed: thanks be to God, and not to me."

"Tell me now," said Justa, "what manner of prayer you used to practice, for it is fitting for this to follow upon the knowledge of yourself you have set forth."

---

34. In one of her books: Teresa of Avila, *The Interior Castle,* vol. 2 of *The Collected Works of St. Teresa of Avila,* Dwelling VI, chap. 10, sec. 7.

35. And that sufficed [Y esto bastaba]: the meaning of this sentence is not entirely clear in the manuscript.

36. That monstrous beast: the devil.

"May it please God that I be able to tell it," said Gracia, "for that is the fear I have, that my pride not make it greater than it was; though by God's mercy, it is not my intention to include anything that I have not felt in my soul.

"Most times that I went to pray, as soon as I got down on my knees (for in the beginning I could not do it any other way), I felt as if I were surrounded by something like a wall of peace and great quiet, and it seemed that my soul withdrew from my body, and it was not what I have felt many other times, which is as if one is entering a very deep place where one is very much closed in. Here it was simply as if I were raised very high and far away from my senses, although I did not lose them entirely. And in that moment, clearly, it is not possible to reason things out or to recall anything by memory; rather, the soul enjoys things that I cannot describe. I will not dare meddle in these matters, as to whether or not the faculties are working;[37] I have no doubt about the will, which is not idle, though I do not know how it works. I only wish to tell what I have been commanded. I have seldom been able to reason while in meditation, for almost always I bore in my mind the presence of Christ on the cross, and I usually began with this reflection. But if I began with another, even if it were of the manger, there would shortly appear before me the cross and His wounds. I am not saying that I would see Him, but that without any attempt on my part, I would soon find that image in my imagination. And during that time when I was experiencing this kind of prayer, I could not—in spite of all my efforts—recite a single lesson in the choir or the refectory in which there was not a mention of the flesh or blood of Our Lord Jesus Christ, or something about the Blessed Sacrament, because of the great strength of that feeling in my spirit.

"I found no better way to have the prayer of quiet than to be before the Holy Sacrament; and in the beginning it was very common, when I was in the choir, for my soul to be recollected to where it felt such great and good things, so that I felt great pity for those who lost the chance to have them. There the Lord let me understand certain things. I can only say that even without any Faith to teach me that there was a God of infinite goodness and wisdom, from that moment I would have given my life confessing His Most Holy Name, and the same for the greatness and truth that are in His Church.

"One time, the Lord granted the favor of giving light to my soul so that I would understand how lofty a thing is His will, and I was filled with great

---

37. I will not dare . . . working: Gracia wisely refrains from speculating on the degree of conscious activity during the prayer of quiet; complete passivity (*dejamiento*) during prayer had been condemned as heretical in 1525.

pleasure for many days when I saw that I had been born to fulfill His most excellent will. At times I was almost beside myself with that exceeding pleasure. In those days I felt that the Devil brought me certain appetites and yearnings for prayer quite different from the true kinds. And the Lord granted me the favor of letting me know which forms of prayer caused a disquiet and despondency in my soul and would leave it empty and sad. In some way, I don't know how, my soul recognized this and shunned the gifts which my senses, deceived by the false appearance of good, were receiving. And I declare that even before seeing the effects, which are very clear to anyone who does not wish to be deceived, my soul knew this right away; I cannot say how, other than to say that I described this to our holy Mother and she said it was so. Even in another person who sees something of this, it seems that my soul understands it. It is no surprise that the Lord should communicate this grace to our souls, for we see that nature grants to animals the ability of each one to know its enemies by their smell; just so, as if by a pestiferous air, I think the soul senses its mortal enemy transformed into an angel of light. And I do not say this because I think the soul has physical nostrils, although, as Father Eliseus says, it does possess five spiritual senses like those of the body, through which, similarly to sight, smell, touch and the rest, it may understand the things of God."[38]

"I would not wish, Sister," said Justa, "for the Devil to deceive you in this way, by your trusting greatly in what you know, and thus play a trick on you, for he is very wily. Consider what Saint Paul says, 'believe not every spirit,'[39] for perhaps the Devil may want to reveal himself to you sometimes so as to deceive you as others."

"I know quite well that I am proud," answered Gracia, "and that he deceives such people, and the more I understand this about myself, the more I fear. Therefore, I am not sure either about what I feel to be bad or what seems good to me, I am distrustful of everything, and I hold fast only to what the Church has taught me. If I am given to understand something in prayer that is already known to be in accordance with God's law, I try to carry it out, not

38. Following Teresa's teaching on the issue, Gracia here expresses confidence in a nun's ability to discern divine ecstasy from its demonic counterpart without reliance on a confessor. On the Discalced Carmelite conception of spiritual discernment see Alison Weber, "Spiritual Administration: Gender and Discernment in the Carmelite Reform," *Sixteenth Century Journal* 31 (2000): 123–46.

39. "Believe not every spirit": this is not Saint Paul, but the First Epistle of Saint John, 4:1 ("Dearly beloved, believe not every spirit, but try the spirits if they be of God: because many false prophets are gone out into the world"), a biblical reflection of the concern for discernment of spirits. Justa, ever cautious, questions Gracia's ability to distinguish between divine and diabolical sensations during prayer.

because it came to me in prayer, but rather because the Church commands it; and I arm myself with the Church both before and after prayer.

"The Lord has almost always brought me by the way I have described, though it is true that the hunger I had at the beginning for that pleasurable prayer was taken from me almost eight years ago, and I was left in great peace, so that now, whether I have prayer or no, I always leave with peace and contentment—I mean, when I do what I can, which is to go to pray, even though nothing pleasurable may be given to me in prayer, I get by with reading and praying vocally and carrying out my acts of devotion. And I never fail to leave satisfied, and with profit as it seems to me, because whatever I may do moves me greatly to praise of God and to contrition, which are two things in which I would like to spend my life. This is the path by which the Lord has brought me ever since His Majesty began to give me light, and this will make understood what I have been commanded to say, without any need to relate more details or feelings. Rather, let us get on with our chief intent."

"You are wrong," said Justa. "Wait just a minute, for you are leaving everything you have said under suspicion; because to have brought you by a path of such consolation and so many gifts, without your having had conflicts and battles, seems to go against God's way, which, if He gives a consolation, is meant to prepare the soul for the struggle. If you have not struggled or had reason to do so, you may fear either that your consolations are not true, or—as you have been given such a great many together—that you are equipping yourself in readiness for a great war."

"It is certainly true, dearest Sister," answered Gracia, "that I have received much and served little and suffered even less, because, as Saint Paul says, 'the sufferings of this time are not worthy to be compared with the glory to come'[40] or even (for this same reason) with the gifts from the beyond that we receive here and now. But who has ever determined to leave the world and the flesh without having to struggle? Or who, among those who have made efforts to join the band of Christ, has not been tempted and afflicted by the Devil? Though I confess that in this matter the Lord has behaved toward me as toward a weak woman, for He has not permitted or consented that I should be greatly tempted up to this time. Yet although I declare this, I should like to know what you call temptations, because it is often very common language among women (please God it may not be so also among men) to go about always complaining of temptations; I fear there are many people who are temptations to themselves, toward whom I feel a natural hatred, and I fear they will not wear as many crowns [in heaven] as they think. And so, as they

40. Romans 8:18.

go searching and planning their lives, and trying to do what God does not want and what cannot even be achieved in this life, they remain uneasy, letting it be known how they suffer, complaining continually of bad fortune and of other people who do not do what they would like. And thus, sad souls will never lack for trials, and whatever worth or merit these possess before the Lord is known only to His Majesty. All this gives rise to such sad and despondent souls that they do not know how to be happy for a single hour. And the opposite gives rise to other souls who do not know a single hour of sadness, because they do not place their soul's good in what appeals to their sensuality, but rather in what God commands. For them, now they are in devotion and now they are not, now they are healthy or sick, now they are held in favor or disfavor. Whatever occurs, they embrace it all as being from the hand of the Lord. And thus we may say that while some souls are always tempted, other souls never are."

"It is quite true," said Justa, "that there are many souls who never undergo temptation. But there are also others whom the Lord wishes to be tormented with various temptations, and as you have no experience of it, you do not know what a torment it is—because I have sometimes heard you say that you have never been tempted bodily, or had temptations of the faith, or been tempted to blasphemy. These three are surely terrible battering rams by which the Devil wages terrible battle against pure souls, aiming three mighty blows against the three powers [of the soul].[41] By depraving the will with sensuality, he tries to darken the understanding; by seeding the understanding with errors against faith, he infects the memory with horrible images that his blasphemies place in the imagination, so that not a single soul would remain standing if God did not assist with His accustomed mercy."

"It is quite true," said Gracia, "that I have not been tempted with temptations like those, by the goodness of the Lord, for which I give Him infinite thanks. And the reason must be, as you said above, that pure souls suffer these temptations. I am not pure, nor do I think there would be virtue in me to resist. As Saint Paul says, 'God is faithful, who will not suffer you to be tempted above that which you are able.'[42] And truly I am of such a sort, that if my

---

41. Three powers of the soul: the three faculties of memory, understanding, and will.

42. 1 Corinthians 10:13. Gracia and Justa are here debating another contested issue in early modern spirituality: whether demonic temptations (sometimes referred to as demonic obsession) constituted an elevated or diminished spiritual state. Many nuns and *beatas* (lay holy women) reported experiencing lascivious demonic temptations, which were considered a consequence of their vows of chastity. Gracia plays down the significance of such temptations and affirms the orthodox doctrine that God does not permit the devil to tempt souls beyond their capacity for resistance.

heart were seized by the way of tenderness and love, I would be in great danger, which is not true for me by way of fear; for I am not defeated by threats or the fear of undergoing trials, but rather, they strengthen me when I ask for them. The most merciful Lord took notice of this weakness in me and did not permit the Devil to tempt me there—I mean with sensuality; for with those other temptations against faith, by the mercy of God, I do not think they could take hold in me. I am persuaded that whatever God wishes, He can do, and it is a great foolishness for me to want to know what is known to Him."

"Well said, Sister," said Justa. "That is how it is, as long as God does not withdraw His light from the soul."

"That is just what I say," said Gracia, "but believe me, only foolish souls have temptations and doubts about the faith."

"Well then, was Saint Augustine foolish," said Justa, "since we know he had doubts and errors in his faith?"

"Yes, Sister," answered Gracia, "very foolish indeed, since he had them, and Your Charity is not very well advised just now to doubt it."

"Now I have fallen into foolishness," said Justa with a smile, insisting that Gracia should tell her what temptations she had had and what trials she had gone through.

Gracia said to her: "I do not know for sure, Sister, what these trials may tell you, if you wish to give them that name—though they have been no such thing for me. All you nuns know about them, for you have all helped me to bear them. And it is no small relief to persons who are afflicted to see that others have compassion for them, in which we clearly see what was said by David, 'how good and pleasant it is for brethren to dwell together in unity,'[43] for with their sweet company, all things pass. How could I, with my weakness, have borne the straits in which I was put each day by those who, with God's permission, were convinced that I was 'Illumined'—or 'Unillumined'[44]—and who on this account had proceedings prepared and had us waiting hourly to be taken off to where faith is purified?[45] I was headed there with not one bit less happiness than is mine in the convent, because the testimony of my own conscience reassured me, and the affront that would be suffered in such a case promised to benefit me greatly. I was only saddened for the honor of our Order, and it hurt me to the depths to see any stain cast

43. Psalms 132:1.

44. "Illumined"—or "Unillumined" [alumbrada o desalumbrada]: María, with Teresa, was accused of the Illuminist heresy, or *alumbradismo*. See introduction, 4.

45. To where faith is purified: that is, before the Inquisition.

on those purest souls of our Father Eliseus and our Mother Angela, who were being defamed with the same crime."

"Is this to say," asked Justa, "that though you have not been tempted, yet you have been persecuted?"

"Yes, Sister," answered Gracia, "and I consider it no little thing to suffer well and commit no offense in such a case, and I have great confidence that our Lord shall grant me the favor—as I have most truly asked Him all my life—to spare me from the three temptations you mentioned earlier, so that not even with His consent may my soul be put in danger; and in place of what I have not suffered with these temptations, to grant that I may serve Him in the midst of all the trials and defamations He desires."

"It seems, Sister," said Justa, "that the Lord has been fulfilling your petition, for He has spared you from those temptations, yet you have been defamed for the very same things. Now it comes back to me how many falsehoods were invented in those days so that people would believe all sorts of depravity of you, although it was done not so much to defame you as because it would redound to the detriment of the pure, chaste heart of Father Eliseus, and that would hurt no less than the injury to oneself."

"No, indeed, but rather much worse," said Gracia. "And the manner in which that was done surely seemed an invention of the Devil, and not to be discussed here; let us pity those folk and thank them for the good they did us. May those who want to go in search of Christ all covered with honor and happiness be undeceived when we remind them of this, for it is impossible to find Him by any such path."

"I would like to know, my Sister," said Justa, "what you felt when, on the one hand, our confessor did not want to absolve you, because you were not confessing what he had believed about you; and next, when the Prelate whom God then gave us behaved so harshly toward you; and when so many servants of God publicly set about rebuking you, for the Prelate had sought them out for no other reason but that, having informed them in advance of his opinion of you. Or how you felt when some of the very nuns you had trained were in agreement with his opinion, which I would think might be very painful indeed, in addition to all the rest. You had no lack of occasions to suffer, and though in the exterior you appeared happy and unperturbed, nevertheless I cannot be convinced that you did not feel some disturbance interiorly."[46]

46. After María was denounced to the Inquisition in 1578, several of the nuns were coerced into testifying against her. See introduction, 4.

"Believe me, dearest Sister," Gracia said to this, "that I am telling you the truth when I say that never in my life was I happier or more encouraged. I am very glad to confess this, and I want all the nuns to know it, so that they may lose their fear of trials and trust in our sweetest Lord, Who sends them and pays the price for[47] the one who determines to undertake such trials for Him. Obviously, this is not the work of any human nature or virtue. For if His Majesty left any room for regret, a woman—who usually puts her honor before her life—would have to regret it quite strongly when she saw her honor being taken from her, with so many people made to believe the thing and so many appearances of truth. As Aristotle says, many times a lie has more of the hue of truth than truth itself. For see here, there was a great deal to regret when they considered me lacking in faith and brought proceedings and witnesses before that very severe tribunal—as just and holy as it is—along with a thousand other things you all know about already, in which the Lord gave me the courage and happiness that I showed in outer ways, with no pretense at all. But given that I did not regret that, does it not seem to you, Sister, that it was a very great affliction to see the entire Order and my Father Eliseus suffering, and the more so because it was on my account? Now, with what I have said here, Sister Justa, be content at last and let us speak of what is more important."

"That cannot be," said Justa. "Instead—and I ask this in the name of charity—you must tell me other particular things that have befallen you in prayer; according to the principles [of prayer], it is not possible that there are no other things worth noting."

"You are terrible, Sister Justa," said Gracia; "I don't know what to tell you, since whatever is in me I consider suspicious; and even if it were not, what fruit could it bear? But I will tell a few things, and try to get them right.

"It has befallen me many times, when I have asked intently for certain things, that I have been given some certainty that it would be granted as I asked. I especially felt this strength one eve of the Feast of the Purification of our Lady,[48] while I was praying to the Virgin herself to move the heart of a young lady to become a nun. We all wanted her, because of a brother of hers who was our confessor, and because the goodness of her nature seemed suited to religious life, though she felt such repugnance for this position that it was impossible to mention it to her. While I was there as I say, it seemed to me that this same young lady appeared before me dressed in the habit, and

47. Pays the price for [hace la costa a]: This phrase may suggest the "purchase" of salvation, as a ransom. See Mark 10:45.
48. Feast of the Purification of our Lady: 2 February.

Our Lady, the Virgin, assured me that she would be a nun. This stayed so strongly in my soul that even though I heard they considered it impossible that she would enter the convent, I never doubted it. I told her brother what I had seen and heard, as he was my confessor. And just four days after that, she asked him with such insistence and fervor to let her join that she was soon given the habit, and she lived most contentedly and died like a saint at the end of five or six years.

"I know our Lady did not do this because of my prayer, for there were many servants of God who were asking for this as insistently as I. But I tell what happened to me so that through this example, a great many things just like it that have happened to me may be understood, for there is no reason to give them all in detail. Ordinarily, the way I understand that something I have asked for in prayer will be granted is by a certain desire with which I ask, and a strength that is felt in the soul quite different from what we usually put into our prayers, however much desire we may feel. And I understand that this is ordinarily the way it is for many souls, and thus when they see their desire fulfilled as they asked, they think they have received a revelation. Yet as I have said it is quite ordinary and true, because the soul feels in its interior that it is given strength to ask, and the consequence the soul earnestly wishes to bring about is good.

"I have been given to understand other things—such as warnings to me or to other nuns, or advice concerning certain serious matters—in another way, when a particular word or verse from Holy Scripture is impressed on me, by which I understand what the Lord wishes to be done, or why something was done as it was.

"When King Sebastian was lost,[49] I was greatly afflicted by that loss, and one day after many others during which I had felt this sadness, still upset during that period by the event, I understood: 'Per me reges regnant, per me principes imperant.'[50] At that moment all my grief was gone and I was left in the greatest consolation, with my soul longing to dissolve in praises to the Lord, and with great pleasure I understood that great good things were to result from this change.

"When the Prelate wished to take me to found a convent, I understood in just the way I have described: 'Take nuns who hold tightly to matters of faith

49. When King Sebastian was lost: In 1578, King Sebastian of Portugal led a disastrous expedition against the Moors of Morocco. In the battle of Alcazarquivir, the young king was killed, leaving his aged uncle, Cardinal Enrique, as heir. After Enrique died in 1580, Philip II of Spain succeeded him, uniting the Iberian peninsula under one crown.

50. Proverbs 8:15–16: "By me kings reign, and lawgivers decree just things, / By me princes rule, and the mighty decree justice."

and who let go of miracles and falsehoods, for in that place there is great need of faith.'[51] These words caused certain effects in me in this matter which shall be left to time to prove whether it was false.

"And with what I have now said, Sister Justa, be satisfied, for I am not obliged to say any more, nor is it right that the soul should tell in public of the particular intimacies that she experiences with God. Nor do I believe that the Lord is served by this, other than by speaking of it with that one who must guide the soul, who is her spiritual Father;[52] nor even then breathes there a soul who would dare to speak of these things, or who possesses a tongue able to speak the words. And though I myself have known no things so lofty they cannot be told, I am a great believer in a doctrine which cannot be bad, which I imagine the most saintly women, deeply favored by the Lord, have kept to. It is this: in just this way, a mighty king of great majesty would not permit revelation of all that he does in secret with his wife, to delight and favor her, when leaving aside all majesty and nobility he lowers himself and makes himself her equal to do the things that only love will suffer, and which to one with no understanding would appear indecent. And so, angered now and in some respect ashamed, a person of no understanding might complain of the looseness of the wife, whom the king permits only to make known the love he bears for her and the favor she thus receives—but to whom he does not give leave to speak of the particular intimacies of love. How great and ardent is the love our great King and Lord has for us! How could one say that with it He commits excesses? And although His Majesty cannot do anything unsuitable to Him, and no one can criticize any such thing in Him, nonetheless it is His pleasure that such things should be received and held in silence with fear and trembling, for the decency of His Most High and Incomprehensible Majesty."

"It seems to me that you are on the wrong track," said Justa. "For how should we know of all the delights and favors the Lord has bestowed on so many sainted women, such as we know occurred with Saint Catherine of Siena, Saint Elizabeth, Saint Brigid, and Angela of Foligno and others, if He were not pleased that such things should be told? Rather, that is why such favors are given, and not solely to benefit those who receive them."

51. In that place . . . of faith: María here refers to the Carmelite foundation at Lisbon; there, authorities deemed deceptive the visions of the famous Dominican nun at the Convent of the Anunciada, Sor María de la Visitación. The latter was also associated with the faction that opposed Spain's annexation of Portugal. María thus draws an implicit distinction between the restrained thaumaturgy of the Carmelites, who supported Philip, and the thaumaturgical excesses of the Dominican prioress, who supported the cause of the Portuguese pretender to the throne.
52. The spiritual Father: that is, the priest or confessor.

"It is true," said Gracia, "that those favors that were written down about those saints—and that our holy Mother wrote about herself—should rightly be told. But do not think that these were the only experiences they had, for that is why Saint Paul came to say, that he 'saw things which it is not granted man to utter.'[53] Saint Catherine, returning from a rapture, often repeated these very words of Saint Paul. And if you read our Mother's books carefully you will find, when telling certain things Our Lord told her and some other matters, that she says the Lord spoke to her with words of such favor that there was no reason to tell them; I heard this from her own mouth, and it is just what I have said. Though it may be permitted to tell the favors that God bestows, it is not granted us to tell all of these favors, far less those excesses of love that are felt and experienced by souls in their sweetest Lord.

"At times there arise such joys and jubilation in the soul that it is really necessary to restrain oneself, and they so overflow to the exterior that they erupt in laughter; thus, it has happened to me that I do not dare enter into prayer where there are other Sisters because of the laughter and impulses that, without my being able to help it, come unbidden. There is a fullness and satisfaction of the soul, a dominion and grandeur that it feels within, so that the things of this world seem but rubbish, not out of scorn but rather because it seems to the soul that it possesses all the riches of God. And with this, a joy is felt that cannot be told. The soul considers itself inferior to all other creatures, because these riches bring with them a firm knowledge that such favor is not obtained through our merit, but through the great love of our good Christ. He knows that I tell the truth when I say that I am often sadly grieved to see how many souls deprive themselves of these true joys, and I would like to shout to them to come and taste 'that the Lord is sweet,' as David says.[54] This [experience] gives rise to other times when the soul goes about most desirous of saying something of what it feels; and though certain fearful and humble souls think this is vainglory or a desire that others should know of their own goodness, it arises from nothing save the desire that others should know of the goodness of God. And it is a great pain to suppress this, because such souls do not always find other souls hurt with the same wound, which is what always gives some rest, because there is no rest save with the person who understands this language. Who can tell of a sweet wound and a pleasurable death by love, in which the soul seems to be undone and strength fails, yet the soul would never wish to be deprived of this pain?

53. 2 Corinthians 12:4 (Douay: "That he . . . heard secret words, which it is not granted to man to utter").
54. Psalms 33:9.

"This is sufficient, dearest Sister, so that there can be some other place in which we tell of the effects that this divine love bestows. Let us each now withdraw for a bit, for the day is leaving us, and it is good that we should spend what remains of it in pondering the things that have been said, and in contemplating the beauty of this great Lord which all of His creatures are displaying to us.[55] Behold the beautiful expressions of this clear fountain we have before us; behold the order and harmony that all creatures keep within themselves, as they proclaim their Creator; for the time is short and life is brief to praise Him for even the least thing that it holds."

And with these words that Gracia spoke, each one went her own way to praise the Lord.

THIRD RECREATION

In which Justa asks Gracia to tell her about Mount Carmel

As the three were returning to the place they had left, they saw in the distance another nun who was coming toward them with her eyes raised to heaven. She was walking among some shrubs, so unconcerned with the road she had taken that at times she strayed from it entirely.

Justa, who was watching the other nun's lack of concern with close attention, said to Gracia: "Who is that coming there who seems so dazed?"

Gracia said, "Don't you know her? That is Sister Cándida. It is only by God's mercy that she hasn't come walking past some little lamp filled with oil where she could dip her fingers, as she often does, mistaking lamp oil for holy water."

"What a pleasure it is to see her," said Justa, "and how she comes walking with an unconcern that is born of proper and fitting concerns."

"We should not be surprised," answered Gracia, "if when she gets here all swept up in observing the little plants and the singing birds, she has forgotten why she came. For certainly solitude, where memory is caught up and employed only on its Creator, plays a great part in awakening the soul to the praises of God. And at the same time, the understanding is satisfied and the will is moved when we see these broad heavens with their birds, the trees, the plants and crags and animals, the little worms, and the temperate wind playing upon the trees with pleasant sounds that join with the sound of the waters that come leaping from the rocks. My soul is gladdened with all this, when I remember what the prophet said: "Your voice, Lord, is like the sound

55. Are displaying to us: the phrase *nos está mostrando*, with the verb in the singular form, appears in the manuscript and is probably a writer's *lapsus* or copyist's error for *están*.

of many waters."[56] And without doubt there is inexpressible majesty in a great stream of waters that show the Majesty by which they were created. Our Mother Angela's books prove that she felt this strongly, for in them we see how this element moved her."

Justa said, "Sister, what could ever fail to move her? In what did she not find a motive for loving and praising God? And that we all may praise and enjoy Him, though it be only by hearsay, tell us something of Mount Carmel and its freshness; for as you know, I have never left this one house, and it will be a great consolation to those of us who have never seen Carmel itself and don't even know where it is located, or any of its particular features, or where our convents are to be found, and other things that you may have seen there."

"Indeed, I have seen such things," said Gracia, "but the one who could best satisfy your desire is Sister Atanasia, who has walked its length and breadth with our Mother Angela. Let us call her, for we have license to speak with whomever we like when we have need of them.[57] If my eyesight does not betray me, I saw her enter the hollow of that rock, because she finds her refuge in openings in rocks just as hedgehogs do, as the rocks are so dear to her. I'll go call her, and you, Sister, pray for us both in the meantime."

Justa, commencing her prayer as Gracia had told her, together raised her hands and eyes and heart to heaven. And she thanked the Lord for having brought her to that spot, where she grew the more inflamed in praising God the closer her Sisters drew to her, because she was moved by the sight of them, especially of Atanasia, who was venerable and manifested clearly what was held in her soul. And when Atanasia had arrived, Justa bowed low before her with the civility that was customary among the nuns, showing with her happy face how the visit pleased her. Having greeted Atanasia, Justa said, "It is time, dearest Sister, for you to speak with us and relate what God conveys to you, so that you may awaken lukewarm nuns like me; it is high time for you to come out of those hollows in the rocks and teach your Sisters and not keep only to yourself. Watch out, or you will be made to give as strict an accounting as the servant who hid the talent that had been given him by his Master.[58]

56. Your voice . . . many waters: Simeón de la Sagrada Familia here cites Psalms 76:18: "Great was the noise of the waters: the clouds sent out a sound." More closely, however, María may be citing any of various passages, such as Ezechiel 43:2, "His voice was like the noise of many waters"; Apocalypse (or Revelation) 1:15, "And his voice as the sound of many waters"; or 14:2, "And I heard a voice from heaven, as the noise of many waters."

57. We have license . . . need of them: The Teresian constitutions permitted nuns to break their vow of silence when they had need of spiritual counsel. At the time María was writing this work, such flexibility was under attack.

58. The talent that had been given him by his Master: Matthew 25:15–30. It is notable that María alludes to these verses as a proof text to counter the prohibitions of I Corinthians 14:34,

For given your age and all the many years you have spent in religious life, there is no reason that you would be subject to the danger of vainglory that can overtake and indeed overthrow those nuns who do not have the experience that you must have of your misery."

At this, having listened with much modesty and silence, Atanasia said, "You have done ill, Sister, for by wanting me as a teacher you keep me from being a disciple and make me lose the lesson I was being taught, which I could use to answer you once I was back in my 'nest,' as you all say. For you quite rightly call me a hedgehog, all ugly and full of quills, as my subsistence is like that of filthy and disgusting little creatures; but I have no resemblance to that animal's good properties. I was confessing my ignorance before the Lord, asking Him to teach me; the Lord answered me: "Cursed be the man that trusteth in man."[59] At once my pride began to judge the answer as unfitting to what I had asked. But at that same instant, divine light—illuminating my understanding, accompanied by a sweet though fearful reprimand— taught me like a true teacher and argued with my madness, showing me both by doctrine and by experience the truth of this statement. I cannot possibly say how true it is other than to say that my soul feels it, and the falls suffered by people who trust in themselves show us how the curse of the Lord more readily includes those who trust in their own knowledge and deeds than in the deeds of others; given that we should always act with the understanding that it is through Christ that our deeds have worth. And this will suffice, Sister, to show that you should neither order me to teach nor take such an office under your own authority; for believe me, at no age or stage of life are we free of the traitor of self-love, which is the little moth that destroys the finest woolen cloth. Well then, order me as to what I must do, for you brought me here."

"You have faithfully fulfilled my desire, Sister," said Justa, "and I must ponder faithfully what you have said. I pray you, have patience and do not weary of answering me, for there are many questions that Sister Gracia and I want to ask you. The first would be to explain to us how you received that answer that you say the Lord gave you: was it a voice that you heard with your corporeal ears, or with the ears of your soul? Tell us, so that anyone who hears you may understand."

"It was not a voice that would be formed in the air or heard with the

---

"Let the women keep silent in the churches." She also explicitly uses the word *enseñar* [to teach] in this passage. This passage offers a fine example of María's dialectical method, by which she breaks down the opposition between learning and teaching.

59. Jeremias (Jeremiah) 17:5.

ears," replied Atanasia. For you to understand me better, I want to bring to mind the ways of speaking that our holy Mother used in her *Interior Castle.*[60] Some voices (she says) seem to come from outside us, others from deep in the interior of the soul, others from the soul's superior part, and others are so exterior that they seem to be heard with the ears of the body. The answer was not given to me in any of these ways because it was not given by a voice, though there were words. And I cannot affirm that it was from God, for in such matters lies the danger with which you are all familiar, and the proof of the true spirit is declared by the effects left by these supernatural things. And so, leaving the examination of this for the proper time, I should like to let you know how it is that there were words although no voice was heard. I know too well that I shall not be able to explain this—what the soul feels and how it knows that God is speaking to it, although it does not, as I say, hear a voice. I can find nothing better as an explanation than what the Lord Himself did, which as Saint John says[61] was to lean down and write on the ground. That is just how it must be in this case: the finger of God writes. There is no need to doubt whether it is His, for as the All-Powerful, His word touches and His touch speaks."

"You have quite satisfied me as to the last question," said Justa. "Now I am left with another doubt, which is how, when you were touched by the finger of God—if it was He that spoke to you—you dared to judge that the answer was unfitting; for as you have just confessed, God does not need and is not tied to the little measure of our circumspection. To touch, one must extend the hands, and to speak, one must use the voice: was it not great audacity to want the answer measured to your judgment?"

Gracia and Atanasia smiled at this, and Atanasia said, "It surely seems, Sister Justa, that the Lord leads you by a straight path and not by extraordinary roads, for you think that His Majesty obligates us, when we hear or see anything that seems good, to believe Him. No, Sister, be undeceived along with all who are deceived. For the Bridegroom possesses patience to call at the door, and is long-suffering to wait, while His hair becomes covered with the dew,[62] and He even likes to find the door shut, and to be asked, "How can such a thing be?" when things seem astonishing, as the Most Blessed Virgin asked when the angel told her that she was to be the Mother of God.[63] I believe that the Treasuress of the Most Holy Trinity asked this question not be-

---

60. Teresa of Avila, *Interior Castle,* Dwelling VI, chap. 3, sec. 1.

61. John 8:6.

62. Canticle of Canticles (Song of Songs) 5:2.

63. Luke 1:34.

cause she did not know that the Son of the Most High was not to be conceived like the rest of us, but to give us an example and testimony of her purity. How much more patient is the Lord when the first movements of the soul are not in our power, and He does not grow angry but rather uses our miserable condition to teach us, as He did in this case; for as I was confessing that I knew nothing, He showed me that I was even more ignorant than I knew. And with that, grant me leave."

"Your words have given me great happiness," said Gracia, "because I cannot endure certain spirits who, as our Mother Angela used to say,[64] scarcely dare draw breath for fear God might leave them, as if He were reluctant to be there and looking for excuses to depart. The worst is that the unfortunate creatures don't dare to obey lest their devotion should leave them; and if the confessor or Prelate, to test their spirit, forbids them [mental] prayer, they think that all is lost.[65] Such people look to me like misers who don't dare use their money for fear of losing it. I should not want any better bill of exchange than what our Lord gives me in the form of obedience, which assures me of recovering my wealth and even doubling my treasure. So let us get on with our story, and you shall tell us very specifically the things you have seen and heard in the convents, which is why we took you from your nest. Fly now to the heights of Carmel, and carry fodder so that you may later gather up and nourish your young, and with your good purpose you will be able to say, like Job,[66] "In my nest I shall die a precious death."

"You tell us first, Gracia," said Justa, "what you know of Carmel, and when your information is not so complete, Sister Atanasia will help you."

To this Gracia answered, "It is a difficult thing you ask, because in order to tell you something it is not enough for me to speak only of the Carmel transplanted here; instead, I should like to start the journey further back and tell of the origins and beginning of this treasure. I know that my forces alone will not suffice, but I shall start with faith in the sovereign princess to whose service and praise this house was built—just as King Solomon did, when he built a house for his bride, the daughter of King Pharaoh."[67]

And falling silent after what she had said, Gracia was left in seeming perplexity. When they had waited for her to go on and saw her cast into si-

---

64. Teresa of Avila, *Interior Castle*, Dwelling V, chap. 3, sec. 11.

65. If the confessor . . . is lost: Gracia is arguing that nuns should not be afraid temporarily to abandon mystical contemplation, especially when ordered to do so. Like Teresa, María advocated a seamless fusion of the active and contemplative life.

66. Job 29:18.

67. 3 Kings (Douay; in other versions, 1 Kings) 7:8–12.

lence, Atanasia and Justa said, "Go on, Sister, and don't abandon what has been begun, for you seem to have lost the courage that you showed just now."

"In part that is true," said Gracia, "because I see how little I serve for such a great undertaking, and the strong impulse and desire I feel to tell of the greatness of this sacred mountain, together with my own insufficiency, robbed me of the power of speech. I should like to see the great Eliseus in possession of the multitude of ideas that occurred to me, along with the desire, or to have him lend me a bit of his wit."

"It seems to me a lack of humility, Sister," replied Justa at this, "to want to speak with as high a style as those who know how to do such things; be simple, and adjust yourself to your limited ability."

"It must of necessity be so," said Gracia, "but it is a shame to see the house and royal building of the Queen Most High receive so little notice, and how little care our forebears have given until now to composing a record of its greatness."

Atanasia said, "You have no further reason to complain that there are no writings on the sacred Carmel, for you see that our Eliseus has left no matter from its beginnings onward on which he has not shed light for us. Both in that admirable history on the origins and beginnings of our Order, and in verse, he has informed us of everything.[68] Now, for you to quiet the hunger you have for these things—since such precious delicacies do not take it from you—all that remains is for you to cook up others, more to your liking and suited to your rough wit, in the style of shepherds and rustic folk, who are happier with garlic and onion than with sweetmeats."

With this said, they arose and withdrew to the convent, which as I said was close by, for it was the hour of compline.

FOURTH RECREATION

In which Gracia continues to tell of the greatness of Mount Carmel

The next morning, when the nuns had recited the divine office and were sitting beside the fountain, Justa said, "Now truly, Sister Gracia, go on with your account, for you must have a great deal to tell us."

"Yes I do," she answered, "but I dare not, because in order to say anything I must cite certain passages that I have read in a great variety of books, espe-

---

68. The first history of the Carmelite order, written by Gracián, to which María refers, has not survived; the second, in verse, was published by Silverio de Santa Teresa in the Biblioteca Mística Carmelitana series, in vol. 3 of *Obras del padre Jerónimo Gracián de la Madre de Dios,* 3 vols. (Burgos: El Monte Carmelo, 1932–33).

cially those of the Holy Bible, which mentions this sacred mountain.[69] And because at the start I appointed you judge, not only are you performing that office, but also that of prosecutor, accusing me whenever I say anything."[70]

They all laughed at this, and Justa gave Gracia license to speak without fear, recalling what she had said above, that Gracia did not know any more than was commonly known to women—"I said that it was not good to write, but you, Sister, who think yourself a lady scholar,[71] which is what we consider you, you certainly will be able to do so."

And so Gracia began, "A short while ago I told you of that great house built by King Solomon for his bride, which Holy Scripture says was a wondrous work, 'all of costly stones, which were cut by a certain rule and measure both within and without, from the foundation to the top of the walls; and the foundations were of precious stones; we are told that the great court was made round, with three rows of hewed stones.'[72] Today we know, as the holy Doctors of the Church tell us, that King Solomon prefigures Our Lord Christ, the eternal King, and that He too has brides who are crowned queens, and that over them all reigns the Queen of virgins. Then it is right that He should build a house for this great Lady and give menservants and maidservants to wait upon her, and that her throne and seat should be prepared for her many years before her birth, for as she says, in the voice of Wisdom, 'I was set up ... before the earth was made';[73] and her throne has been established 'on a mountain,' as Isaias says, for 'the mountain of the house of the Lord shall be prepared on the top of mountains,'[74] and David says that 'it is a craggy mountain, a fat mountain.'[75]

---

69. The Indexes of Prohibited Books issued by the Inquisition in 1551, 1554, and 1559 all prohibited the publication of bibles in the vernacular. María may have had access to a Vulgate Bible or read portions of the Bible incorporated in vernacular devotional books. For María's knowledge of biblical texts, see the introduction, 11.

70. But also that of prosecutor, accusing . . . anything: María may here be alluding to the Inquisition's prosecuting attorneys (*fiscales*), who were known to ask for the harshest possible sentences from the inquisitional tribunals.

71. Who think yourself a lady scholar: The Spanish phrase, "que presumes de bachillera," makes fun of Gracia's "pretensions"; as Gracia's learning becomes evident, the humor doubles back ironically against those who think women unfit for study and discussion of sacred texts.

72. All of costly stones . . . of hewn stones: This passage cites directly the description of the house Solomon built, in 3 Kings (Douay; elsewhere 1 Kings) 7:8–12.

73. Proverbs 8:23. In this chapter of Proverbs, "Wisdom" is personified and speaks as female. The complete verse is, "I was set up from eternity, and of old before the earth was made."

74. Isaias (Isaiah) 2:2.

75. It is a craggy mountain, a fat mountain [es monte enriscado y lleno de grosura]: Psalms 67:16 in the Douay version (which follows the Latin Vulgate that was familiar to María) reads, "The mountain of God is a curdled mountain, a fat mountain." Other English versions, in which this is Psalms 68:16, vary widely in their renderings of this passage.

"A fitting thing it was that the dwelling to be built for her who is loftier and more exalted than any other pure creature should be placed on the summit that stands above all other mountains, and that a tabernacle should be built for the Mother of the Lord upon the mountain of the house of the Lord. And it was right that this should be a craggy mountain, so that the foundations might be strong, for this place was built for her, the mightiest of the mighty, so strong that she cracked the head of Lucifer. Within this stronghold are raised up people trained in the Lord's militia, with which this woman, Captain of God's army, does affront His enemies.

"I do not, exalted Lady, highest Empress, *semper augusta,* Mother of the eternal fatherland, place you in a fortress and tower because you require walls to defend you, or guards to keep guard over you; for upon your arm you bear the shield and the strength of Zion, and you are the sovereign Queen, the tower of Lebanon, which looks out over Damascus, and the tower of David, upon which hang a thousand shields of gold.[76] Rather, I know that it pleases you to be enclosed and to have the women who follow you be so as well, placing before themselves a rampart. Never were you pleased, Virgin most pure, to be found among the noise and tumult of the worldly. Nor have I, to honor you, called you by such names as those by which mortals are honored, for full well do I know your names, which are lofty, as your epithets are eternal, for you are Mother of our eternal God, who desires that you should be guarded by 'threescore valiant ones of the most valiant of Israel,' for you are the flowery bed of the divine Solomon.[77]

"May the great Elias be the captain of them all,[78] for you appointed him valiant protector of the honor of your beloved Solomon, through the fears of nighttime when in darkness his entire people adored foreign gods, and through fears in the night when others spoke against your purity. He took a vow of chastity to make known that he was dedicated to the defense of your most spotless bed. And your sixty valiant Carmelites have defended you no less bravely, like Saint Cyril, the Patriarch of Alexandria, in the Council of Ephesus,[79] and many others whose names need not be left to silence, for they

---

76. Canticle of Canticles (Song of Songs) 4:4 is echoed here; Douay gives "bucklers" for shields, but we have maintained the latter as the more familiar term for Spanish "escudos."

77. Canticle of Canticles 3:7.

78. May the great Elias be the captain of them all: The Carmelites of this period believed Elias (alternate spelling: Elijah) the ninth-century Hebrew prophet, to be their founder, whereas modern historians place the origins of the order in the second half of the twelfth century.

79. Saint Cyril, the fifth-century Patriarch of Alexandria, considered a defender of the church against heresy. María may have confused him with Cyril of Constantinople (d. 1235), a Carmelite general and the presumed author of a letter connecting the order with the prophets of the Old Law.

are inscribed on your banner, and I do not think my Sisters would allow me to let them slip by unmentioned."

Justa and Atanasia promptly said, "You will give us great pleasure by noting them; it was only because we didn't want to interrupt what you were saying that we did not ask you to do so."

"The book of Numbers tells,"[80] said Gracia, "of the fighting men who went out from Egypt, whom the Lord ordered to assemble in orderly squadrons, each of which was to gather with its standard round about the tabernacle of the covenant wherein dwelt the Lord.[81] And each standard was to be placed before the precious stone that was of the same color; these stones were upon the breast of the high priest. This figure, which we must use to represent our own camp, appears most fittingly, for this camp of ours surrounds God's tabernacle in the same orderly and harmonious way that God commanded their camp should be arrayed around the sanctuary. This figure is our blessed Virgin, upon whom shine in the highest degree of perfection the three costly stones of chastity, obedience, and poverty, and in their brilliance our army makes camp in the great round courtyard that, as we said, was made by Solomon for his bride, setting within it three rows of hewn stones, just as it is here.

"Here we must set a painting of a circle, and within it a triangle, with the names of the saints, martyrs, virgins, and confessors of the Order. At each point of the triangle, as it says here, is one of our captains, and at their feet, the world, the flesh, and the Devil. There is another circle in the middle of this triangle, which must contain our Lady giving Elias flames of fire to eat, as his father saw in a vision.[82] All are arrayed for war, armed with the weapons named by the Apostle[83] just as our Rule commands us:[84] the breastplate of justice, the shield of faith, the helmet of health and grace, the sword of the word of God. This army is placed on three points against three enemies: the world, the Devil, and the flesh.

---

80. The book of Numbers tells: Numbers 1 and following chapters. It is interesting to note that in this passage María draws parallels between female monasticism and defensive military maneuvers. The nuns are compared to soldiers protecting the fortress of their lady captain, the Virgin Mary. In other words, María suggests that the Discalced nuns are playing an important role in the defense of a besieged church.

81. The tabernacle of the covenant: Numbers 2:2.

82. Flames . . . vision: an obscure reference to Carmelite iconography.

83. Ephesians 6:11–17: "The armour of God . . . your loins girt about with truth . . . the breastplate of justice . . . your feet shod with the preparation of the gospel of peace . . . the shield of faith . . . the helmet of salvation, and the sword of the spirit (which is the word of God)."

84. Carmelite Rule, *Exhortations*, http://www.ocd.pnc.net/regola.htm.

"The martyrs form one point set against the world, scorning it with their bodies and their lives; the great John the Baptist stands as captain of this squadron.

"The virgins stand at the second point, against the flesh, headed by their captain, the glorious Eliseus.

"The confessors stand at the third point against the third enemy, which is the Devil; as their captain they have the mighty Jerome.

"The ark of the testament and the tabernacle of God, which is the archive of the Most Holy Trinity and the flowery bed of the bride, stands in the midst of these armies surrounded by the three points that form a triangle, because all of these people fight in the name and power of the Most Blessed Trinity.

"The captain general of the entire army is the great Elias. His life and deeds are proof of whether he be strong and reliable for such an undertaking, for indeed, he was chosen by the Virgin in a vision his father had, where the most beautiful damsel gave him flames of fire to eat; and thus his deeds were inflamed, as Ecclesiasticus says: "And Elias the prophet stood up, as a fire, and his words burnt like a torch."[85] By blood and by fire he carried away the enemies of God, just as He was seen to descend from heaven upon the sacrifice, and with his own hand in one day Elias beheaded four hundred and fifty prophets of Baal.[86] Twice he ordered fire to descend from the heavens to burn the soldiers, together with their captains, that were sent to him by King Ozias.[87] Elias was taken up in a chariot of fire.[88] His word served to open and close the heavens, and the heavens gave the dew as he willed it. Holy Scripture tells of such great deeds by this great Father that I do not doubt, dearest Sisters, that it would give you the greatest pleasure to hear them, were I not afraid to relate them.[89] I shall only tell you, for your consolation, that Eccle-

---

85. Ecclesiasticus 48:1.

86. Four hundred and fifty prophets of Baal: I Kings 16–18. Under the influence of his Tyrian wife Jezebel, King Achab of Israel erected a temple to the Tyrian god Baal and introduced a multitude of foreign priests. Elias exhorted the faithful to return to the worship of Yahweh and on Mount Carmel incited a great crowd to slay the priests of Baal. The end of a two-year drought that had afflicted the land was attributed to Elias's intercessory prayers. At his death the prophet ascended to heaven in a chariot of fire (Ecclesiasticus 48:1).

87. King Ozias (c. 791–739 b.c.): also spelled Uzziah and Ocias, king of Judah. 2 Paralipomenon 26 (in Douay; in other versions 2 Chronicles 26) tells of the prosperity and military expansion that characterized his reign.

88. Ecclesiasticus 48:9.

89. I do not doubt . . . were I not afraid to relate them [no dudo . . . sino que os daría gran contento no me atreviera yo aquí a referirlas]: conjectural reading of an obscure passage; an example of María's use of *reticencia*, the rhetorical ploy of pretending not to relate what one is in fact relating.

siasticus tells of him, in the passage cited above: "Who can glory like to thee?[90] and who will have the power to do such things?" And a bit further on it says: "Blessed are they that saw you, and were honoured with thy friendship."[91]

"As to whether there are crags and rocks and fountains on this sacred mountain, this has been firmly established in that the word of the sacred prophet had such strength."

While Gracia was wanting to proceed, Justa said, "As to Elias's being our Father and founder, Sister, we have no doubts, nor do I think you need to inform us further. But tell us how you can say that Saint John the Baptist and Saint Jerome were."

"I did not think," said Atanasia, "that you were so backward in your knowledge of these matters. Taking as much pride as you do in being the Daughter of our Eliseus, have you not read the history of our Order that he wrote, where this truth is so well established?"

"If you were thought, Sister Justa," said Gracia, "to be of the spiritual sort, like Sister Cándida, we would understand that that was why you were so forgetful. I did not say all the above about our Father Eliseus to prove that he was a member of our Order, nor did I think it necessary to bring proof concerning the other saints about whom you have doubts. But as you do not know, read the history our Sister is telling you of, and you shall find out how Saint John the Patriarch of Jerusalem, and Saint Ambrose, Saint John Chrysostom, Saint Jerome, and many others write that Saint John the Baptist followed the Order of Elias.[92] As proof of this, let what Our Lord Christ says be enough for us, that John came in the spirit and power of Elias,[93] and that if they wish to receive him as Elias they may well do so. And a Pope proclaims in a papal bull that John was a saint of the Carmelite Order. Who would dare to say this? As to whether Saint Jerome was, he himself says that he keeps the Rule of Elias. And in a letter to Paulus[94] he says: Our prince is Elias, and our captain is Eliseus."

90. Ecclesiasticus 48:4.

91. Ecclesiasticus 48:11.

92. Saint John . . . Order of Elias: Since Saint John the Baptist spent nearly the whole of his life in the desert and gathered around him a number of disciples, Carmelite tradition has claimed him as one of the fathers of the order.

93. Luke 1:17.

94. Paulus Venatus: Theologian of the Hermits of the Order of Saint Augustine, c. 1368–1428. Saint Jerome represented Elias and Eliseus as the models of religious perfection and the patrons of hermits and monks. This led to the Carmelite tradition that claims Jerome as an early member of their order.

"You have done well, Sister, in removing my doubts about this and the doubts of other persons, who must number more than a few."

"I know well," replied Gracia, "that there are and have been a great many who have not known these things, and who mock our Order. To them, we can say what Jerome himself did in defense of this high mountain that God chose as His dwelling: 'Why do you fight against this mountain, why do you envy and try to vanquish it? This is the mountain that God chose for His dwelling and in which He is pleased to dwell forever.'

"I know full well that the saint makes this defense for an even higher purpose. But as it is true that the saints themselves are called mountains, certainly the Congregation of saints can still better be called by that name. And Holy Scripture, which speaks thus of Our Lord Christ—that same Lord who gave Himself entirely to us—also allows us to honor His saints with the same terms, and above all, to honor the things that among all the Orders are dedicated and consecrated to the saintliest of saints, Our Lady. For which Order can glory in such a high distinction as does ours, in naming itself after the Mother of God?[95] Certainly it is an honor to belong to great Benedict and glorious Augustine, and they have much to be proud of who follow in the tracks of such distinguished Fathers as Saint Dominic and Saint Francis and the other saints who founded religious Orders, which are high mountains. But the peak raised above the summit of all mountains, clearly, is the one offered to our sovereign Virgin, who has the moon beneath her feet and is clothed with the sun and is crowned with stars."[96]

"As far as Saint John the Baptist and Saint Jerome's being members of our sacred Order," said Justa, "I am satisfied with the reasons you have given. But I am still left with my greatest doubt, which is for what reason this Order more than any other is said to belong to Our Lady. For although you have brought up the house built by Solomon and everything you said on that subject, your reasons do not carry very much weight, for nowhere in Scripture does it explicitly say that this Order was instituted in her name. If you can prove this to me with reliable testimonies, that will suffice to make me believe any other great things you may tell me about."

"I am happy to do so," said Gracia, "and I am confident of satisfying you. Let the first proof be what His Holiness Pope Gregory XIII says at the beginning of the papal bull that he granted us a short time ago,[97] reaffirming our

95. Naming itself after the Mother of God: The formal name of the order is Our Lady of Mount Carmel.

96. Apocalypse (Revelation) 12:1.

97. The bull titled *Ut laudes* was dated September 18, 1577. Gregory XIII (1502–85) was elected pope in 1572. During the Middle Ages, the Carmelite friars of Europe claimed that the Virgin Mary would liberate them from purgatory on the Saturday following their death, an indulgence

ancient indulgences so as to leave in effect what was granted by other Pontiffs who addressed the matter, along with the grace granted by the Council of Ephesus at Saint Cyril's request, of which you must have heard. Our Pontiff, then, says the following: 'So that the human tongue may never cease to sing the praises of our most glorious Virgin Mary, who produced the author of our salvation, but rather may venerate her, honoring her most holy name with pious devotion, it seems to us that the sacred Order invoking the Virgin Mary herself should be embraced with special grace: that is, Our Lady of Mount Carmel. The Virgin herself—most beautiful, and adorned with the flowers of all virtues—brought this Order to light and beautified it with the title of her own name. It has thus been approved by many Roman Pontiffs, our predecessors, and since times long past has been adorned with privileges and faculties. From ancient times, fertile fruits have sprung up in the Lord's field, and no fewer now are harvested every day. Therefore we cherish with particular favors and graces this same Order and its monks and nuns, who shine with special brightness as a model of religious life among the others who profess in those regular Orders that belong to the Catholic Church, and who descend directly from the holy prophets Elias and Eliseus and Enoch and other holy Fathers, who lived on Mount Carmel near the fountain of Elias.'"

"Sister Gracia has done well," said Atanasia, "in fulfilling what she promised you; the testimony she has brought you is sufficient,[98] for not only does it possess such reliability and authority that no one would dare to contradict it, but with this one answer she has confirmed everything she said."

"Wait, Sister," said Gracia, "for I still have a great deal to say on this matter."

"Tell us, Sister, tell us," said Justa, who was listening with great attention.

And Gracia went on, saying, "Wait, and you shall see how ancient a legacy and possession of the Virgin is this Order. Isaias, in chapter 35, says that 'the glory of Lebanon is given to it [and] the beauty of Carmel.'[99] And when Jeremias in his second chapter speaks in the name of the Virgin as the Lady of this holy mountain—who, in addressing her Order, reminds them that she took them out of the desert and the shadow of death and brought them to the land of Carmel 'to eat the fruit thereof and the best things

---

known as the Sabbatine Privilege. This indulgence, supposedly ratified by John XXII in 1322, was widely disputed by orders hostile to the Carmelites. *Ut laudes*, ratified by Gregory XIII ("our Pontiff," of whom María speaks immediately below) in 1577, permitted the Carmelites to continue to preach their belief in Mary's particular intercession on their behalf.

98. Is sufficient [basta el]: Simeón de la Sagrada Familia thus corrects the manuscript, which here reads "is all" [sólo es].

99. Isaias (Isaiah) 35:2; the Douay bible gives "Lebanon" as "Libanus." In this sentence of María's text, Simeón de la Sagrada Familia corrects "será de" in the manuscript with "se le dió."

thereof'—this passage, complaining of their ingratitude, says: 'you defiled my land, and made my inheritance an abomination.'"[100]

Justa was astonished by this, as she showed by raising her eyebrows. She held out her hand and stopped Gracia, who was about to go on, to say, "Tell me, dearest, is it possible that there in that prophet is found our Queen's complaint, which we have with our own eyes so clearly seen fulfilled? Because the reasons that have just been presented now leave no room to doubt that Carmel is hers, or that she is the one speaking there."

"Wait, Justa," said Gracia, "for I have said nothing in comparison with what you shall hear further on, when I speak of the destruction of this mountain. And for now let us go on with its greatness.

"And how well was the Virgin established in this place! The angel found her here when he brought her news that she was to conceive God, for the city of Nazareth was on the summit of this mountain, as it says in our "Courier of the Holy Land." Our Lord Christ went up this mountain many times to pray. On this mountain, the Lord healed the daughter of the woman from Cana; on His way down from this mountain He cured a leper, and the centurion asked Him to restore his boy to health. It was here that, going into Saint Peter's house, He cured the saint's sister-in-law, as well as a great multitude of the ill and possessed, for on this mountain were founded the cities of Tyre and Sidon and Capernaum and the sea of Tiberias. It was on the slopes of this mountain that the Lord fed five thousand men with five loaves and two fishes, and worked many other miracles. Because as a good and obedient son, He did not leave His mother's house, by which it is well proven that He is pleased to dwell in it. And she, the most serene Princess, gave her word to her servant Saint Peter Thomas that this shall be so forever.[101] While he was praying to her to let our sacred Order increase and continue forever, she told him in a miraculous vision: 'Have faith, my son, and do not fear, for the Carmelite Order shall remain until the end of the world, because Elias, its founder, has asked my Son for this.' This seems just as it should be if only so that, while the Master lives, He should not be left without disciples. And as the mighty Captain Elias is kept to wage war against the fierce beast of which

100. Jeremias (Jeremiah) 2:7.

101. Saint Peter Thomas (c.1305–66), bishop and confessor. He was "revered by medieval members of his Order who regarded him as the ideal Carmelite, combining in his life the two prophetic elements of contemplation and apostolic engagement" (Peter-Thomas Rohrbach, *Journey to Carith: The Story of the Carmelite Order* [Garden City, N.Y.: Doubleday, 1966], 89). The account of his celebrated vision states that he had been praying to the Virgin Mary on behalf of the Carmelite order when he heard her say, "Have confidence, Peter, for the Carmelite Order will last until the end of the world. Elijah, its founder, obtained it a long time ago from my Son."

Saint John speaks,[102] obviously he must have soldiers to follow his zeal for the glory and honor of God.

"We have clearly seen how the Virgin has cared for this Order whenever it has been in need. For being the Mother of God, when she knew that the Holy Land was to be destroyed she revealed to the Provincials, who were in the general chapter of Mount Carmel, that it would be right to go and found monasteries in Europe. There, by the mercy of the Lord, the Order now flourishes in its primitive austerity, because the sovereign Queen has taken her servant Angela to be her mediator; in Angela we see fulfilled what David says, that '[she] is as a fruitful vine, and we see her covered with new shoots; above Lebanon shall the fruit thereof be exalted.'[103] And Isaias, in the chapter we mentioned not long ago, writes, 'The land that was desolate and impassable shall be glad, and the wilderness shall rejoice, and shall flourish like the lily.'[104] These passages prove that Carmel is a 'fat mountain,' for where is greater abundance and wealth possessed than by those who adhere to their devotion to the Most Blessed Virgin, who is the keeper of the treasury of graces?"[105]

"It is very clear indeed, Sister," said Justa, "that there is no doubt that Mount Carmel holds an advantage over all other mountains, which, prostrating themselves, should venerate the mountain dedicated to the Queen of Heaven. But they are not sure of this, and as we know they have envied it. Therefore, to speak clearly of this mountain [is to refer] to that passage written by Saint Jerome that you recently quoted, for the other mountains have managed to overthrow and undo this one. It now remains to be seen whether it is a greater glory for the Virgin to have one Order in particular established for her service and worship, since all the Orders, though they be named for other saints, are also hers because she is universal Mother and Lady of the Church."

Gracia answered this by saying, "Although a Queen may be given ladies of honor and maidservants to attend her and wait on her in her chambers, it

---

102. The fierce beast of which Saint John speaks: in many passages of Apocalypse (Revelation).

103. These citations include Psalms 127:3 (128:3) and 71:16 (72:16).

104. Isaias (Isaiah) 35:1.

105. María's emphasis on the Virgin's patronage and Teresa's role as her prophesied mediator may be attributed to the author's wish to underscore women's roles in the history of the order at the time when the Disclaced general, Nicolás Doria, was threatening to curtail the autonomy of the nuns. It has been suggested that conversos like Teresa and possibly María de San José were attracted to the Carmelite order because they saw in it the continuity of a Judeo-Christian heritage. It is notable that María gives ample attention to the Marian as well as the Hebraic traditions of the order.

is not therefore thought that this deprives her of the command of all the other women of her kingdom, as Lady of all the land. Nor is it thought that because her own ladies and serving women obey her like vassals, she should therefore have no others save those who are employed solely in her service. We know full well that blind heathendom, who adored and served the demons though they mistakenly named them gods, as such offered and dedicated special priests to them, in the manner they thought pleasing to their gods. The Gallic priests were dedicated to the goddess Verecintia, whom they called the mother of the gods,[106] and these priests wore white vestments. The Vestal virgins were dedicated to the goddess Vesta. Thus were the heathen temples filled with priests and priestesses. And though it is repugnant to me to introduce things that are so vain and full of superstition in support of things so true and holy, I remember having read that many customs followed by the Gentiles in their temples are now practiced by our Christian religion, though with all the difference that exists between the false and the true, the sacred and the profane. I mean that the priests in white vestments were one day to be dedicated not to the mother of the vain gods, but to the Mother of the true God; and that their virgins, who in their temple, preserved the fire of the love of God, were dedicated to the goddess Vesta, which means 'fire.'"

Justa now grew somewhat scandalized, as is the way with women who know very little, to hear that certain practices observed by the Gentiles were used in the Church. And understanding this, Atanasia said, "I will answer her question so that you, Sister, may rest; for it does not astonish me that you might be tired and vexed with enduring Sister Justa and all her scruples."

"You will be doing me a great kindness," said Gracia, "for she has quite worn me out."

"You must know, Sister Justa," said Atanasia, "that the Gentiles, though they erred in adoring many gods, were able to guess and sniff out that there must be some deity; and accordingly, they performed services and offered certain just and honorable sacrifices to it, though others that they made were hideous. But leaving that aside, let us consider how they made sacrifices of cattle and clean offerings, which men also offered up to the true God. This

---

106. The author is here speaking of the goddess Cybele, "the great mother-goddess of Anatolia, . . . primarily she is a goddess of fertility, but also cures (and sends) disease, gives oracles, and . . . protects her people in war. . . . [S]he is also mistress of wild nature . . . " (*Oxford Classical Dictionary*, 303). Known in Greece by the fifth century, she was associated with Demeter. Berecynthia was the mountain sacred to Cybele; Virgil, in the Aeneid, refers to the goddess using the name of the mountain.

kind of offering has now stopped under the law of grace, but offering incense has not, and having lamps and fonts, such as we see used today."

"As to that," said Justa, "why should I have to say that the Church takes such things from the time of the Gentiles, or learned these things from them, if they have been known much longer under the Old Law?"[107]

"That is a good question," said Atanasia, "but I shall tell you something that the Church uses that it did not learn from the synagogue, and that is the consecration of virgins. Do not think it any offense to holy things to say how ancient is this sacrifice, which is so pleasing to the eyes of God. And although it lacked any value in a blind people who acted without any light of faith, do not think that it occurred entirely without the will of the universal Lord as Creator of all things, even though they did not know Him. Here we may see how thoroughly the heretics condemn themselves.[108] Oh, if you only knew the virtues possessed by many of those Gentiles, and how the holy Doctors of the Church confound us with those very virtues! It gives me great shame when I remember what Plutarch wrote in the life of Numa Pompilius,[109] using these words: 'Having laid waste to the cities, Numa then began to converse very little with men, spending his time in the fields and in the contemplation of divine things; there, in the silence of the deserted fields, far from the vexatious hindrance of human company, he considered the works of God, in contemplation of which he was often elevated and without knowing it carried off in ecstasy.'

"Let this be enough for us to take away two things: first, what shame it brings those of us who take pride in being solitary nuns that a Gentile without the light of faith should have such advantages over us; and second, how little attention we should give to ecstasies, for when the Gentiles contemplated natural things they were carried off in ecstasy without the grace of God, and thus we should fear that our ecstasies might be like that. That, Sister Justa, is what I want you to take away from this, since I do not know if you will be satisfied. Now let us go to the convent, for the Lord's voice is calling us by means of that little bell."[110]

---

107. The Old Law: that is, the Old Testament or Hebraic law.

108. How thoroughly the heretics condemn themselves: The meaning of this sentence is unclear. María may be referring to the Protestant rejection of monasticism, her point being that even the ancient gentiles knew that virginity was pleasing to God.

109. Plutarch, *Lives*, Numa, 4.1. Numa Pompilius was the legendary Sabine king who, after Romulus, ruled Rome from 715 to 673 B.C.E.

110. There follows in the manuscript, "List of the Captain and soldiers who should be placed at the three points of the squadron."

FIFTH RECREATION

In which Gracia continues to tell of the greatness of Mount Carmel

"Go on with your story," Atanasia said to Gracia, when they had returned to their spot the next day.

"With pleasure, Sister, but on one condition: that Sister Justa not act scandalized at what I say."

"That is entirely up to you," said Justa, "so long as you tell me nothing about the Gentiles, for I won't hear such things."

"By that I see, Sister," answered Gracia, "that you possess even less wit than I had thought. Calm down, for I shall say nothing on that subject at present; what Atanasia said earlier was enough for our purpose.

"And now let us return to our mountain, and I'll tell what Isaias, Jeremias, and Amos say about Carmel—always understanding that we have no wish to reduce or abridge the mysteries of that vast sea of the spirit of God that stirs in holy letters, for their least part is full of such mysteries.

"Isaias, then, says in chapter 16, 'And gladness and joy shall be taken away from Carmel, and there shall be no rejoicing nor shouting in the vineyards.'[111] It must be understood that 'Carmel' means 'abundance of wine,' so that not without mystery do we speak of 'the vineyard of Carmel,' while all the prophets foresaw the destruction of this sacred mountain; and Isaias himself says, in chapter 33, 'The land hath mourned [. . .]: Lebanon is confounded, and become foul, and [. . .] as a desert: and Basan and Carmel are shaken, and there I shall destroy and cut down the high cedars.'[112] And Jeremias, in chapter 4: 'I looked upon the mountains, and behold they trembled: and all the hills were troubled. I beheld, and lo there was no man: and all the birds of the air were gone. I looked, and behold Carmel was a wilderness.' [113] Amos, chapter 1: 'and the beautiful places of the shepherds have mourned, and the top of Carmel is withered.' [114] Nahum, chapter 1: 'Basan languisheth, and Carmel.'[115]

"Now let Sister Atanasia make known to us what these passages tell us about our mountain."

"The meaning is clear," said Atanasia, "and indeed, all the threats made against our mountain have been fulfilled: true gladness and joy were taken

111. Isaias (Isaiah) 16:10.

112. Isaias 33:9. María's passage does not correspond to the Douay translation or any Bible we have located, in that the final phrase, "and there I shall destroy and cut down the high cedars," does not appear.

113. Jeremias (Jeremiah) 4:24–26.

114. Amos 1:2.

115. Nahum 1:4.

away when the monks and nuns sought their consolation here on earth. They forgot to eat their bread and were not happy with the fruit of the vine and trampling of the grapes; as true charity cooled, Lebanon was left confounded and dark, losing the whiteness of chastity; Saron was left a desert, empty of the praises of God, because this signified how Basan and Carmel were laid waste by insatiable ambition, losing their sweet sleep, quiet, and repose. And later it says in Jeremias, 'I looked upon the mountains and behold, they [that] trembled [were the largest]: and all the hills were troubled. I beheld, and lo there was no man: and all the birds of the air were gone.' Now this passage will be understood to refer to the contemplatives, and therefore Carmel was left deserted and mourning for the beautiful places of the shepherds and the green fields. With no one to be nourished by grazing there, the summit of Carmel withered.

"Look ahead now, Gracia, and tell what you have twice been about to start when Justa stopped you."

"She must have been afraid," replied Gracia, "that I might say something about the past, or mention the Devil, which seems to frighten her as it does Sister Basiana, who crosses herself a thousand times during the reading in refectory whenever his name is mentioned."

"I'm not so timid as to be scared by that," said Justa, "but I am afraid, when you make ready to loose your reason upon us, that you may say something foolish."

"Is that what you're afraid of?" said Gracia. "By now you should have lost your fear and taken up arms against the many foolish things you've already heard, for most likely you have them all counted up for us."

"No, by now I've lost count," said Justa.

"This is no time to set us laughing," said Gracia, "for it is time for nothing but tears when we consider such a fall, though the heart takes courage once more on reaching the point where, with yet another prophecy from Isaias, our Carmel is to rise again. So that you may see clearly, Sister, that it is not by chance but rather entirely by God's design that this loss was restored by women, hear what Isaias says in chapter thirty-two, 'Rise up, ye rich women, and hear my voice; ye confident daughters, give ear to my speech; [. . .] for the vintage is at an end, the gathering shall come no more [and all shall be destroyed]. . . . Then the fruitful field shall become as a desert, and judgment shall dwell in the wilderness, and justice shall sit in the fruitful field of Carmel. And the work of justice shall be peace, and the service of justice quietness.'"[116]

116. Isaias (Isaiah) 32: 9–10, 15–17, adapted to account for disparities between María's and other biblical translations.

"Wait," said Justa, "go no further; what you just said about 'the service of justice' is right there in Isaias?"

"Yes, Sister," answered Gracia, "would I make things up out of my head?"

"A wondrous thing," said Justa. "Do you not see the very words of our own Rule,[117] by which Isaias seems to wish to inspire those women whom he is calling?"

"Just so," said Gracia, "wait, and you will see how he leads them, to bring them to that justice and peace, because further on he says, 'and [for your] security for ever [. . .] my people shall sit in the beauty of peace, and in the tabernacles of confidence'[118]—which is another point in our Rule—when he has first told them to gird their loins and mourn for the breasts, for the destruction of that fruitful vineyard;[119] so that we were not wrong in calling it 'a fat mountain,' for there have been shepherds, pastures, and sheep that were sacrificed there, as were the glorious Saint Anastasius and many others along with him, in countless numbers both before and after, ravaged by those ravening wolves, the Devil's disciples. As the direct opponent of anything belonging to the Most Blessed Virgin, the Devil tries to darken and tear down the stars of our sky with his serpent's tail, tearing down the true spirit of poverty with possession, and humility with pride; resisting God and His Prelates with self-will, and abstinence with immoderation; and tearing down charity with ambition.

"When these foundations were pulled from under the building, it began to go to ruin and would have fallen to the ground, had not she who was its protector and shelter extended her hand and taken to the roads to appease the true David, who came in anger against Nabal.[120] Like another Abigail, she offered him two hundred loaves, which is the number of priests who were engaged in this reform when His Holiness Pope Gregory XIII granted us the papal bull; and they can quite properly be offered up in place of the bread and wine offered up by Abigail, for they are priests after the Order of Melchisedek.[121] But this divine Abigail brought slain and dressed the five

117. The very words of our own Rule: Carmelite Rule, *Silence.*

118. Isaias (Isaiah) 32: 17–18.

119. To gird their loins . . . that fruitful vineyard: Paraphrase of Isaias 32:11–12.

120. 1 Kings 25: 23–35 (and 25:18 is cited in the next sentence). Nabal is described (in Douay) as a wealthy man whose "possessions were in Carmel . . . and the name of his wife was Abigail. And she was a prudent and very comely woman, but her husband was churlish" (1 Kings 25:2, 3).

121. Priests after the Order of Melchisedek: María is making a complex typological allusion here; weaving together two biblical texts: Psalms 109:4 (110:4), "Thou art a priest for ever according to the order of Melchisedek"; and Genesis 14:18, "Melchisedek, the king of Salem, [brought] forth bread and wine, for he was the priest of the most high God."

kids that had destroyed Carmel, which are the five vices we have named, and a hundred clusters of raisins, which are the nuns joined together in charity who have undergone mortification. And at this our sovereign David, clearly appeased, sent blessings and thanks by way of his vicar-general here on earth.

"And with that," said Gracia, "you go on, Sister Atanasia, for I have come thus far."

"It would be a pity, Sister," said Atanasia, "for you to cut this thread for a woman who will be so poor at tying it up."

"It seems to me it's already cut," said Justa, "for by what Gracia has said, that great Carmel of the past has already come to an end; this one will have to be built from another start."

"You are deceived," said Gracia, "for that one has not now come to an end nor is this one now beginning, but rather, it is the same now as it was."

"How can it possibly be the same?" said Justa. "For those regions where the hermit saints once dwelled have come to an end, and they are no longer ours; and it is impossible to say that those mountains moved to this place."

"Impossible, Sister?" replied Gracia. "That would be true for those who have no faith, but for those of us who do it is not necessarily so. Don't you know what the Lord says in the Gospel? 'If you have faith as a grain of mustard seed, you shall say to this mountain, Remove from hence hither, and it shall remove'?[122] Well then, where is such lively faith to be found as in our Spain? It moved the great Carmelite Order here; here the Order sent forth new shoots where it is now established in the midst of that faith, which is its basis. Our Carmel is set in the northern reaches, in the midst of this fortunate and cherished province of Spain, with the greater part of it transplanted at present between the west and the north, extending toward the south through the east.

"And so that you may understand that it is one and the same Carmel, I shall go back to say, with the passage from David, that it is a fat mountain because it is full of wealth and pastures and everything that can be found on mountainsides. God did not leave this dwelling empty, as it is 'a mountain in which God is well pleased to dwell: for there the Lord shall dwell unto the end.'[123] And it is not surprising that it should be rich and full of good things, because Micheas says in his seventh chapter, 'Feed thy people with thy rod, the flock of thy inheritance, them that dwell alone in the forest, in the midst

122. Matthew 17:19.
123. Psalms 67:16–17.

of Carmel.'[124] 'Blessed is the nation whose God is the Lord,' we might add here, 'the people whom He hath chosen for His inheritance.'[125]

"And because I am tired, and our Sister Atanasia is no longer here, although we still see her body before us, let us allow her to retreat to her little cave, for I don't think she will give us much of an explanation of what we have said."

"Don't leave off your conversation for my sake," said Atanasia, "for you do not disturb me just because I am engaged in certain devotions; conversations like this are like music to the ears, to enliven the spirit."

"Be that as it may," said Gracia, "it would be well for us to retire, for it is time."

SIXTH RECREATION

In which they discuss the riches and precious stones of Mount Carmel

The next day, when Justa and Gracia had come to Atanasia's hermitage, they found her prostrate upon the ground; and though it caused her great mortification, she went with them because it was a matter of obedience, which the Lord desires more than He does sacrifice.[126] Nevertheless, in order to provide her Sisters with some recreation, she said to them, "You are short on prayer but long on conversation, for you have arrived at daybreak."

"Have no doubt, Sister," said Gracia, "but that it is quite natural for women to talk a great deal. I think this springs from the fact that, as we know very little, we need a great many words to make ourselves understood. And now sit down, and we will return to our story.

"It is fitting that we first give water to our mountain, for water is the element most necessary to human life, without which we could not live; and rivers and fountains beautify and fertilize the earth. And to show how God attends to such things, I will tell you what is written in Deuteronomy, chapter 8. There Moses says, in speaking to the people of God, 'For the Lord thy God will bring thee into a good land, of brooks and of waters, and of fountains: in the plains of which and the hills deep rivers break out.'[127] And Isaias says in chapter 41, 'I will open rivers in the high hills, and fountains in the midst of the plains: I will turn the desert into pools of waters, and the impass-

---

124. Michaes (Micah) 7:14.
125. Psalms 32:12.
126. 1 Kings 15:22: "For obedience is better than sacrifices."
127. Deuteronomy 8:7.

able land into streams of waters.'[128] The rivers in our own province of Spain are not unworthy of admiration, as their waters possess great virtue and delicacy. For as I have said, our province lies to the north, so that our running waters are more wholesome and light because they are refined by the northerly winds of the septentrion and freed from the southerly winds of the meridian, which thicken the waters and fill them with vapors. And although counting and praising the multitude of rivers and springs would be a difficult task, I shall not fail further on to record them when I speak of the establishment of our monasteries, many of which are on the banks of mighty and distinguished rivers.

"Now I come to our purpose, to begin telling of the spiritual properties of this mountain: there is no lack of water where one may contemplate and speak of God's law, for as David says, 'And he shall be like a tree which is planted near the running waters, which shall bring forth its fruit, in due season. And his leaf shall not fall off.'[129] And Job says, 'my root is opened beside the waters, and dew shall continue in my harvest.'[130] Above all, this mountain is in the midst of that river that Saint John saw, 'proceeding from the throne . . . of the Lamb'[131] and that fountain of living water from which Our Lord Christ invited the Samaritan woman to partake.[132] Here the Lord calls to all who are thirsty; here are the waters of Siloe[133] that flow in silence; here is where water is drawn from the stone. Oh, sweetest Jesus! Rightly do you endow us with water, the thing most necessary to human life. For indeed, most blessed Source and Spring, there is no life in our works if they be not showered by the water of your grace; we must seek you by roads and paths of water, for as your prophet says, 'thy way is in the sea, and thy paths in many waters.'[134] You are the life, the truth, and the way, and this way must lead through the waters of tribulation; and thus, Sisters, it is not right that tribulations should be lacking in Carmel. For we do not praise and cherish Carmel on account of its great age, or for the many favors of the nobility that have been bestowed upon it, or because we dress in sackcloth, or because ours is the habit of the most blessed Virgin. All this would profit us little if we did not live here in imitation of Christ. *This* is the true way. Walk in Him, says our

128. Isaias (Isaiah) 41:18.
129. Psalms 1:3.
130. Job 29:19 (this passage is incorrectly identified by Simeón de la Sagrada Familia).
131. Apocalypse 22:1.
132. John 4:10.
133. John 9:7.
134. Psalms 76:20.

Rule.[135] And may no one suppose that we boast of being Discalced or of wearing coarse cloth, for neither these things nor anything else we might do would be enough for us to reach the prize given to the righteous, without a true imitation of Our Lord Jesus Christ. Such an imitation consists of abiding by His law, and of holding the divine Sun in highest regard while contemplating ourselves in Him, and of buying the gold of true wisdom, which is a mine of holy metals, wherein lies that precious pearl for which wise merchants exchange all earthly goods in order to possess Christ, a pearl of great price.[136]

"This is the lodestone that raises hearts laden and shackled with faults[137] to the hope of eternal life; it is the carbuncle that shines resplendent through our tribulations, expelling from the heart that owns it all venom and mistrust, which in my judgment are the means by which demons poison and harry those who attempt prayer and recollection; it is jacinth,[138] which wards off the bolts of the wrath of God; it is turquoise, which keeps one from falling; the diamond, which strengthens the heart to stand where it is and gives it courage, drawing to it those who see it—as Isaias says of the face of God that draws others to it like the diamond;[139] it is coral and chalcedony, which protect against falling sickness;[140] it is jasper, which stanches the blood; it is topaz, which engenders charity in anyone who carries it; it is chrysolite, which works against madness and drives away visions and fantasies; it is crystal, which clears the sight, and sapphire, which pleases the sight of those who carry these stones and makes them well loved; it is an emerald, which makes the heart happy and rids it of melancholy; it is the amethyst stone, which drives away demons; it is the heliotrope stone, which makes men faithful and invisible, and bestows long life; it is the stone called selenite, which has the form of the moon and waxes and wanes just as she does. I shall do no wrong by applying this last stone to You, for You, my Lord, do greatly resemble it. You have the likeness of our Queen and Mother, our Lady, who is called by the name of moon, and your mercies grow according to the measure of her

135. Carmelite Rule, *Exhortations.*

136. Matthew 13:45–46.

137. Hearts laden and shackled with faults [los corazones pesados y cargados de hierros]: Here there is a play on words, as *hierros* (irons, shackles) and *yerros* (errors, faults, sins) are homonyms in Spanish.

138. Jacinth: a reddish or cinnamon-colored variety of transparent zircon, used as a gemstone; also called "hyacinth."

139. Isaias (Isaiah) 50:6–7 (Douay, "I have not turned my face away from them that rebuked me, and spit upon me. / The Lord God is my helper, therefore am I not confounded: therefore have I set my face as a most hard rock ").

140. Falling sickness [el morbo caduco]: epilepsy.

good will and will diminish on the judgment day, when she has no more good will toward sinners. You, my God, are the agate stone[141] that attracts all other stones and encloses in itself all their virtues, like a true sun from whose virtues are derived all the virtues transmitted to all other creatures, and in whose divine rays, just as those of the sun infuse virtue into gold, so yours engender the virtue of charity, which you have placed in this sacred mountain, where there is also the silver of wisdom."

"You have pleased us greatly," said Justa, with all you have said of these stones. But I want to know if what you have said of them are their own virtues, or if you meant to apply the virtues to our Lord, suiting the stones either by their color, or for some other reason, to those effects which our divine Lord works in the soul where He is found."

"You answer this, Atanasia," said Gracia, "for now I am tired; and it is right that one should also speak who must know this better—if only so that she not tell us that we are talking a great deal."

"You tell it yourself," said Justa, "and leave our Sister alone; don't hinder her."

"You must know, Sister," said Gracia, "since you want to hear it from me, that this virtue is possessed not only by the stones we have mentioned, but by many others that I omit so as not to go on too long in this matter—a brevity that goes quite a bit against my liking, because great good can be found in the contemplation of all creatures. And as the glorious Saint Paul says, 'for the invisible things . . . are clearly seen, being understood by the things that are made,'[142] because in truth visible things are like steps by which one ascends to a knowledge of God as if on a stairway. And since stones, trees, birds, and animals and all other things created have so many virtues and qualities, all of which are gathered together in humankind, then what a high and perfect creature the human must be, and how clearly shown to be beloved by the Lord, Who placed in the human all the graces and virtues of all other creatures and above all created humankind in the Creator's own image, bestowing the seal of His divinity.

"Once we see, dearest Sisters, the treasure of the divine miner who is Christ Our Lord, do not think that He is avaricious and wants it all for Himself; for as His Majesty says through Saint Matthew, this treasure is hidden in the field so that we all may benefit from it,[143] as many do from this sacred mountain. The virtue of the lodestone is enjoyed by those who, leaving off

---

141. Agate stone: the identification of this stone is not entirely clear. María's manuscript reads "pantaura," perhaps for *pantera,* a type of agate.

142. Romans 1:20.

143. Matthew 13:44: "The kingdom of Heaven is like a treasure hidden in a field."

concern for earthly things that weigh them down, rise and let themselves be carried by Christ to high and eternal things."

"I have noticed something about that stone," said Justa, "which is that it will not draw any metal to itself except for iron, and I wanted to know why."

"There must be some natural cause, which I don't know," answered Gracia, "but what we can take from this to suit our purpose is that it draws nothing to itself, as we were saying just now, except for the irons and fetters of faults and sins.

"The splendor of the carbuncle is enjoyed by those who embrace the Cross and trials of their Lord, their souls filled with joy; they possess peace of heart, with all venom expelled from it.

"From the bolts and fury of the wrath of God, jacinths defend those who walk always in their fear, fulfilling what David says, 'Serve ye the Lord with fear: and rejoice unto Him with trembling.'[144]

"The virtue of the diamond draws to it those who do not withdraw from the Law of God and who find sustenance in His word, which is a dish that never causes illness, unlike the fruit that sickened our first parents.

"The virtue of the diamond draws to it those who walk in the presence of God, as did our father Elias, and thus it makes them be valiant and strong of heart as was that holy prophet, and as are many of his children.

"The virtue of coral and chalcedony has been transmitted to others who with their holy counsel cure all those afflicted with falling sickness.

"Jasper draws those who, detached from flesh and blood, serve the spirit.

"Topazes draw the chaste and the clean.

"The virtue of crystal is enjoyed by those who have plain and simple sight and do not judge harshly by what they see.

"Chrysolites are those who, free of madness, have dispelled the memory of the visions and fantasies of this world.

"Sapphires and rubies are the truly humble, whose sight is pleasing because God places His eyes on them, and they are well-loved because they offend no one, though offense may be done to them.

"The emerald that gladdens the hearts of its brothers is the merciful man, who with emerald freed the unhappy from their melancholy.

"The truly obedient have the virtue of amethysts, to drive away demons, for there is nothing that drives them away more than obedience; they know that it was on account of this virtue that they were stripped and cast out of the kingdom which they had tyrannized.

"Those who speak truly in prayer, who adore the Father in spirit and in truth, are the heliotrope stone, whose virtue, as has been said, is to make men

144. Psalms 2:11.

faithful and invisible and long lived. What virtue does this stone have to make us faithful, like that of prayer? And what exercise to make men invisible and forgetful of the weight and coarseness of their bodies, so that they may be raised, not only in spirit but with their very bodies, toward invisible things? For so we read of a great many saints, and indeed, we know this to be true of our own Mother Angela. That this quality gives long life is quite clear, for it thus anticipates the life eternal, beginning from this day on to enjoy its good.

"The selenite stone, which has the form of the moon and waxes and wanes with her, represents those who, contemplating how little stability there is in all things, receive prosperity and adversity alike, with no disturbance of their spirits.

"The agate stone is those who possess true charity, which is the foundation of all things and virtues. And we would do well to hear of this sovereign virtue from Sister Atanasia, while I shall be silent, for I have spoken a great deal without knowing a single thing about virtue from my own experience."

"Well said," said Justa. "Let our Sister, who is well practiced in charity, tell us something about it; for it is right for a person to speak on such a virtue who has put it to work."

Atanasia, who had been quiet all this time, now said, "Justa has judged wisely that we should hear from one who has charity; I know of no one who has accomplished this deed as well as our dear Christ; let us go to Him, for He is a good teacher. Stop hunting down other petty means, for I am going back to my little cave."

"I shall go look at the sky," said Gracia.

"Well I shall go look at the earth," said Justa; "and although I choose what is lowliest, I firmly believe that if I knew how to benefit from it I could find great charity from our God, who came down to this earth for love. And with that, dearest Sisters, so that we may begin with charity, let our prayers be for each other."

"Well and good," they answered.

And with that they left one another.

SEVENTH RECREATION

In which all three nuns discuss the properties of prayer, and the practice of the same

When their prayers were done, all three returned to the place where they had spoken earlier. And Atanasia, whom they regarded as their teacher, greeted them and said, "We have all made our prayers, and in the prayer of each one of us the others participated as well. Well then, it is fitting that each should tell just how she has prayed, so that like the charity we shared, this may be common to all. And let Gracia begin."

"I was trembling to think you might order me to go first," said Justa. "Blessed be the Lord, that someone who knows something about it is going to begin. For I don't know what prayer is. I have never understood it, nor do I know what to say about myself, for I don't have those experiences that all of you have; and however hard I work at it, all I accomplish is to make my head dizzy and my heart sadder than night itself."

"I am glad indeed that you have spoken your mind," said Atanasia, "for this is just what I was after. It seems to me a great pity when I see how few there are who exert themselves in the heavenly practice of prayer, and of these few, how many waste their time to no advantage because they do not fully comprehend this matter. I can't understand what we imagine these inventions or tricks of prayer to be, for they are enough to frighten our spirits and to drive poor women mad. And this does not surprise me in their case, for we women are ignorant. But I am astonished when I think how many years I went about half foolish from conversing with people who are most greatly renowned for their way of prayer, and yet when they spoke to me about it they always left me confused until Our Lord made me understand. In order to know what prayer is, I don't know what more we could want than to see what the Lord Jesus Christ taught to His disciples when they asked Him, "Lord, teach us to pray, as John also taught his disciples," and His Majesty taught them the Our Father.[145] I could not wish for a better rule to tell me what prayer is. May the Lord bless me! If His Majesty teaches us to sanctify the name of God as a prayer, commanding us to call Him Father and to ask Him for whatever is necessary to us, just as we do in that holy prayer, then why do we go hither and thither making ourselves dizzy, with some people saying that they must not rock back and forth, and others that they should not open their eyes, and still others that they should visualize hither and yon whatever they are thinking about, and that on no account should they move from certain thoughts or meditations to different ones? It may well be that those who teach such things know what they are talking about, but I think there are few who understand them. I myself have seen certain people who you would think had been ordered to enter purgatory when they have to do one hour of prayer all in the dark and are obliged to think according to a pattern they have devised or one that others have devised for them."

"How happy it makes me to hear you say that," said Justa, "for that is literally what happens to me. And I don't know what I am looking for there, but my spirit grows tired and fearful so that I tremble at having to go back to the

145. Luke 11:1–4.

place of prayer. Now, what you have said about the Our Father comforts me. I shall rest happy with that, understanding that praising God is prayer, as well as asking forgiveness for our sins, and glorifying the Lord, and loving and obeying Him—regardless of whether this all be mixed together at one moment or if there be more of one thing or of another. So long as one's understanding is concerned with things that move the will to follow what is good and abhor what is wicked, then it is prayer."

"Yes, Sister," said Atanasia, "that is what I consider prayer to be, and I do not think there is any other kind. Let us leave aside the high and sovereign matters that God often communicates, which our holy Mother calls supernatural things, because they are not in our hands nor are they given to us whenever we might wish. Nor should greedy appetite for them bring us to prayer, because, as our holy Mother says, wanting them will of itself prevent their coming. And because we have gone on too long, let Gracia speak now."

"By now I had thought I was free of your command," answered Gracia, "which was no small relief to me, because I know less than Justa of this matter. But, as we are never to contradict what obedience orders, I shall tell—if I manage to make clear, as it was shown to my soul—how greatly God is pleased by the prayer we make on behalf of our brothers and sisters. Indeed, I have seen this clearly in the very prayer Our Lord taught us. There all He commanded us to ask was not for each one alone, but rather for all together, for we say: May Thy kingdom come *to us*, give *us* our daily bread, forgive *us* our trespasses. From this I have taken a mighty resolve never to ask anything for myself alone, because the Lord is so greatly pleased when our prayers are made with love of our neighbor—without which we may as well take our leave of the love of God."

"Oh, may the Lord bless me," said Atanasia, "how I am put out by souls who are so self-absorbed, that if they are asked for a Hail Mary they squeeze it to the very last drop. You'd think that God will deny them His heaven because they're just a penny short!"

"I don't think that is why they are like that," said Justa, "but rather from humility, because they believe they are worthless and God will not hear them."

"A fine humility," answered Gracia. "To me it looks like enormous ignorance, and I'm not sure I shouldn't say arrogance—to think that we should be heard for the sake of our merits. It is for the sake of Christ's merits that we are to ask, whether we are asking for ourselves or for others; and we should do so with great trust, for God is neither stingy nor miserly, as miserable souls think. And now let us get back to our Mount Carmel and its greatness."

At this Justa cut her off, saying, "Wait, Sister, for we are missing the best part; let Sister Atanasia have her say, since we have already spoken."

"Let me say," answered Atanasia, "that there's nothing in me that would be of any use."

"Have no fear," argued Justa, "for we shall forgive you."

"So be it," said Atanasia. "Ordinarily I begin praying with the Prayer of King Manasses,[146] which to me is one of the prayers that best satisfies my spirit. For I find in it what my soul desires to find in prayer; which is to praise God, confess sins, and trust—three things without which prayer seems unrewarding to me. Because (with deference to any opinion sounder than mine) all perfection is contained in these three parts; and because the beginning of this prayer starts out by saying: 'Lord God omnipotent, Creator of the heavens and all that is in them, whose word the sea obeys,' and it goes on like that telling of God's greatness and of His great goodness and mercy, by which He arranged for penitence for the sinner. And here King Manasses begins to tell of his sin, repeating many times and in many ways that he did sin, which is why he is prostrate and heavily fettered. Now it seems to me that in these two things—God's goodness and mercy—lies the constant exercise which he preaches we all should maintain: we are to present ourselves to the Lord at all times, pondering who He is and who we are ourselves. And these two extremes[147] prayer joins with that great trust with which it ends, promising always to praise Him. With this, Sister Gracia, continue what you began and let's not waste any more time."

"Have patience, Sister," said Justa, "because what you have said has stirred more doubts in me. Do not think it is a waste of time to discuss these things. After all, what matters most to the spiritual life is prayer. Just as the body without physical nourishment faints away, so the soul without the nourishment of prayer loses its strength for virtue—that's why it is no waste of time for you to tell us about it."

"Not only do I consider it misspent time to speak of what you say," answered Atanasia, "but when there are so many books of prayer written by such learned and holy men, it is temerity and boldness to look for a woman's rules for prayer, especially from a woman such as I."

"Now drop all these expressions of humility," said Justa; "I know perfectly well what you are. And as to what you say about books already written,

---

146. The prayer of King Manasses: an apocryphal text referred to in Douay, 2 Paralipomenon 33:12 ("And after that he was in distress he prayed to the Lord his God: and did penance exceedingly before the God of his fathers") and 19 ("His prayer also, and his being heard . . . are written in the words of Hozai"). Manasses (Manasseh, in King James), a king of Judah in the seventh century B.C.E., having sinned extensively, fell prisoner to the Assyrians and repented.

147. These two extremes: that is, human lowliness and divine greatness; and confidence in God's mercy joins the two.

I know that too, and in important and essential matters we would do well not to stray from them. But I am of the opinion that men miss the mark in the tiny and tangential little things to which, as it happens, we women are subject through our weak and imperfect nature. For having no experience of such things, men are not likely to come to them by study, just as we see that great physicians often err in prescribing a cure for women's ailments, while another woman gets it right."

"Well, as you still stubbornly insist that I should say something," said Atanasia, "tell me what your infirmity is, and we'll apply some remedy. However lowly and common it may be—as our remedies usually are—it may possibly do you some good, as you say."

"My infirmity," said Justa, "is what I said earlier, that I have no prayer nor do I know what it is, nor what I should do to have it. And although what you told me made me very happy—that asking forgiveness for sins is prayer, and desiring that God's will be done, and other such things—still, since so much is written about prayer, there should be more to it than that. And they say it should have seven parts, which are preparation, reading, meditation, contemplation, thanksgiving, petition, and epilogue."

"Just so," said Atanasia, "prayer has all those parts, and it is my belief that not one of them is missing in any true prayer, however brief it may be, as we shall say further on.

"But first it would be well for you to tell us how you act and exert yourself in all these parts. And be brief, so that we don't distract ourselves and wander far afield from the history of our mountain."

"I pray God that I may get it right," said Justa. "For it can't do any harm to tell all the ways I am ignorant, so that other women who I imagine are like me may escape from this ignorance.

"First, I go to the place of prayer, and many times as gloomily as if they were taking me to dig in the fields; indeed, it seems to me I'd set off more willingly for that. When I get there, I cross myself and say certain prayers by way of preparation. Then I read in a book the passage on which I am to meditate, and at times I go on reading and meditating because my distracted imagination allows for no more than that.

"When meditation is finished—sometimes by itself and sometimes accompanied by reading—I try to go on to contemplation. This is the most difficult part. The others seem more like the very first stitches we are taught, where we know more or less how to count and how to go; but once here, there is no keeping count, nor do I know where I'm going. I shut my eyes and try to force the faculties of my soul to quiet down, and sometimes, when it seems to me that even breathing obstructs the calm that I'd like and that I picture contemplation to be, I hold my breath. Whether this does me any good or not, you can tell me later, because now I want to go on to the act of thanksgiving, which is lukewarm and uneven.

"And next I begin my petition. But what happens is that by pressing ahead to finish the task, I distract myself and wander away from even the little bit of quiet I have gained, for I think that nothing has been accomplished if it has not been done in order.

"After having made my petition, I think about how I have wasted my time, and in thinking that, I waste another little bit. With this I come and go, and though at times my soul may incline toward something else, I neither dare to let it do so nor find any satisfaction in what I'm doing. Now for the sake of brevity, I cannot spell out a thousand things that come into this matter."

"For that very reason," said Atanasia, "it is difficult to leave these matters entirely clear, for each one of them holds an infinite number of difficulties. But we shall say whatever we can in response to what you have said.

"With regard to the first point, about going to your place of prayer, this is the most important thing. I would go so far as to promise that whoever persists in going to pray will emerge victorious without fail so long as it is done in pursuit of the true goal, which is to seek God. For without Him everything is done in error. And there is no need to pay any heed to whether you go gloomily or not, for sometimes that condition is caused by some indisposition and other times by the Devil. Most commonly people with no habit of prayer feel this distaste, but once they practice prayer, it goes away.

"Crossing yourself and saying a few prayers to make yourself ready is fine, but do not think that this alone is all the preparation that is necessary. For unless preparation is made in the soul with such a cleanness of conscience and modesty of heart that no room is left for anything that could be a sin, there is no reason to think that there will be any quiet in the prayer. I do not mean that sinners cannot have quiet, for if they persist with prayer, they will emerge from sin. This persistence is a most efficacious remedy. But in speaking of the true preparation that the soul must carry out before prayer, I mean that it must occur long before one prays, with a good conscience; and when that is in place, the soul quickly finds itself well disposed for prayer, and at times becomes recollected even before having occasion to make the sign of the cross."

"If that is the case," said Justa, "I do not have a good conscience, for I never end up recollected."

"I am not saying," said Atanasia, "that a person with a good conscience becomes recollected immediately upon arriving at prayer, but I do say that sleep does not come more quickly to the eyes of the sleepy than recollection to whoever has a good conscience and the habit of prayer."

"That is not always true," said Gracia, "because no matter how spiritual a person may be, it is not [always?] possible, on this earth, for these things to exist in one being."[148]

"That is so," replied Atanasia, "but just as recollection is slow in coming, if at all, to those who are not accustomed to prayer, just so distraction comes to those who are proficient in it."

"So this preparation consists of a good conscience, and practice?" said Justa.

"Indeed, Sister," said Atanasia, "and that is the first part. And I say it is the first, because the other parts that you strive so mightily to maintain do not always happen in order, because many times thanksgiving follows right after preparation, without waiting for meditation and the rest of it, and in the same way the other parts come according to how the Lord moves the soul. That is *poras sdf* why it is said that the Holy Spirit is the teacher. There may be many teachers, but all they can do is to tell us of the treasures that lie in prayer and warn us of the dangers so that we can protect ourselves. As for teaching us what the experience of prayer is like, I consider that impossible. And this shows how excellent this divine practice is, for only the Holy Spirit teaches it. Thus there is no reason to tie down one's spirit lest it be lifted up before entering into prayer.

"When they say that reading is the second part, it is understood that just as one takes a guide so as not to wander about lost, so any meditation we undertake should be something that is read in and taught by the holy doctors of the Church. But it is not always necessarily required that one read, especially for those proficient in prayer who are already informed in these matters; in their case, when they are least concerned about it some word from a certain passage will occur to them, which they have heard from God, and they take that as a basis for prayer. I speak in regard to the second part, which is reading; but again, people proficient in spiritual matters often do not leave it out. Indeed, our holy Mother Angela always did read.

"Next follows meditating, either on what has been read, or what the soul already carries in its memory, or what the Lord suggests to it. For it often happens that those with experience intend to meditate on a particular thing but receive another which they could not set aside even if they wanted to. Meditation serves to persuade and move the will of those who have not been per-

---

148. No matter how . . . in one being [por muy espiritual que uno sea no es posible, en la tierra, estar esas cosas en un ser]: The meaning of this passage is not clear; it may be a lapsus.

suaded and are unmoved, which is why it is more necessary for beginners who should spend more time on this part than people who are already experienced and accustomed to prayer, and who require no more than to touch upon the first notice of any matter to be awakened. What I am saying does not apply to meditation during times of temptations when everything is needful and nothing suffices save only the mercy of our Lord, who helps anyone who calls on Him. But because there are a thousand remedies already written down for such times, there is no call for us to linger over this.

"Let us just speak of the difference that lies between the meditation of those who are experienced in prayer and those who are not, because I am afraid that here is where a great many people stumble and waste time. Because, as I shall explain later, the soul that is moved by the first thing that comes to its notice as being from God makes of its will a captive. At times the will is incited to dissolve in praises of God, and at others to marvel at God's greatness and infinite goodness while abasing itself in the abyss of its own wretchedness, which it sees before it. And how could the soul be able or willing to leave either of these states without a great effort? But on the other hand, we have the soul's own ignorance as well as the Devil, who helps the soul leave these states and go back to its meditation. For the soul believes that if it does not continue meditating, it is doing nothing and wasting time. Yet the truth is quite the opposite. Indeed, the soul loses a thousand benefits, as the Devil knows full well. So he uses his wiles to snatch away this part of prayer so that the soul will fail to reach the next part, which is contemplation. Once people are in contemplation, the Devil is hard pressed to harm them, because here the soul receives greater light, and the Holy Spirit now extends His hand with greater fervor (I mean that at this point the Holy Spirit alone is working, and it is no longer a matter of our own effort, nor indeed is there any work on our part—for it is there in our effort that the Devil can interfere and get involved). Therefore the Devil sets all his traps, and though he cannot utterly harm souls who are going toward God as their goal, he contents himself at the very least with hindering them as much as he can, so that they cannot receive the delicate and very gentle anointing by the Holy Spirit that is given through contemplation. It is here, in contemplation, that this anointing is granted by the Holy Spirit Himself, without whose permission souls can do nothing; and at times it is granted either for our sins or to make us humble.[149]

149. It is granted . . . to make us humble: This passage, which is somewhat obscure, seems to suggest that contemplation is sometimes granted as a complete gift, even when the soul is most sinful, as a way of increasing the soul's humility.

"I should like to make known the delicate smoke that rises in the soul from this sacrifice, which to me seems the most apt comparison; for in speaking of the golden bowls full of incense that the ancients held before the altar of the lamb, the glorious Saint John says that they were 'the prayers of the saints.'[150]

"And to start from the beginning to explain what contemplation is, let us suppose that our preparation—which is the first part of prayer, as we have said, and the foundation underlying all the rest—is similar to the arrangements we might make to create a fragrant pomander box. To do this, we first mix an essence of fragrant waters with other aromatic spices. Then we place it upon glowing coals where there are also ashes to bank the coals. The materials we have used determine the scent that is released there either quickly or more slowly, depending on the fire—which we know to be the love of God, and the ashes are humility. Thus these are the parts that must make up our preparation: cleanness, which is the precious water, a high goal in the love of God, and humility.

"By *reading*, we understand these materials brought together and arranged so as to be burned; *meditation* is that fomentation and activity of the fire, whose heat raises a delicate and very gentle vapor, which I see as *contemplation*. I do not call it smoke, as this vapor is more subtle and gently penetrates the senses; just so, a soul is instantly infused with sweetness without knowing how or what the sensation is that has been transmitted to it, because nothing there is so coarse that the senses could perceive it. When some time has passed in which the soul is seemingly suspended and its faculties are almost though not entirely lost, there arises the impulse of *thanksgiving* consistent with the mystery or mysteries that the soul pondered or the Lord communicated to it in contemplation. For many times the soul best understands the favor it has received—indeed, this is most often so—through the effects with which it is left. Thanksgiving in turn prompts the soul to make a *petition* with confidence and to recall what it has received, which is its summary or *epilogue*. In this way, the soul is like a wife who has received many caresses and favors from her husband; while she is receiving them, she has her attention focused more on the love with which they are given than on the specific words or deeds that she receives, which she will ponder later in detail and carry in her heart.

"That is why this memory is said to be the last part of prayer, because if it does not remain in the soul, one might fear either that the prayer was of little profit or that what was received in prayer—though it seemed to the re-

150. Apocalypse 5:8.

cipient to be many pleasures and caresses—must have proceeded from that person's own sensuality. Clear proof of the latter appears when the soul is left empty, and everything seems to have vanished like smoke. Such is not the case when the suspension and uplifting of the spirit that has occurred comes from God, for though it may be as brief as a blink of the eyes, it remains in the soul with weight and substance—though there are greater and lesser degrees in these things, consistent with the disposition each person brings and the grace the Lord wishes to transmit. At times a person is left with a plenitude and filling of the faculties of the soul, at others with a sense of marveling at a great majesty, as we have already said; for as the Lord is so rich, He has much to bestow. It sorrows me sometimes, when I see the deception that has befallen some people (and would to God that they were only women) who think that they are not true contemplatives and are not engaging in prayer if they don't go into rapture at every step or have visions. I think this deception gives rise to the taste for contemplations,[151] though there are many in our day who do go into rapture at every step. As this subject is lengthy and not one for me, I will leave it. And now what has been said must suffice."

"But see here, I'm not yet satisfied," said Justa, "because everything you have said is for people already profiting from and accustomed to prayer; tell me something so that I may profit by it."

"I have already told you the first and fundamental thing, that without preparation nothing can be done; you already know how it should be done. In all the rest, as I said, the Holy Spirit, who is the teacher, instructs bit by bit. Keep on with righteous intention, which will bring you to His Majesty and a safe harbor, even through the midst of the kinds of ignorance that we have mentioned. Be very careful not to let yourself hold your breath at the exhalation or inhalation, because I know for certain that some ignorant people have lost their health and their heads by that path; it is barbaric and ill advised to think that one can attain a state of prayer in that way. There must be few people indeed of those who pursue this way as a remedy who truly understand it, and it cannot be bad to say so here. Women must fall into this most often, although I have seen a man or two who, thinking to achieve the interior quiet that is so highly recommended, believe that even their breathing disturbs them and that in order to heed whatever happens in their interior, they must hold their breath. What happens is that, by holding their breath, they decrease that air which is life itself—and which, were it entirely

---

151. Contemplations: Simeón de la Sagrada Familia follows the earlier edition in using this word, which is unclear in the manuscript. In colloquial Spanish of this period, pluralizing a normally singular abstract noun adds a disparaging connotation.

stopped, would suffice in a short time to end life. But instead they slow it down, thus suffocating the heart and taking from it the cooling that as a very warm organ of the body it needs at all times, so that smoke immediately rises to the chimney, which is to say the brain, and puts the senses to sleep. This they believe is prayer. The heart that is thus afflicted and fatigued shows itself at times so driven by impulse and sorely affected that different and disturbing expressions are seen on the exterior; then such people deceive themselves and others, believing these expressions to be impulses of prayer.

"In such matters I do indeed have something to say. I know I am not deceiving myself, because more than one person has communicated that they would like their ecstasies[152] examined—for so they call them, though without the slightest cause, for true ecstasies are just as different in substance as they are in their incidental aspects and form. And if such people do not wish to be deceived, as we have said, it is all made clear by the benefits that remain in the soul. Therefore, let anyone who wishes to examine such impulses speak with these souls and it will be seen that these impulses hold nothing substantial once the souls have left their so-called ecstasy.

"Because it is high time, let us finish with this subject on which I have lingered longer than I intended, and may God grant that Sister Justa may at last be satisfied."

"So I shall," answered Justa, "and I know how much truth you speak in your bits of ignorance, as one who has experience in the matter. Now it is time for Sister Gracia to go on with her story, for we have let her rest."

"I need no rest, for I do not grow tired of telling of Mount Carmel," replied Gracia, "and thus I would go back with good grace to what still lies before us in the way of flowers and plants and a thousand other things. So that you may not think that displaying the virtues of this mountain by a resemblance to precious stones or flowers or meadows is just the work of my imagination, listen to what our glorious Saint Jerome says in writing to Praesidio: 'Not long since, while traveling through the desert plains of Egypt, you saw quite fully the blessed company of angels that is spread throughout them. I am sure you contemplated the infinite number of flowers to be gathered here, the great and rich variety of precious stones and pearls found in these hills, and the meadows, green and blossoming the year round.'[153] In-

---

152. Ecstasies: María uses the negatively marked term for ecstasies [*arrobamientos*]. Here we see evidence that María, like Teresa, attributed most false ecstasies to physiological rather than demonic causes.

153. Jerome, *Ad Praesidium, de cereo paschali*, in *Patrilogiae cursus completus . . . Series latina* (known as *Patrilogiae Latinae*), ed. J[acques]-P[aul] Migne, 221 vols., 30:185 (Paris, 1846).

deed, there are pearls and precious stones, as our glorious Saint Jerome says and as we have already seen. It now remains for us to see the variety of flowers and trees and highly beneficial plants that grow on this blessed mountain, encircled by the crystalline river flowing from paradise that makes it fertile and abundant and irrigates it with mild and peaceable waters. There is no summer or winter to wither these holy flowers, interwoven[154] with a variety that composes the most beautiful places of hermitage, where those who dwell therein defend themselves from the wild beasts of the vices, which are enemies to all virtue; where the whiteness and fragrance of the chaste lilies chases away the stench of lewdness; where the sweetness and lovely color of the roses, which signify chastity, give value to their deeds; where pride is banished with the humble violets; and where the variety of all the other flowers serves to destroy the deadly weeds of the vices.

"There are palms where fruit is plucked; there are cedars and ash trees, laurels and ivy—these trees that remain evergreen; there are blackberries, which have the property of alleviating inflamations of the flesh. Here, deer that have been bitten by poisonous spiders find the plants *litamo*[155] and celandine. Here the swallows, heralds of the spring, find what they need to heal the eyes of their blind young ones. Here is sage, too, for those affected by palsy; indeed, great remedies for that disease are found on our mountain. Here is agaric and the wild climbing rose, and other things effective against bad humors; here is myrrh, balsam, and incense. And just as on Mount Lebanon (where according to Saint Jerome there are no venomous beasts because the smell of the cedars and their incense drives away serpents), so on our Mount Carmel they are put to flight; and the fleet deer upon this mountain assist by killing, with their breath, the snakes whose nature it is to pursue the clothed man but to flee from the naked one. But I do not want to moralize each of these things lest I go on too long, because they themselves explain what they are, and what has been explained is quite clear. For just as no thief will pursue a naked man, so the Devil, that old serpent, will not pursue the monk whom he sees to be naked and stripped of wealth. Against the little foxes that destroy the ripe fields of grain,[156] there are eagles to pursue

154. Interwoven: Simeón de la Sagrada Familia corrects the manuscript, which gives "entreteniéndose" [entertaining each other], to "entretejiéndose" [interwoven], a reading we accept here. If the former is correct, however, it might suggest the "entertainment" that the nuns provide each other in recreation, albeit in the literal and figurative "hermitages" of convent life.

155. Litamo: We have been unable to ascertain the identity of this plant. The word may be a coypist's misspelling or a regionalism. By ellision it might indicate *litocálamo*, or fossilized reed; *cálamo aromático*, the calamus or sweet flag root, was used in the preparation of theriac, an ancient antidote to bites by poisonous animals.

156. Cf. Canticle of Canticles (Song of Solomon) 2:15: "Catch us the little foxes that destroy the vines: for our vineyard hath flourished."

and banish them; against elephants, there are lambs that make them tremble. There are the turtledoves, who lament in solitude and whom the crows often pursue—against whom in turn there are the birds of prey called kites. The royal eagles are enemies of the cackling goose. Our illustrious mountain is full of these eagles, and when one grows old and her feathers adhere to her and her sight grows weak, she comes down to the fountain where she bathes and is renewed. Where better can man be renewed when he finds himself grown old in vices than in the fountain of living waters that is Christ Our Lord? In Him, too, these birds make their nest, for He is also the stone with rays as of a divine sun, by which their eyesight is restored. And here one learns the wisdom of the serpent, as the Lord commands.[157] Those who find themselves ill with vices make a fast for forty days, just as the serpent does when it enters a narrow hole in a rock to shed its old and ugly skin. Here are found the whitest swans and an infinite number of guileless doves, and all other things that make the fields beautiful and abundant; here too, as is right in our mountain, there is no lack of the little ants to whom Solomon sent sluggards.[158] For the ants live in a very well ordered republic and without having any king help one another in the summer toward the winter, living with a prudence and instinct greater than those of irrational animals. Nor is our mountain deprived of the beneficial work of the bees and their sweet labor, for when Saint Jerome writes to the virgin Eustochium about the multitude of monks in the deserts, he calls them swarms of bees.[159] We might do well to call them so, or to put this better, we cannot take away from our Carmelites a name they so well deserve for their continual practice of prayer and meditation. Isaiah, in chapter 41, says: 'In the name of the Lord, I will open rivers in the high hills,' and all the rest that we have said above when we spoke of water; and he goes on to say: 'I will plant in the wilderness the cedar, and the thorn, and the myrtle, and the olive tree.'[160] And he says this: 'That they may see and know, and consider, and understand together that the hand of the Lord has done this, and the Holy One of Israel hath created it.'[161]

"According to this, my dearest Sisters, it is neither vain nor beside the point to bring these things we have mentioned to your mind, for you find them in this mountain not only in the sense in which we have spoken of

---

157. Matthew 10:16: "Be therefore wise as serpents, and guileless as doves."

158. Proverbs 6:6: "Go to the ant, O sluggard, and consider her ways, and learn wisdom."

159. Jerome, *Commentariorum In Isaiam Prophetam* (Isaiah 19:24–25) in *Patrilogiae cursus completus . . . Series latina* (known as *Patrilogiae Latinae*), ed. J[acques]-P[aul] Migne, 221 vols., 24:193 (Paris: 1865).

160. Simeón de la Sagrada Familia points out that these last words must be arrived at from the context rather than read, given the poor condition of the manuscript here.

161. Isaias (Isaiah) 41:18, 19, 20.

them, which is spiritual, but indeed, you enjoy here an infinite number of herbs and plants and flowers. Be grateful and bear this in mind, for as we have seen in what Isaiah says, the Lord is pleased with this and He would wish us to suffer, if we did not by these means come to know His love and greatness.

"And now as we have made a very long pause, let us go on to our Angela."

"But certainly, Sister Gracia," said Justa, "though I want to hear about our Mother, I wish you would finish telling of the greatness of Carmel, for that gives me great contentment."

"I have not finished," said Gracia, "rather, let us now climb to its very summit, where this true Carmelite nun is to be found. And after we have spoken of her, we shall walk about our mountain, and I shall tell of all the monasteries that she founded—for I have not forgotten your desire."

EIGHTH RECREATION

Which tells of the life of the holy Mother Teresa of Jesus and of her birth and parents,
calling her by the name of Angela, and sums up the favors that God granted her,
as she relates them in her books

"After having discussed the greatness and riches of this mountain, it is only right that we should not forget the woman who caused it to be restored; this is all the more true as our chief purpose in this discussion is to record the life and wondrous virtues of our great Angela. I know no better place to include these than here, where we discuss the glory and splendor of this heaven. Let us make known and recognized the luminous star that shines so brilliantly in this sky; let the wise woman who discovered this field full of treasures appear among the pearls and precious stones of this deep mine. Since we have mentioned the eagles that are found here, let us look to this one who flies so high; for making her nest on the unbroken flint of the highest peaks, she inspires her children to flight, dividing the prey with them all, as is the nature of true eagles. Again, she is the whitest swan who, when plunged in dark waters of tribulation, preserves her purity and considers suffering to be a delight.

"Having come this far, dearest Sisters, the flimsy little boat of my limited wit dares not set out to sea, as if it foundered in an abyss; but putting down the oar of my own efforts, I offer myself up to divine aid, trusting in the Holy Spirit, which will blow with its divine breath if this effort of mine can serve it in any way.

"I shall begin by presenting an image that the Holy Spirit itself presents [in Scripture] when it portrays the worthy wife,[162] because from the time I

162. Proverbs 31:10 ff.

began to speak with this holy woman [Angela], I saw that she had undertaken the role of worthy wife with great perfection, so that few women who have been in God's Church can better be called by that name than she. And although many women have resembled that same strong woman in many respects, our Mother does so in all ways, as shall be seen if the grace of the Lord is with me and if you assist me with your prayers."

Said Justa, "We are glad to see what a good path you have taken, because truly the woman of whom we speak is the very same strong woman, but it frightens me to see such great and lofty mysteries in your hands. And I would not want you to think that the things the Holy Spirit says through Solomon are as homely and everyday as they sound in the literal sense, for as [the Holy Spirit] is speaking there of Our Lord Jesus Christ and His Church, it seems audacious for you to jump right in. Of course it is true that, as you said earlier, the same Lord who gave us and daily gives us the Blessed Sacrament, also allows His holy women to be honored with that by which He is honored,[163] and as far as what may be applied to our Holy Mother, do not think that you are to penetrate the lofty and hidden mysteries that lie in these sacred letters—and I don't know that it wouldn't be better to let it alone, for it is a great audacity and a forbidden thing for women like you to set about explicating Scripture or speaking of it."

"Now," said Gracia, "don't you be afraid that I will think you are being overly fearful as in the past. For what you are saying is right, and no good can come of women daring to do such things—and so I said to you at the outset. You gave me license then, and you may do so again now, for I would have you know that I am opposed to all extremes."

"And what do you call extremes?" asked Justa.

"I shall tell you," said Gracia. "I consider an extreme, Sister, what men so frequently use against poor women; for when they see women speaking of God, they are scandalized and put fear into the women. I consider certain women to be extreme who are falsely bookish and bold, meddling in what they know nothing about. And between these two extremes I see Our Lord and Treasure, who shows us the middle way as our true path. Our sweet Master acted in favor of women with that kindness He showed them when He did not disdain to hold a long and lofty conversation with the Samaritan woman; for the Lord allowed her to pursue the question of what was the

---

163. The same Lord . . . also allows his holy women to be honored with that by which He is honored [el mismo Señor . . . da licencia para que se honren sus santas con lo que él se honra]: an obscure passage. A possible interpretation is that although Justa warns Gracia not to engage in scriptural exegesis, she does concede that God permits "holy women" knowledge of Scripture. Despite her disclaimers, Gracia is treading perilously close to an anagogical interpretation of Proverbs 31, implying that the virtuous woman of these verses prefigures Teresa.

proper place in which to adore God, with His Majesty teaching her and making her the one to divulge His holy word.[164] We also know that He first revealed the most high mystery of His Resurrection to Mary Magdalene and
the other Marys and commanded them to announce it to their brothers.[165]
So there is no reason for us to be excluded from speaking and communicating
with God, nor should we be kept from telling of His greatness or from wanting to know of the teachings; and in this lies what should serve as a bridle to
curb bold women. I say that we should speak and know of the teachings, not
that we should teach. I believe the Lord Himself showed Mary Magdalene
this point when, after having revealed to her a mystery so high and so necessary to our faith, and having commanded her to be the messenger of this
good news to the grieving apostles, He did not allow her to come to Him,
saying, 'Touch me not.'[166] For in this we can see that, although we may be allowed to tell of God's greatness and to help our brothers, it is not ours to pry
into mysteries, as you said. Thus you may know that I will only set down the
words and tell of the affairs of our Mother, so that every person may see
whether we can in truth call her that, as soon as we begin this history.

"In the name of Jesus and Mary."

'The first things that must be told are the parents, lineage, and birthplace of this saint; her countenance and stature; when and how it was that the
Lord called her; which monastery was the first she founded and the names of
all the rest; along with other matters necessary to shed light on the virtues
she possessed, of which we shall be speaking. It is true that in the *Book of Her
Life* and in the books others have written about her, she told everything at
length, and others have given their explanations. Yet because the saint wrote
her book at the command of her confessors so that they could use it to examine her spirit, she tends to put in many trifling details and to stray from what
she is saying toward the contemplation of her sins. For as she was truly
humble, these came to her mind at every turn. At such times she leaves the
subject she has begun and utters many exclamations, now about how
wretched she has been and how the Lord could have put up with her, and
again, about the grandeur of God. These two matters continually occupied
her memory and so she did not know how to move on to other things, which
makes what she is saying somewhat obscure."

"That seems to me exactly like someone who puts a jeweler's foil in back
of pearls and precious stones," said Atanasia. "The plain, humble words she

164. John 4:7–42.
165. Matthew 28:7–8.
166. John 20:17.

uses to write of the great things God showed to her soul bear witness to how true her spirit was."

"That is so," Gracia said. "It is the common language of saints when they tell of their own excellent qualities (which they cannot silence entirely), as it was also her custom, to diminish themselves as our saint does in everything that she writes. This shows that her writing is a true mine of precious stones, because it is covered with the earth of humility. Then it is necessary to dig away the earth so that the content may shine. Very aptly do we speak of the saints as hidden mines and treasures. For just as gold and precious stones cannot shine when they lie deep in the mines, because they are mixed in with the earth, in the same way the virtues and graces that saints tell of themselves are covered up with the earth of humility. Thus it is well that their writings be given to others who can uncover their clarity. And although I am in no way a good lapidary, nevertheless I know that it will give pleasure to those who wish to learn in brief about the life of our Mother and the favors the Lord gave her, to find it all here in summary.

"She was a native of the city of Avila. It is fitting that one whose shining virtues would illuminate our times should spring up in that famous and most Christian birthplace, for Avila is a sepulcher of saints and a blessed land that produces such plants. She had illustrious ancestry; her grandfather on her father's side was called Juan Sánchez de Cepeda, and her grandmother, Doña Inés de Toledo; her maternal grandparents were Mateo de Ahumada and Doña Teresa de Tapia, daughter of the purser Diego de Tapia, residents of the city of Avila. They are buried there in the Church of Saint John.

"Her father's name was Alonso Sánchez de Cepeda. He was twice married, the first time to Doña Catalina de Peso, with whom he had only one daughter, named Doña María de Cepeda. She is the sister whom the holy Mother says she dearly loved, although she was only a half sister, and the one the Lord ordered our Mother to warn that she was to die suddenly. Her mother's name was Doña Beatriz de Ahumada, with whom her father had eight sons and two daughters. The oldest of the daughters was our holy Mother, who in the world was called Doña Teresa de Ahumada; the other daughter, Doña Juana de Ahumada, married Juan de Ovalle.

"Being the fortunate brothers of this blessed Mother, it is fitting that the names of her brothers be remembered in perpetuity, as their courage and deeds also warrant. They are as follows: the oldest, called Juan de Cepeda, died in Africa as a captain in the infantry. The second, Rodrigo de Cepeda, is the one the holy Mother says was her companion in childhood, because they were nearly the same age and both born on the same day, the twenty-eighth of March. Rodrigo was born in 1511, and our Mother in 1515, so that he was four years older than she. The saint says that Rodrigo shared in her conversations and desires. He went to the Río de la Plata as a captain, and he died proving at the end of his life the good beginnings he had had. I have heard our Mother say that she considered him a martyr because he died defending the faith, although I don't know where or on what occasion. Fernando de Ahumada, Lorenzo de Cepeda, Jerónimo de Cepeda, Agustín de Ahumada, Pedro de Ahumada, and Antonio de Ahumada—these brothers went to Peru and took part in the battle under the command of the Viceroy Blasco Núñez Vela, where they served His Majesty the King. Antonio de Ahumada died in that battle. Lorenzo, the oldest of the brothers, was the King's treasurer in the city of Quito, where he had an allotment of lands, which was inherited in turn by his second son, Lorenzo de Cepeda, who is married and lives in Madrid with the daughter of Don Francisco de Mendoza and Doña Beatriz de Castilla.

"I am obliged to give a particular account of the life of the gentleman Lorenzo de Cepeda. For not only is he the brother of our holy Mother and the one she loved best and father of the good Teresa de Jesús, a nun of our Order, professed in Avila, who gives us hope that through her virtue and courage she will revive that of her ancestors and of the holy Mother whose name she bears. In addition, I am obliged to him for another reason beside these, for he was the second founder of the convent in Seville. I am greatly obliged, because it happened that when our Mother went to found the convent in Seville, that same year the flotilla arrived from Peru, and with it came Lorenzo de Cepeda, his two sons, and the second Teresa, a girl of ten whom we immediately accepted into our monastery, out of devotion to our Mother.[167] Her father spent a great deal on founding the house, which was just in its early days and very poor, and when we left the house that we had rented for another that we purchased, he very generously gave us everything needed to make it suitable for a convent—materials, workmen, and food for everyone—helping in person with the labor and anything else that was necessary. With this and with other things he gave for the Blessed Sacrament, he freed us from want and guaranteed the loan on the house we bought, for since we were strangers in that city and unknown to anyone, we suffered

167. Lorenzo's daughter Teresita (1566–1610) was born in Quito and arrived in Spain with her father in 1575. She lived with the nuns in the Seville convent and later moved to Saint Joseph's in Avila, where she made her profession in 1582. See E. Allison Peers, *Handbook to the Life and Times of St. Teresa and St. John of the Cross* (London: Burns and Oates, 1954), 224. Although the Council of Trent prohibited girls under sixteen years of age from taking monastic vows, young girls sometimes lived in convents with relatives who were nuns. As María reveals below, Teresa opposed this practice, although an exception was made for Teresita.

many trials, more than in any other foundation, as our Mother recounts in *The Book of Her Foundations*.[168] Thus, it seemed a miracle that he had arrived at such a moment, having spent thirty years in the Indies.

"I could go on at length in praising his great virtues and the many spiritual exercises to which he dedicated himself after he had returned to Spain and communicated with our holy Mother. He had always been virtuous and much given to charity, since he was so good natured and because he had a delicate wit and generous heart. Yet as a result of his conversations with our Mother and the help she gave him, he began to grow a great deal. As I know from letters that our Mother sent me—his own letters, in which he gave her an account of his progress in prayer—the Lord gave him many favors, and in a short time he achieved the prayer of quiet. He prepared all matters relating to his soul very well, providing for his sons (for, as we have said, he gave the oldest his inheritance in Spain, and he sent the second to attend to all that the King had given him in the Indies for his services, which were great, for he distinguished himself fighting in the wars and revolts there). For himself, he only wanted his two Teresas: our Mother, whom he accompanied and followed as much as he could, and the cherished and best loved of all his children, Teresa de Jesús. To show how much he loved his daughter, he would deliver her only to the hands of that good and faithful Bridegroom who is in heaven. Because I helped him in this matter to persuade our Mother (who was opposed to it because the girl was so young and her relative, and because she did not want to introduce the custom of accepting girls into the convent at such a young age), he showed gratitude to me as long as he lived and made particular benefactions to the convent. I could not think how else to repay him except by putting him on this blessed mountain and at its summit, which he deserves as brother of such a sister and because from the time he returned to Spain he lived and died in our habit and according to our ways (although in his own home), for which he deserves the name of Carmelite. I believe him not to be one of the least glorified; our Carmel is glorified by having him as its son.

"And so that we may conclude with her brothers, Agustín de Ahumada is governor of Los Quijos in Peru; Jerónimo died during the journey back to Spain with his brother Lorenzo; and there is Pedro de Ahumada, who is still living.

"Our Mother records nine siblings in her book. What I have put down here is taken from old documents that state that her grandparents were

168. Teresa of Avila, *Book of Her Foundations*, vol. 3 of *The Collected Works of St. Teresa of Avila*, chaps. 23–26.

parishioners of San Juan, where the *hijosdalgos* cast their lots,[169] as indeed her parents and grandparents did. I have not found mention of any other brothers or sisters, nor did her father record the birth of any others than the eight sons and three daughters I have mentioned. I have in my possession the sheet of paper where this is written, as I have said, in our Mother's father's hand. As for Fernando, I have not been able to discover when or where he died, but I know he is no longer alive. Of all eleven children, the only ones still living are Pedro and Agustín de Ahumada, and Doña Juana de Ahumada, the mother of our dear Sister.

"On Wednesday the twenty-eighth of March, the eve of the feast day of Saint Bertoldo, Carmelite, this holy Mother was born; and by the great providence of the highest Lord this was the year 1515, a little less than three years before the ill-fated Luther declared his apostasy. For it is the custom of His Divine Majesty to foresee the remedy for misfortune. And since this son of perdition has not only been the cause of an infinite number of men being lost, but has also perverted and taken away Christ's consecrated virgins from the society of the Church and from His nuptial bed, it is just that, having sent saintly men, He should also send saintly women to repair the wrongs done to them. For He does not hold women in little esteem. Among them, as I believe is shown in her life, the saint was chosen for this purpose, as we shall say later.

"With this zeal she began to found convents three years before the decrees of the Holy Council of Trent were published. Thus might the times, the works, and the name of Teresa show us that the Holy Trinity chose her so as to delight in her with the favors and gifts that she received through the consideration and communication of these three divine Persons, as our Lord Jesus Christ told her and shall be seen later, and through the particular devotion and spiritual exercise that she dedicated to the Trinity.

"From the time she was seven years old, God began to awaken her to virtue; she was also moved by the example of her parents, who were God-fearing people. All her brothers and sisters loved her, and her parents loved her more than their other children, because of the many graces the Lord had bestowed on her. Many were natural graces and others, which the Lord communicated to her through her many holy exercises, were supernatural.

"At that tender age of seven she would withdraw with her brother Rodrigo to read saints' lives, and when they saw the martyrdom that the saints

169. *Hijosdalgos* were members of the lesser nobility who, unlike commoners (*pecheros*), were exempt from paying taxes. In 1522 Teresa's father and her uncles, like many other wealthy *converso* merchants, successfully won a suit claiming this noble status after bribing a number of witnesses. Although María affirms the Cepeda family's status as *hidalgos*, it is notable that she never claims that they were "Old Christians" of "pure" (i.e., non-Jewish) blood.

suffered, they thought the saints paid very cheaply for going to enjoy God, and they longed to die in the same way. Considering how they might achieve this, they agreed to go off to the land of the Moors and beg for the love of God that they make them martyrs over there. It seemed to them that having parents was a great obstacle to their desire, and when they saw they could not carry off this plan, they agreed to be hermits in a kitchen garden at their house. As best they could they used to make hermitages out of little rocks, which would fall down immediately, and the children would be sad since they could find no way to fulfill their desires. They were very frightened to hear that hell pains and glory are forever, and they used to spend a great deal of time together talking this over, repeating the word to each other: 'Forever, Teresa.' And she would answer: 'Forever, Rodrigo.' This truth, so worthy of consideration—that hell pain or glory is forever—so amazed the souls of these holy children that they would pronounce it very slowly, repeating it many times. With such lofty exercises in such pure souls, how much their virtues must have grown! And so this holy girl, from the time mentioned until the age of twelve, when her mother died, practiced giving alms, reciting her prayers and withdrawing in solitude (of which she was very fond). After her mother died, she went to Our Lady in grief over that loss and took her as her mother, and the saint says from that hour she felt that Our Lady protected her and assisted her in all her needs.

"When she grew older and began to mix with some pleasure-seeking company, as she tells it, she began to forget her first exercises and fervor and to give herself over to finery and strike up friendships, which she laments a great deal. She says she believes that until the age of fourteen and even later she had not offended the Lord mortally, although she always lets it be understood that the fear of God persisted in her soul, and that she never did anything knowingly that she understood to be a mortal sin. This way of life and these friendships gave rise to an affection which, although outwardly she always behaved with all modesty and honor, as a discreet and wise daughter worthy of her father, inwardly wreaked the havoc that such things do, tearing down all her spiritual foundation by cooling her love for God. In the end this matter resulted in certain rumors, and it was the cause of her father's taking her to a convent where persons of her quality were educated. Although on first arriving she was very distressed, with her gentle disposition she became consoled and made herself loved by all. Through her friendship with those holy nuns, she began to take to the idea of being a nun, a condition she had previously abhorred. Because she was so wise and the nuns removed the occasions of sin that had taken her away from her first fervent devotions, she returned to the latter and began persuading herself what a good and secure condition that of a nun was. Thus, moved more by reason than enthusiasm, she made up her mind. She says that when it came time to take leave of her father's house, to which she had returned from the convent as a result of having fallen ill, it pained her so much that it seemed her bones were being pulled asunder, and that she could not feel greater pain if she were dying. If the Lord had not helped her, her reasoning would have been insufficient.

"With that help she vanquished herself at last and chose to be a nun in the Convent of the Incarnation, because she had a great friend there. The chief cause, I believe, was that the Holy Virgin had chosen her for this good purpose. And so at about nineteen, more or less, she took the habit of the Virgin of Carmel under Mitigated Rule, according to which she lived for twenty-eight years. During that time the Lord gave her many favors, which I shall summarize here, having taken them from the *Book of Her Life*. In order to give more pleasure, I will use the very words that the saint put down, although I will leave out, as I have said, the matters she mixes in and exclamations she makes.[170] But they cannot be put in order, because she does not do so; instead, she puts earlier things last and later things first. For example, one notes that as she is writing when she was in the Convent of Saint Joseph in Avila, which was the first convent she founded, she happens to remember some favors that the Lord had given her, and she says: 'they called me to go to see a sick man,' or 'while I was in such-and-such a church,' and so forth, which could imply that she used to leave the convent. This shows that it happened before she made the foundation, at a time when she was permitted by her prelates to go out, or that it was because of illness or some other reason, since before the Council of Trent permission was easily granted.[171]

"She was indeed often outside the convent, as she writes in the account of her life, which was very full of trials and terrible illnesses. To seek a cure for these illnesses she left the convent during her novitiate, and it happened that while she was in a village where she had gone for the cure, there was an important cleric, and since the saint was beautiful and full of wit and charm, he became fond of her. And it seemed to her that she should reciprocate his

170. Despite her claims to tell the foundress's story in her own words, a comparison with *Book of Her Life* reveals that María condenses, paraphrases, and reorders Teresa's words considerably. See introduction, 21. Readers who wish to compare María's retelling with Teresa's account should consult *The Book of Her Life*, trans. Kieran Kavanaugh and Otilio Rodríguez, vol. 1 of *The Collected Works of St. Teresa of Avila* (Washington, D.C., Institute of Carmelite Studies, 1976). This translation includes an informative introduction and notes on the historical and theological context of Teresa's spiritual autobiography. To facilitate comparisons with Teresa's *Life*, we have attempted to employ a mystical vocabulary consistent with the one developed by Kavanaugh and Rodríguez; chapter subdivisions are also consistent with those used in this translation.

171. María here takes pains to defend Teresa against accusations that she did not observe the Tridentine mandates on strict enclosure.

friendship out of gratitude, the more so because he was her confessor and had told her that certain things were not a sin. Because she was deceived in this, the saint endured what she would not have endured had she known it was a sin, for she says that for all the world she would not commit a mortal sin if she knew that it was one. But from this wrong God drew something very good. For seven years this priest had been living in sin with a woman from the village, and he was saying Mass. The woman had put spells into a little copper image that she had begged him to wear around his neck as a token of love for her. No one had the power to get it away from him. As a result of the great love he felt for the saint, he gave her the image and made her throw it into a river. Once he had taken it off, like someone waking from a deep sleep, he gradually began to remember all that he had done during those years. Frightened of himself, and distressed over his perdition, he began to abhor the woman and left her at once. Within a year he died very much in the service of God, who in His mercy gave the saint to that man so that the excessive love he felt for her might bring about the salvation of his soul. And His Divine Majesty permitted a somewhat unseemly friendship with His own dear bride, in exchange for which this man's soul might be saved.[172]

"God did these things through the saint in that village, and she returned from it to her father's house in terrible pain and sickness, greater than when she had departed. For four days a paroxysm seized her, so that they were ready to bury her. She returned to her convent and remained there paralyzed for a long time. Her patience, as well as the charm and love with which she treated everyone, was extraordinary. She recovered from that pain and illness as a result of her devotion to Saint Joseph, whose intervention has been so beneficial to so many souls in the convents that she founded in his name. Thus, God returned her to health. Since she was young and, as we have said, beautiful and charming and very neat and clean in her appearance (for despite her many spiritual exercises, she maintained her fastidiousness), and since in such a large convent there were many opportunities for conversing at the grill, she again became involved in these conversations, deceived by the fact that her confessor had told her it was not a sin.[173] Until one day, when she was entertaining herself in one of these diversions at the grill (not one of those to which God would call her), she and those with her there saw a large toad.[174] Through it she understood the sins she had committed in those

---

172. Teresa of Avila, *Life*, chap. 5.

173. Under the mitigated rule in the Convent of the Incarnation, nuns frequently received visitors, of both sexes, with whom they conversed through a wooden grill. Sometimes nuns developed flirtatious relationships with their male visitors, who were known as *devotos de monjas*.

174. Teresa of Avila, *Life*, chap. 7.

friendships, and when she discussed the matter with learned men and servants of God they disabused her of her error. God fortified her soul through many favors He was giving her, and she returned to mental prayer, which she had abandoned for those friendships. Yet she always inspired in all her acquaintances a love for prayer, and thus she initiated her father in that holy practice, to the great benefit of his soul. He died a holy death.

"Leaving aside the other things that happened in the span of the twenty-eight years and more that she was a nun at the Convent of the Incarnation, I will only relate the favors and visions the Lord gave her until she founded her first convent. From there we will set down the other foundations, as she went about establishing them, until the Lord took her from this life.

"The saint writes: 'The first time that the Lord gave me the favor of a rapture I understood these words: "No longer do I want you to converse with men, but with angels." From that time when the Lord spoke to me, the interior locutions were continuous.

"'One day when I was very afflicted because many learned men had come together to discuss my spiritual state, and all had decided that my experience came from the Devil, I was experiencing the greatest distress and torment imaginable. The Lord said to me: "Be not afraid, daughter, that I will abandon you. It is I, do not fear." Instantly I became calm and greatly consoled, with strength, with courage, with assurance, with calm, with light. And at that instant I saw my soul transformed, and it seems to me I could argue with all the world that the voice was God.[175]

"'Many times the Lord set my sins before me, and it seemed to me I was in the Last Judgment. This was especially so when the Lord was about to give me some notable favor. Many other times He warned me of dangers that lay in store for me, and for other persons, some two or three or four years further on. Many times when I was very much afflicted by the fears others put into me, the Lord said to me, "What do you fear? Do you not know that I am all-powerful? I will fulfill what I promised."[176] One day when I was very sad because they had taken away some books that I liked to read, the Lord said to me in Latin, "Do not be sad, for I shall give you a living book."[177] How well has He fulfilled His word, and how much have I been able to read in it about

---

175. Ibid., chap. 25, secs. 14, 18.

176. Ibid., chap. 26, sec. 2.

177. Ibid., chap. 26, sec. 5. The Index of Prohibited Books, published in 1559 by the inquisitor general Fernando de Valdés, banned guides to mental prayer written in the vernacular. Here, María (or perhaps the copyist) has misread Teresa's text, which does not state that God speaks in Latin. Teresa's text, in the Kavanaugh and Rodríguez translation, states, "I felt that prohibition very much because reading some of [the books] was an enjoyment for me, and I could no longer do so since only the Latin editions were allowed. The Lord said to me, 'Do not be sad . . .'" (172).

the wounds of Christ! Once in prayer on the feast of the glorious Saint Peter, I felt our Lord Christ beside me, and I felt it was He who was speaking to me. He was always on my right side, and He was the witness of what I said, and whenever I was recollected, I found Him near me; I knew this through an intellectual vision.[178]

"'While in prayer another time the Lord wished to show me only His hands, which were beautiful beyond comparison, and a few days later I also saw that divine face, which left me completely absorbed. I could not understand why the Lord was showing Himself to me little by little. Afterward I understood that He was leading me according to my weakness, because these were the first times that He appeared to me in an imaginative vision.[179]

"'Another day, when I was extremely grieved because it seemed to me that my confessor did not believe me, the Lord told me not to be weary, for that sorrow would soon be over. I rejoiced greatly, thinking that I was to die soon, and I was very happy when I thought about it. Afterward, I clearly saw His words meant the arrival of a rector of the Society of Jesus, who helped in every way and told my confessor not to lead me by such a severe path but to let the spirit of the Lord work. For at times it seemed that with these great impulses of the spirit my soul could scarcely breathe.[180]

"'It once happened, when I was with a certain person, that she mentioned to me and to some others that we could be nuns in the manner of the Discalced nuns of Saint Francis in Madrid, and that it was possible to found a convent of that kind. Since I already had the same desires, I started having conversations about it with one of my friends, although we thought that our plan was not going anywhere. One day after communion, His Majesty ordered me to strive for this with all my strength, making great promises that the convent would be founded without fail and would be of great service to Him. He said it should be called Saint Joseph, who would protect us at one door while Our Lady protected the other, and Christ would walk among us, and the convent would be a star that would shine with great splendor. He said that even when the nuns followed a mitigated rule, they should not think He was little served by them, for what would become of the world if not for

---

178. Teresa of Avila, *Life,* chap. 27, sec. 2. Teresa distinguished three kinds of visions: the corporeal (perceived with the physical senses), the imaginative (bypassing the physical senses and imprinted on the imagination, though not in the conventional sense of "imaginary"), and the intellectual, like the one described here, which were intuitive rather than representational. For further explanation of the three kinds of visions, see Kathleen A. Myers and Amanda Powell, *A Wild Country Out in the Garden: The Spiritual Journals of a Colonial Mexican Nun* (Bloomington: Indiana University Press, 1999), 282–83.

179. Teresa of Avila, *Life,* chap. 28, sec. 1.

180. Ibid., chap. 33, sec. 8.

nuns and friars? And I should tell my confessor everything that He had told me and beg him not to oppose or obstruct me in this. This vision had such great effects, and the locution was of such a manner, that I could not doubt it was the Lord. The Lord spoke to me of this matter many times, always ordering me to do it. One time He told me: "Here you will see how the saints who founded religious Orders suffered," and He told me that I had to suffer much more persecution than I could imagine. He also told me some things to tell my companion. When the house for the convent was bought, and it seemed small to me, the Lord told me to enter as best I could, that I would see what His Majesty was doing, as I have indeed seen.[181]

"'One day after communion, the Lord said to me: "I have already told you to enter as best you can." And in exclamatory style He added: "Oh, the covetousness of human kind! You think that you will lack even a plot of ground! How many times did I sleep in the night dew because I had nowhere else to go!" Because when I saw the house was so small, I still doubted that we could make a convent in it.[182]

"'One time, when I was in such need that I did not know what to do or how to pay some workmen, Saint Joseph, my true father and lord, appeared to me and let me know that I would not be in want, and I should hire them. So I did, without a single penny, and the Lord provided for me in ways that astonished those who saw it.[183]

"'One day on the feast of Saint Peter when I was in the convent,[184] the most sacred Humanity of Christ Our Lord was represented to me, as He is depicted in paintings of the Resurrection, with such great beauty and majesty that, if there were nothing else in heaven to delight the eyes than the great beauty of glorified bodies, seeing this would be the greatest glory, especially the vision of the Humanity of Christ Our Lord. If even here below His Majesty shows Himself according to what our miserable state can bear, how glorious must this sight be where such a blessing is enjoyed completely![185]

"'For some two years the Lord appeared to me in this way, and afterward He replaced this vision with another more exalted one. Often I would look at

---

181. Ibid., chap. 32, secs. 10–11, 14. On Teresa's concept of a reformed religious life, see Jodi Bilinkoff, *The Avila of Saint Teresa: Religious Reform in a Sixteenth-Century City* (Ithaca, N.Y.: Cornell University Press, 1989), 122–51.

182. Teresa of Avila, *Life*, chap. 33, sec. 12.

183. Ibid.

184. María's text reads "estando en casa" [while at home, or in this case, in the convent], but Teresa's *Life* reads "estando en misa" [while at Mass].

185. Teresa of Avila, *Life*, chap. 28, sec. 3. Although María abbreviates the description of this vision, she retains much of the tangled syntax of the original.

His great beauty and the gentleness with which He spoke those words with His beautiful and divine mouth; other times He also spoke with severity. I felt a strong desire to see the color of His eyes and how tall He was, so that I might know how to describe these things. I have never deserved to see this, nor was it any use for me to seek to do so, although sometimes I saw that He was looking at me with pity. But this vision is so powerful that the soul cannot bear it and is swept up in such an exalted rapture that in order to enjoy it more completely, it loses this beautiful sight. And thus there is no question of wanting or not wanting, for one clearly sees that the Lord wants there to be nothing but humility and shame, and that we accept whatever is given and praise Him who gives it. This is true of all visions without exception: for we cannot see any more or any less, nor can we do or leave anything undone, through our own effort.[186]

"'At other times the Lord appeared to me on the cross, or at others He would be carrying the cross either in the Garden of Gethsemane or with the crown of thorns, and He would show me His wounds. He appeared to me in this way on occasions when I was distressed, in order to console me, because at other times it was more ordinary for him to appear to me as risen, as I have said.'[187]

"After that the saint goes on to say, 'I have suffered many affronts and trials in telling of these things, and a great many fears and persecutions. Some persons were so certain that the visions were from the Devil that they wanted to exorcise me. They ordered me, whenever I was in prayer, to cross myself, and to do so I used to hold a cross in the hand that I keep on my rosary. One day when I was in prayer the Lord took this cross in His own hand, and when He returned it to me it was made of four large stones, more precious than diamonds and beyond compare. It bore the five wounds, of very pretty workmanship. And the Lord told me that I would see the cross this way from then on, which was so, for I do not see the wood it is made of but rather these stones, although no one sees them but me.[188]

"'Sometimes when I was swept up in those great impulses of love for God that leave me in the extreme state that was explained, the Lord wished for me sometimes to see this vision: I would see an angel on my left side in bodily form, and though not very large he was beautiful, and his face so much aflame that he resembled the very exalted angels that seemed to be completely afire.

186. Ibid., chap. 29, secs. 2, 3.
187. Ibid., chap. 29, sec. 4.
188. Ibid., chap. 29, secs. 4–7.

He held in his hands a long, golden dart, and at the iron point there seemed to me to be a little fire. He seemed to thrust this into my heart at times so that it reached my entrails, and when he withdrew the dart, it brought them out with it and left me afire with love. Oh great God! So great was the pain that it made me moan, and so excessive was the gentleness that caused this pain, that there is no desiring for it to be taken away, nor can the soul be content with less than God.[189] Sometimes the tribulations and torments that the Devil gave me, with the Lord's permission, were so great that it seemed to me a picture of hell, and thus in a vision the Lord made me understand that my soul was burning, without knowing who was burning it.[190]

"'When the Convent of Saint Joseph in Avila was founded in poverty and without an income, everyone opposed it. One day when I was commending the convent to the Lord, He told me that in no way should I fail to found it in poverty, for that was His will and His Father's, and He would help me. Another time He told me that an income would be a source of embarrassment and trouble, and He told me many other things in praise of poverty, assuring me that whoever served Him would not lack what was necessary to live.[191]

"'When a brother-in-law of mine died suddenly, and I was very sorrowful because he was not in the habit of going to confession, I was told through prayer that my sister would die that way, and I should go to her and try to make her prepare herself for it. I told my confessor about it, and since he did not let me go, I heard the message another time. When he saw this he told me to go to her, for there was nothing to lose. I went and began to enlighten her as best I could and got her into the habit of going to confession often and putting her soul in order. Four or five years after she adopted this practice, she died without anyone coming to see her and without being able to confess. But since she had that habit, only eight days had passed since her last confession. The news of the way she died made me very happy. She spent very little time in purgatory; I don't think more than a week had passed when, just after I had taken communion, the Lord appeared before me and wanted me to see that He was taking her to heaven. In all these years, from the time

---

189. Ibid., chap. 29, sec. 13. This is a description of the transverberation commemorated by Bernini's sculpture *Saint Teresa in Ecstasy* in Santa Maria della Vittoria in Rome. According to Covarrubias's 1611 dictionary, *Tesoro de la Lengua Castellana o Española*, "entrails" (entrañas) could be used metaphorically for "what is most hidden . . . profound." Hence, Kavanaugh and Rodríguez translate the passage as "he was carrying off with him the deepest part of me" (194).

190. Teresa of Avila, *Life*, chap. 32, sec. 1.

191. Ibid., chap. 35, sec. 6 . On the opposition to Teresa's plan to make a foundation without an income, see Bilinkoff, *The Avila of Saint Teresa*, 123–37.

that I was forewarned until she died, I did not forget what He had given me to understand. Praise be to God forever![192]

"'Around that time came the feast of the Assumption of our Lady, while I was in a convent of the Order of the glorious Saint Dominic. I was contemplating the many sins and things about my wretched life that I had confessed in that house in the past; there came over me such a great rapture that it almost took me out of myself. I sat down, and it seems to me that I could not even see the elevation of the Host or hear Mass. Afterward I felt a scruple about that. Being in this state, it seemed that I saw myself dressed in a shining white robe, and at first I did not see who was dressing me. Afterward I saw our Lady on my right side and my father Saint Joseph on my left, putting that robe on me. I understood that I was now cleansed of my sins.[193]

"'When they had finished dressing me, and I was in a state of glorious delight, our Lady seemed to grasp me by the hands. She told me it made her very happy that I was serving our glorious Saint Joseph, and I should believe that what I was striving for with the convent would be accomplished, for the Lord, Saint Joseph, and she would be greatly served by it. I should not fear, for it would never fail, although the obedience that was to be given might not be to my liking, because they would protect us, and her Son had already promised to walk with us. As a sign that this would be true she was giving me a jewel. It seemed to me she put around my neck a beautiful gold necklace with a cross of great value affixed to it. That gold and those stones are so different from the ones here below that there is no comparison, because their beauty is very different from what we can imagine here. Our minds cannot grasp what the garment was made of or imagine how white the Lord makes it appear, for everything here below seems like a sketch made with charcoal.[194]

"'The beauty I saw in our Lady was very great, although I could not make out any particular feature. Rather, I saw the beauty of her face in its entirety, and how she was dressed in brilliant white, not dazzling but soft. I did not see the glorious Saint Joseph so clearly, although I did see that he was there as in the visions I have had, which as I have explained are not seen; our Lady seemed to me to be a young girl. They stayed with me a little while like this, while it seemed to me I was in a state of greater glory and happiness than I have ever experienced, so that I never wanted to come out of that state. It seemed that I saw them rise to heaven with a multitude of angels, and I was

192. Ibid., chap. 34, sec. 19. The reference is to María de Cepeda, Teresa's half sister.
193. Ibid., chap. 33, sec. 4.
194. Ibid., chap. 33, sec. 14.

left very much alone, although I felt so consoled, exalted, recollected in prayer, and moved with tenderness that I remained for some time without being able to stir or speak; rather, I was almost outside of myself. I was left with a great impulse to be dissolved in love for God, and with the effects I have named. Everything happened in such a way that I could never doubt that the experience was from God. It left me greatly consoled and in great peace.[195]

"'As to what the Queen of the Angels said about obedience, it was because I was troubled not to render obedience to the Order, but the Lord had told me that it was not fitting for me to give obedience to them. He told me reasons why it was in no way fitting for it to be done. Rather, I should petition Rome by a certain means that He also told me, and He would assure a favorable response from there. And so it happened, by the means the Lord told me, whereas we hadn't succeeded in the negotiations ourselves. It turned out very well, and with what has happened since, it was very fitting to give obedience to the bishop. But at that time I did not know him, nor did I even know which prelate he would be. Because of the great opposition there has been against the foundation, the Lord was pleased to have him be so good and favor this house as much as has been necessary to put it in its present state. Blessed be He who has accomplished everything this way, amen![196]

"'The Lord ordained that a brother-in-law of mine should fall ill, and that gave reason for me to leave the Convent of the Incarnation. It was astonishing that he was ill not a moment longer than was necessary for me to finish the business for which the Lord had brought me, which was to plan the conversion of the house into the convent. So the Lord gave him health and he cleared out the house, and he was astonished at his sudden recovery.'[197]

"Our holy Mother suffered innumerable trials during the foundation of this first convent from her confessors, who opposed her and believed the Devil caused her visions; from her own nuns and friars, who opposed her for attempting it; and after the foundation, from the entire city and all kinds of people. We will tell about that elsewhere, because this is a brief summary of the marvels the Lord worked in order to found these convents.[198]

"As we have said, the first foundation was Saint Joseph's of Avila, which was founded in 1562 on the feast of glorious Saint Bartholomew. And while

195. Ibid., chap. 33, sec. 15.

196. Ibid., chap. 33, sec. 16.

197. Ibid., chap. 36, sec. 3. Saint Joseph's was placed under the jurisdiction of the bishop of Avila, Alvaro de Mendoza, instead of the Carmelite order.

198. On the opposition to the foundation of Saint Joseph's in Avila, see Bilinkoff, 137–51.

the saint was very happy, having reserved the Blessed Sacrament in the convent, she says that the Lord permitted her to experience a spiritual battle in which it seemed that all the devils had banded together to torment her with the greatest unhappiness over what she had done. As she says in her own words: 'A short time before it seemed I would not exchange my happiness with anyone on earth, and the very reason for my happiness now tormented me so that I did not know what to do. I went before the Blessed Sacrament, and the Lord did not let His poor servant suffer long, because He never failed to help me in my tribulations. He did so then, for He gave me a little light to see that it was the Devil, and so that I could understand the truth. I promised before the Blessed Sacrament to do everything I could to obtain permission from my prelate to come to live in the recently founded convent, and to observe enclosure once permission was granted.'[199]

"The saint did that because, since she was under the jurisdiction of the Order while the convent was under that of the bishop, whether she should stay in the convent was not in her power. Instead, her prelates immediately ordered her to return to the Convent of the Incarnation, where another war was going on in its own right. She says that the moment she made the vow we have described, the Devil fled and she was left calm and happy. Afterward, her prelates gave her permission to return to her new convent. This was a great surprise to those who had seen her removed from it with such great fury, and how she had been rebuked as a scandalous woman, and other names that had been given to her work, with God's permission. And with that same divine permission, she was allowed to return to the place where her young plants were left clamoring, like sheep without their shepherd. She says that upon returning to the convent, 'The day I entered the convent, being almost in rapture, I saw Christ, who seemed to be greeting me with great love and placing a crown on my head, thanking me for what I had done for His Mother. Another time, when we were all praying in the choir after compline, I saw our Lady in the greatest glory clothed in a white mantle, and it seemed that she sheltered all of us beneath it. I understood what a high degree of glory the Lord would give the nuns of this convent.[200]

"'While going to communion on the feast of Saint Clare, this very saint herself appeared to me with great beauty. She told me to strive to go forward with what I had begun, for she would help me. I became very devoted to her

---

199. Teresa of Avila, *Life*, chap. 36, secs. 7–9. This passage provides a good example of María's willingness to condense Teresa's words. What Teresa expresses in approximately eight hundred words is reduced in María's version to a little over one hundred words.

200. Teresa of Avila, *Life*, chap. 36, sec. 24.

and her words have turned out to be very true, for a convent of her Order near this one helps to support us. Moreover, little by little she has brought to such perfection my desire for the poverty that the blessed saint practiced in her house, that the same poverty is observed in this one, for we live on alms, and the Lord does more; it must be thanks to the prayers of this blessed saint, for without our making any requests, His Majesty provides us very fully with what is necessary. May He be blessed for everything, amen.'[201]

"Since the Devil must have guessed, from the marvelous things that the Lord was working in the foundation of that humble little convent, that the good work would not end there, he began to invent every sort of scandal imaginable to obstruct that work, and thus the saint suffered great trials. When she returned to her convent, there was much meeting and talking in the city about wanting to dissolve the convent, and the greatest pressure they brought to bear was to argue that if the convent were not dissolved, at least it should not be founded in poverty; and the saint says the Lord told her, when she was feeling very weary, 'Don't you know that I am powerful? What do you fear?' And He assured me that the convent would not be dissolved. And with this I was left greatly consoled. This battering lasted almost half a year; it would take a long time to describe in detail the trials that were suffered.'[202]

"'I was amazed at how the Devil struggled to defeat a few weak women. Since he wanted the convent to have an income—and being imperfect I thought perhaps that was what the Lord wanted, because without an income we could not go forward with our plans—I came to accept this compromise. While I was in prayer the night before this matter was to be discussed, the Lord told me I should do no such thing, for if we started by receiving an income, we would not be allowed to give it up later, and He told me some other things as well. That same night the holy friar Peter of Alcántara appeared to me.[203] I had seen him already twice after his death, and I had seen his great glory, so that I was not afraid of him. Rather, I was very glad, because he always appeared to me in his glorified body full of great glory, and it gave me

201. Ibid., chap. 33, sec. 13. Teresa was inspired in her reform by the Franciscan model of voluntary poverty. As this passage indicates, Saint Joseph's also received some material assistance from a convent of Poor Clares in Avila.

202. Ibid., chap. 36, sec. 16.

203. Peter of Alcántara (1499–1562, canonized 1669): the Franciscan ascetic and founder of the Discalced Friars Minor. He had supported Teresa during the period when her confessors thought her possessed. Despite the bitter struggle to found Saint Joseph's in poverty, in some subsequent foundations Teresa found it necessary to accept an income.

the greatest sensation of glory to see him. I remember that he told me the first time I saw him, among other things, as he was telling me of his great joy in heaven, that it was a blessed penance that he had done, because he had won such a reward through it. This time he was severe with me. He told me that in no way should I accept an income and asked me why I did not want to take his advice, and then he disappeared immediately. While he was alive this saint had written me three times, persuading me not to accept an income. One year before the saint died, he appeared to me while absent, and I knew that he was to die. A year later he did die, having been forewarned by me, and when he expired he appeared to me and told me what I have said above. He consoles me and advises me more since his death than when he was alive; I have seen him many times in the greatest glory, and our Lord told me He would not fail to concede anything requested in this saint's name, and indeed, I have seen many things fulfilled that I asked for in his name.[204]

"'It is hard for me to say more than I have already about the favors the Lord has given me, and even these are too many to believe they would be given to such a wretched person, but out of obligation to obey the Lord who has commanded me, and for His glory, I will say something.[205]

"'Since the Lord has given me to understand the difference that there is in heaven between the joy that some experience and the joy of others, I see clearly that here too on earth there is no limit to what the Lord gives, when He is pleased to do so. Thus, I would not want to limit myself in serving His Majesty and employing all my life, strength, and health in doing so.[206]

"'It should be noted also that with every favor the Lord gave me, whether vision or revelation, my soul was left with some gain, which after some visions was very great indeed. From seeing Christ, I was left clearly impressed by His great beauty, and that impression remains today, because just one experience was sufficient. How much more so considering how often the Lord grants me this favor![207]

"'One night when I was so ill that I wanted to excuse myself from mental prayer, I took up my rosary to occupy myself in vocal prayer, trying not to become recollected in my mind, although in my exterior body I was recol-

---

204. Teresa of Avila, *Life,* chap. 36, secs. 19–20; chap. 27, sec. 19. This passage provides another example of how María has reorganized Teresa's text, grouping together references to visions of Peter of Alcántara from different chapters of the *Life.*

205. Ibid., chap. 37, sec. 1. Apparent omissions in María's text have been supplemented with interpolations from the *Life.*

206. Ibid., chap. 37, sec. 2.

207. Ibid., chap. 37, sec. 4.

lected in an oratory. When the Lord so wishes, these efforts are of little use. I was in this state a little while, and a rapture came upon me with such force that there was no resisting it. It seemed to me that I was set down in heaven, and the first people I saw there were my father and mother, and such great things happened in no more than the time it takes to recite a Hail Mary, although it may have been longer, but the time seemed short.[208]

"'I would like to explain at least a little of what I came to know, and in thinking how I might do so, I find it impossible. For even in the difference between the light we see on earth and the light in heaven, although both are light, there is no comparison, because the brilliance of the sun seems something very ordinary. In short, the imagination, no matter how subtle it is, cannot paint or sketch what heavenly light is like, or any of the things the Lord allows me to understand with such supreme delight, because all my senses find joy to such degree and with such gentleness that the experience cannot be exaggerated, so that it is better to say no more.[209]

"'I had been in this state with the Lord for more than an hour, while He told me marvelous things, for it seemed to me that He did not move from my side, and He told me: "See, daughter, what those who oppose me lose. Do not fail to tell them of this."[210]

"'One day after Mass, on the eve of Pentecost, I went to a very secluded place where I often prayed, and I began to read about this feast in a volume by the Carthusian.[211] I was reading about the signs that those who practice prayer—the beginners, the adept, and the perfect—must have in order to understand whether the Holy Spirit is with them. Having read about these three stages, it seemed to me that by the goodness of God, the Holy Spirit did not fail to be with me, as far as I could tell. While I was praising God I remembered another time I had read this passage, when I had been lacking everything. I clearly knew my lack then, just as now I knew the opposite about myself.[212] Thus, I recognized that the Lord had given me a very great favor. I began to reflect on how I deserved a place in hell because of my sins,

208. Ibid., chap. 38, sec. 1.

209. Ibid., chap. 38, sec. 2.

210. Ibid., chap. 38, sec. 3.

211. Carthusian: Ludolph of Saxony. His *Life of Christ*, written originally in Latin, appeared in a four-volume Spanish translation in 1502. This is one of the works that Teresa recommends for nuns in her constitutions.

212. Teresa of Avila, *Life*, chap. 38, sec. 9. This is an obscure passage in the original Teresian text, as well as in María's close paraphrase. The bracketed words indicate our conjectural interpolations.

and I thanked God because it seemed to me I couldn't recognize my own soul, it was so changed. While I was reflecting on this, a great impulse came over me without my understanding what caused it. It seemed my soul did not fit in my body and wanted to leave it, nor could it see if it was capable of so much good. The impulse was so extreme that I felt helpless. In my opinion it was different from other times, for I understood neither what was happening to my soul nor what it wanted, it was so agitated. I leaned over, for although I was seated I could not sit upright, because my natural strength failed me completely. While in this state I see a dove over my head,[213] very different from the kind here on earth. It did not have feathers but rather wings covered with little shells that gave off great brilliance. It was larger than a dove. It seems to me I heard the sound of its wings fluttering for the length of a Hail Mary. My soul was in such a state that in losing itself, it lost sight of the dove. My spirit was calmed by such a good guest, for in my opinion such an amazing favor as this should have frightened my soul; but as I began to enjoy the favor, my soul lost its fear and quietude began to accompany the joy. Enraptured, I spent the rest of Pentecost stupefied, so much so that I did not know what to do or how such a great gift and favor had befallen me. I could neither hear nor see, in a manner of speaking, from my great interior joy. After that day I understood that I had benefited greatly from the vision and had been left with a more exalted love for God and with my virtues fortified. May He be blessed and praised forever, amen.[214]

"'Another time I saw the same dove over the head of a Dominican Father, except that it seemed to me that the rays and brilliance of its wings extended much further. I understood that he was to bring souls to God.[215]

"'Another time I saw our Lady putting a very white mantle on a Presentee of this same Order, whom I have spoken of several times. She told me that in honor of the service this friar had rendered in helping to found the convent, she was giving him the mantle as a sign that she would keep his soul pure from that time forward and he would not fall into mortal sin. I am certain it turned out to be so, for he died a few years later, and in both his death and the rest of the time he lived, his life was so penitential and his death so holy, that insofar as one can know, there is no reason to doubt. A friar who was present at his death told me that this Presentee, before he expired, had told him that Saint Thomas was with him and that he was dying with great joy and de-

---

213. María reproduces Teresa's shift from past to present tense.

214. Teresa of Avila, *Life*, chap. 38, secs. 9–11.

215. Ibid., chap. 38, sec. 12.

sire to leave this exile. Afterward he appeared to me in great glory; he told me a few things. This servant of the Lord had so many raptures and so much prayer that a little before he died he wrote me asking me what he should do, because when he finished saying Mass he would be taken up in great raptures that lasted a long time, without being able to prevent this.[216]

"'As for the Rector of the Society of Jesus, whom I have sometimes mentioned, I have seen something of the great favors that the Lord granted him, which I will not put down here in order not to make this too long. Once a great trial befell him, in which he was severely persecuted and he found himself greatly afflicted. One day when I was hearing Mass, during the elevation of the host, I saw Christ on the cross. He told me a few words of consolation that I should tell the rector along with other words to warn him of what was to come, reminding him of what Christ had suffered for him and telling him to prepare to suffer. These words gave the rector consolation and courage, and everything has happened since just as the Lord told me.[217]

"'I have seen great things concerning members of this Father's Order, the Society of Jesus. I saw them in heaven carrying white banners and other marvelous things. And thus I hold this order in great veneration, because I have had many dealings with them and I see that their way of life conforms with what the Lord has given me to understand about them.[218]

"'One night while I was in prayer, the Lord began to say a few words to remind me of what a bad life I had led. This filled me with shame and sorrow, because even if such words are not spoken harshly, one is undone with regret and sorrow. A few words like this do more good than many days spent reflecting on our own wretchedness, because this experience carries engraved within it a truth that we cannot deny. He represented to me the affections that I had so vainly entertained. He told me I should esteem the desire to place my will, which I had employed so poorly, in Him, and that He would accept it. Other times He told me to remember when I apparently thought it honorable to go against His honor; at others, He reminded me of what I owed Him, and that when I was striking hardest against Him, He was giving me the greatest favors. If I have any faults at all—and they are more than a few—His Majesty makes me understand them in such a way that it seems I

216. Ibid., chap. 38, sec. 13. This Dominican father has been identified as Pedro Ibáñez (d. 1565). He initially opposed founding Saint Joseph's without an income but became reconciled to this part of Teresa's plan. See Peers, *Handbook*, 167–68.

217. Teresa of Avila, *Life*, chap. 38, sec. 14. This Jesuit has been identified as Gaspar de Salazar (1529–93).

218. Ibid., chap. 38, sec. 15.

am entirely undone. And my faults being so many, this happens often. Indeed, when my confessor reprimanded me and I wanted to find consolation in prayer, there I would find my true reprimand.[219]

"'Well, as I was saying, the Lord began to remind me of my wretched life. Since I had done nothing at that time, in my opinion, I wondered in the midst of my tears if He wanted to give me some favor. This is because it often happens that when I receive some particular favor from the Lord I have first become undone within myself so that I see more clearly how far I am from being worthy of His favors.[220] For a little while my spirit was so enraptured that it almost seemed it was outside my body. At least, there is no sense that it lives in the body. I saw Christ's most Sacred Humanity in more exalted glory than I had ever seen before. It was shown to me with the clear and amazing knowledge that it was placed within the bosom of the Father. I cannot describe how this is so, because without seeing myself it seemed that I saw myself in the presence of that divinity. I was so amazed that it seems that several days went by in which I couldn't return to myself, while I seemed always to go about in the presence of that majesty of the Son of God, although no longer like the very first time. I understood this clearly, for this vision remained so inscribed in my imagination that, however brief it had been, I could not dispel it. This vision brings plentiful consolation and benefit. I have seen it at other times, and in my opinion this is the most exalted favor that the Lord has granted me to see. The vision brings with it very great benefits. I believe it purifies the soul greatly and almost entirely takes away the strength of this sensuous nature of ours.[221] It is a great flame that seems to burn up and annihilate all the desires of this life. Since, glory be to God, I no longer desired vain things, I was clearly shown that all is vanity. When I went to take communion and would recall how I had seen His Most Sublime Majesty, and considered that it was He who was in the Blessed Sacrament (for the Lord often allows me to see Him in the Host), my hair would stand on end, and I seemed to be entirely annihilated. Oh, my Lord, if You did not conceal Your greatness, who would dare approach the altar so often to join something so dirty and miserable with such great Majesty! May You be blessed, and may the angels and all creatures praise you, for You set the measure of things to our weakness in

219. Ibid., chap. 38, sec. 16.

220. María's text reads "para que veamos claro" [so that we may clearly see], which we correct according to Teresa's text as "para que vea más claro" [so that I may see more clearly].

221. María, following Teresa, uses the word *sensualidad*, which in Teresa's vocabulary refers broadly to what is perceived by the senses.

such a way that Your great power does not terrify us while we are enjoying Your sovereign favors.[222]

"'When I see such a great Majesty concealed in something so little as the Host, I don't know how I have the courage and strength to approach Him. If He who has granted and grants me such great favors did not give me this courage and strength, it would not be possible for me to conceal this and keep from shouting such great marvels aloud. For what should a miserable thing like me feel—weighed down with abominations, who has spent her life with so little fear of God—upon seeing herself approach a Lord of such greatness and majesty, when He wants my soul to see Him? And how can a mouth that has spoken so many words against this very Lord then join with His glorious body which is so full of purity? And the soul is more afflicted by having failed to serve Him with the same love shown on that Face that is so full of beauty, tenderness, and kindness, than by a fear of the majesty that is seen there. And what could I possibly have felt, the two times I saw what I am about to describe?[223]

"'Once when I was approaching the altar to take communion, I saw with the eyes of my soul, more clearly than with the eyes of my body, two demons of most abominable appearance. It seemed to me that their horns encircled the priest's throat, and I saw my Lord placed in those hands, with all the majesty I have described, in the form that the priest was about to give me. I understood that those hands had offended the Lord, and that the priest's soul was in mortal sin. Who, my Lord, could imagine seeing Your beauty amidst such abominable figures! They were trembling from the fear of being before You, for it seems that they would willingly have fled if You had let them go. I was so disturbed that I don't know how I was able to take communion. I was terrified, thinking that if the vision truly were from God, He would not permit me to see the evil state that soul was in. The Lord told me to pray for the priest, and that He had permitted me to see this so that I might understand the power that the words of the consecration of the Host have. For God would not fail to be there, no matter how evil the priest who said those words might be. And He said He had done this so that I might see His goodness, knowing that He puts Himself in the hands of His enemy for our good. I understood clearly the obligation that priests have to be good, and what a violent thing it is to receive the Blessed Sacrament unworthily, and how the Devil rules a soul in mortal sin.[224]

222. Ibid., chap. 38, secs. 17–19.

223. Ibid., chap. 38, sec. 21.

224. Ibid., chap. 38, sec. 23. Mariá's departure from the meaning of Teresa's text here is notable

"'Another time I saw a similar vision. I was in a place where a person who had lived a bad life had died. Although he had been ill for two years, and in some ways he seemed to have made amends, he died without confession. In spite of all this it did not seem to me that he was going to be condemned. As they were wrapping his body in a shroud, I saw many demons take the body, and they seemed to be playing with it and punishing it a great deal, which terrified me, for they were passing him from one demon to another with great hooks. Since I saw that he was being taken to be buried with the same honor and ceremony as others, I was thinking of the goodness of God and how He did not want that soul to be defamed, but rather, He was concealing that the man had been His enemy. I was half stupefied from what I had seen. During the entire Mass I did not see any more demons. Afterward, when they put his body in the tomb, there were so many of them in it ready to take it that I was beside myself with the sight of it, and I needed no little courage to conceal my fear. I reflected on what those demons would do to the soul if they ruled over the poor body that way. Would to God that all whose souls are in a bad state might see what I saw, and that it might be enough to make them live a virtuous life.[225]

"They told me that one of our Provincials, to whom I was indebted for certain good deeds, had died. His death made me very sad and distressed, because I feared for his salvation, since he had been a superior for twenty years. This is something I greatly fear, because it clearly seems to me to be very dangerous.[226] And thus with much anguish I went to an oratory. I offered him all the good I had done in my life, which was very little, and so I asked the Lord to supply with His merits whatever was lacking for that soul to leave purgatory. While I was asking for this, it seemed to me that his soul emerged from the depths of the earth on my right side and I saw it rise to heaven with great happiness. He was quite old, but I saw him as if he were thirty, with a shining face. This vision was quickly over, but I was so greatly consoled that this mat-

---

and apparently intentional. The equivalent passage in the *Life* reads: "entendí bien cuán más obligados están los sacerdotes a ser buenos que otros" [I understood clearly how much more priests are obligated to be good than are others]. María is careful—even more than Teresa—to avoid the heterodox implication that the Communion wafer cannot be sanctified by a priest in mortal sin.

225. Ibid., chap. 38, secs. 24–25.

226. Teresa's text, which María has abbreviated, clarifies the meaning here: 'This is something I greatly fear, indeed, because it seems to me to be a very dangerous thing to be entrusted with others' souls." The implication, which María perhaps wished to soften, is that the friar had seriously failed in his duties as superior.

ter does not sadden me any more. He had been dead two weeks when I saw this.[227]

"'In our convent a nun had died, a great servant of God. She had been dead for a day and a half, and while I was in the choir reciting a reading from the office of the dead for her, in the middle of the reading I saw her come out on my right side and rise to heaven.[228]

"'Another nun died, a great servant of God and devoted to the choir, who for some eighteen or twenty years had always been ill. I thought that she would not go to purgatory because she had suffered so many illnesses. While we were reciting the hours of the office before her burial—she had been dead for four hours—I saw her come out from purgatory and go to heaven.[229]

"'While I was at a college of the Society of Jesus, a Brother of that house died. As another Father was saying Mass for him, I saw that Brother rise to heaven, and while I was in a great rapture I saw the Lord with him. I understood that this Brother was going with the Lord by special favor, and that his soul was departing in great glory.[230]

"'Concerning another friar of our Order, a very good friar, when I was at Mass I became recollected and I saw that he was dead, and I saw him go to heaven without entering purgatory. I understood that since he had kept the vows of his profession well, he had profited from the Bulls given the Order so as not to enter purgatory.[231]

"'Until now I have seen only those three souls who have not entered purgatory: this friar, our holy Father Friar Peter of Alcántara and the Dominican I have described. With some souls, it has pleased the Lord to let me see the degrees of glory that each one has, which was shown to me by the place each one occupies, for the difference between some places and others is great.'[232]

"'Once I was entreating the Lord to restore sight to a person to whom I bore an obligation, who had become almost entirely blind, and for whom I felt great pity.'"[233]

227. Ibid., chap. 38, secs. 26–27.

228. Ibid., chap. 38, sec. 28.

229. Ibid., chap. 38, sec. 29.

230. Ibid., chap. 38, sec. 30. For modern editors of Teresa's text, "by special favor" modifies "I understood." Thus, Kavanaugh and Rodríguez's translation of the equivalent Teresian text reads: "By special favor I understood it was His Majesty going with him" (266). María evidently read the phrasing in Teresa's text differently.

231. Teresa of Avila, *Life*, chap. 38, sec. 31. The passage refers to the bull *Ut laudes*. See "Fourth Recreation," n. 97.

232. Ibid., chap. 38, sec. 32.

233. Ibid., chap. 39, sec. 1. María's citation of this passage from Teresa remains incomplete.

"Everything said here and many other things that are omitted for the sake of brevity our holy Mother left written down in the *Book of Her Life*, which she wrote at the beginning of the foundation of the convent in Avila so that her spirit might be understood, as I said, along with another book called *Way of Perfection*, which is addressed only to the nuns of Saint Joseph, for at that time there were no other Discalced nuns. Since the foundation of that convent was successful and the things she wrote about were clearly and manifestly fulfilled, our Mother herself as well as her confessors were satisfied that her spirit was truly of God. And since she was pleased with this, she no longer worried about writing down many wonders that the Lord manifested to her, as I learned from our Mother herself, and afterward our Lord even ordered her to do so. She began to relate other revelations in a little notebook, which is labeled 'year of 1575,' when she was in the foundation of Beas and she and Father Eliseus met and she gave him a vow of obedience at the command of the Lord, as we will see later. Then she took up writing again about things that were happening to her so as to give an account to that Father about what befell them during the foundation of the Seville convent. This is not to mention other accounts that have been lost.[234] In particular, we know that an important Dominican friar, to whom she used to make her confession, during the time of the great upheavals and controversies regarding our Mother and our convents, burned some papers that belonged to her, for which he is now sorry.

"After some twenty-eight years, more or less,[235] as we have said, in 1562 she founded the first convent in Avila, the second in Medina del Campo, the third in Malagón, the fourth in Valladolid, the fifth in Toledo, the sixth in Pastrana (which lasted almost five years before our Mother, with just cause, dissolved it, because it seemed to her that the Princess of Eboli, who had joined the nuns after becoming a widow, was not going to allow the life of enclosure and perfection to be lived there as it was in the other convents; in doing this our Mother amazed everyone with her zeal and rigor, because she dissolved the convent against the wishes of the princess, whereby she showed no less courage than in the foundation of the other convents); the seventh was in Salamanca and the eighth in Alba: these two were founded in 1571. I mention this year because in it our holy Mother solemnly renounced the Mitigated Rule in the presence of Father Mariano and his companion Friar Juan de la Miseria and Francisco Salcedo (a gentleman priest whom the

---

234. Conjectural reading of an obscure passage.

235. María refers to the years 1536–62, during which Teresa lived under the mitigated Carmelite rule in the Convent of the Incarnation in Avila.

Mother mentions in her book), Master Daza, and Julián de Avila, the chaplain of Saint Joseph's of Avila, where our Mother resided at this time.

"The tenor of the renunciation is this, taken from the warrant in our Mother's very own handwriting that I have in my possession: 'Say I, Teresa de Jesús, nun of Our Lady of Carmen, professed in the Convent of the Incarnation of Avila, who am now present in Saint Joseph's of Avila, where the Primitive Rule is kept, which until now I have kept here with the permission of our Father Friar General Juan Bautista, who also permitted me to keep it at the Incarnation should my prelates order me to return there: it is my will to keep the Primitive Rule all my life and so I promise to do. And I renounce all briefs that the pontiffs may have given for the mitigation of the aforementioned Primitive Rule which, with our Lord's favor, I intend and promise to keep until death. Because this is true, I affirm it with my name. July 13, 1571. Teresa de Jesús, Carmelite.'

"This very warrant, written and signed by our Mother, bears the signatures of the Fathers I named above as witnesses, and in the same paper there also appears the confirmation of Father Friar Pedro Fernández, which says: 'I, Friar Pedro Fernández, Apostolic Commissary for the visitation of Castile of the Carmelite Order, accept said renunciation made at the petition of said Mother. As her prelate, I remove her from the conventuality of the Incarnation and make her a conventual of the convents of the Primitive Rule, and I now assign her to and make her conventual of the Discalced Nuns of Salamanca. And by whatever means she should finish her term of office as prioress of the Incarnation which she presently occupies, I revoke her residency in the latter monastery and make her a resident of the convent of Salamanca. And during the said term of office I also wish that insomuch as she belongs to the conventuality of the said convent of Salamanca, by this I do not remove her from the office of prioress of the Incarnation, which I am well able to do since her conventuality belongs to Salamanca; and if perchance in the Order of Carmen there is a law to the contrary, on this occasion I revoke it and with my authority I do what is stated. Medina del Campo on the Ninth of October of 1571. Fray Pedro Fernández, Apostolic Commissary.'

"Even if it were not as necessary as it is to put here this confirmation for the clarification of certain matters, I would seek an opportunity to remember this excellent man to whom we owe so much, and for whom our Mother felt great friendship. He was of the Order of the glorious Saint Dominic and served as our Visitator[236] in the reform that His Holiness Father Pius V commanded for several religious Orders in Spain, among them the Order of Car-

---

236. Visitators were friars who inspected monasteries and convents to insure that the communities were observing monastic rules and constitutions.

men, during the time that our Primitive Rule arose. Our reform was assisted to no small degree by this holy and very learned man, and by Friar Francisco de Vargas in the province of Andalusia, from that same Order of preachers, and with his favor our Discalced Fathers began to found there. Our holy Mother was fond of this Father and greatly saddened by his death, which was in the year 1580, when His Holiness Father Gregory XIII had ordered him in a Brief to separate our province. Because of the death of that Father it was necessary for His Holiness to name Master Juan de las Cuevas, so that it was he who presided at our first Chapter. And of the many benefits our Order has received from our most Christian King, for which he should be thanked and served, not least is having ordered that the business pertaining to our province was to be placed in the hand of this pious and learned Father, who demonstrated as much zeal and ardor for the good of our Order as any of our own holy Fathers in the past. I would like to have sufficient skill to express any of the great good that I desire for him and he deserves, but as my pen cannot, may his perpetual memory rest in our hearts, and there may we find written the peace, prudence, humility, and charity with which he conducted himself and the fatherly affection that he shows us now, in return for which we all obey him as our superior. The Virgin has a reward in store for him, and his memory will be eternal in Carmel.

"And let us return to our Mother's story, though we do not stray from her liking when we pause to express our gratitude, for that virtue shone so brightly in her that she will be pleased to let the thread of our argument be broken.

"Since the first convent was in Avila and she was residing in it, it is necessary for us to go back a little to explain why Friar Pedro Fernández assigned her to the one in Salamanca.

"I believe that it has already been made clear how when the first Discalced convent was founded it was necessary to place it under obedience to the Bishop, and why the Order did not want to accept that convent, and how Our Lord wanted it that way, as it seems from the way He consoled her for the pain she suffered, as we have seen. In order not to leave her subject to the Bishop and unable to respond to opportunities that might present themselves to found new convents, He wished to make her free from this subjection and from that which she might suffer at the hands of the Fathers of the Mitigated Rule to whom she was subject, being a professed nun of their Order in the Incarnation and prioress there, named to that position by the Apostolic Visitator himself to accomplish the reform of that house. All of this was remedied by making her a conventual of Salamanca, which was subject to the Visitator, who as we have said was so much in our favor.

"It seems to me that another question remains that I want to satisfy, which is why, nine years after the first convent had been founded, with eight more already founded, our Mother now renounces the Mitigated Rule and promises to live according to the Primitive Rule, and why in her renunciation she does not recall that she founded or initiated this way of life. The answer to the last question is her great humility; to the first, I say that she had already renounced [the Mitigated Rule] from the beginning, as can be inferred from the very first warrant of renunciation. It was done by permission of our Reverend Father General Juan Bautista de Ravena [Rubeo], who had been in Spain at the beginning of the foundation of the first Discalced convent.[237] The foundation made him very happy, and he showed great love and favor to our Mother and the nuns of the convent. He was very saintly and desiring of the reform of the Order of the Virgin, to whom he was deeply devoted as a true son of our holy Mother, although he regretted seeing the Order subject to the Bishop, and he reprimanded the friars for not wanting to accept it. But, to remedy this pain, and it was a great pain for him to have the house that he called a sanctuary outside his obedience, he gave our Mother power to found wherever the opportunity arose, and he obligated her with the order that she should not fail to consider any possible foundation that arose in any of the regions of Spain. And to conclude, as far as now renouncing the Mitigated Rule, it was because our Father Visitor had decreed that any of the nuns of the Mitigation who wanted to remain in our Discalced convents, being obligated to keep the Primitive Rule, should make a public renunciation of the Mitigated Rule, which is what our Mother did.

"At this time, as has been explained, she was Prioress at the Incarnation, where she was placed by the Father Visitor to reform that house. And when she went to it, it seems our Mother felt some reluctance, according to these words that the Lord told her which are found in a little notebook that she left written in her own hand.

"She says: 'One day, after the octave of the feast of the Visitation, when I was in a hermitage of Mount Carmel praying to God for one of my brothers, I said to the Lord (I don't know whether in my thoughts or aloud) because my brother is in a place where his salvation is in danger: "If Lord, I saw one of your brothers in this danger, what would I not do to remedy it? It seems to me that there is nothing that, if I could do it, I would fail to do." The Lord replied: "Oh, daughter, these nuns of the Incarnation are my Sisters, and you delay! Well, take courage, for I wish it, and it is not as difficult as it seems to

---

237. Rubeo: Giovanni Battisti Rossi, 1507–78. As apostolic visitator, in 1567 he gave Teresa licences to found further convents in Castile. See Peers, *Handbook*, 218–19.

you, and whereas you think that those other convents will lose, all will gain. Do not resist, for my power is great.'"238

"This great power of the Lord was seen clearly in this work, because even with the nuns resisting and the friars working to impede the desired reform, in the end the Visitor took her to the convent. He had to use all the power he had and all the power that the King had given him for the reform, for both were necessary because of the strength of the opposition to accepting her as prioress. This was not because she wasn't loved by all and well received in person, for she was well known there for her great discretion and gentleness, but because of that word 'reform' which, for our sins, is even today so feared. Since the Devil helped, fearing the good that was to follow when that saint entered there, there arose such a great scandal and uproar that the convent was about to go under, and her greatest friends and acquaintances at that time did not recognize her and everyone resisted her, which was no small war.

"And something very amusing happened that our Mother told me, laughing about her bad memory, and it was that having entered the convent with the force that we have described, with the Visitor himself accompanying her and the magistrates helping to quiet the shouting and resistance, with some nuns dishonoring her and others cursing her, at last they brought her to the choir. And when she entered it, forgetting where she was going, she went to the place where she used to sit when she was a nun there, without remembering that she went there to be a Prioress. And so, concealing her laughter which was even greater than her sorrow, she went to her stall where she put a statue of Our Lady, telling the nuns that the Virgin was their Prioress and not she, and with this and her great discretion and the grace that Our Lord gave her, she quieted them and put them in order.

"The same year she entered that convent she saw a vision, on the day of the feast of Saint Sebastian, while she was saying the Salve Regina. Our Lady appeared to her with a great multitude of angels on the cornice of the choir stalls and above the railing, not in corporeal form, for this was an intellectual vision. She held this vision during all of the Salve, and Our Lady told her: 'You did right to put me here; I will be present for all the praises given to my Son and I will offer them to Him.'239

"It is clearly seen how changed these nuns were from the beginning and

238. Teresa of Avila, "Spiritual Testimonies," no. 16. In the course of her life, Teresa wrote for her confessors a number of short accounts of her spiritual favors, known as *relaciones* or *cuentas de conciencia*. They appear as "Spiritual Testimonies" in volume 1 of *The Collected Works of St. Teresa*, trans. Kieran Kavanaugh and Otilio Rodríguez.

239. Teresa of Avila, "Spiritual Testimonies," no. 21.

how calm, through the favor that the Lord gave them. Our Mother found still more help from some nuns from the same convent who had left to help found ours, and some of them had returned because they weren't strong enough or for other legitimate reasons. Many of these still wore the habit of our coarse cloth and went without shoes, still keeping the exercises of prayer and mortification that they had learned in our Discalced convents.

"I am glad to find occasion to remember these favors. To them we owe the good order and ceremonies of the choir and many other things that they knew as nuns, and since our holy Mother took them as her helpers, it is right that we recognize them for having been our teachers and that we render due thanks to them, acknowledging their holy House as our mother and progenitor. As mother of so many daughters, that house deserves a glorious memory, for one Daughter alone whom she engendered was enough to give her eternal fame, which will be hers, as she glories in having raised the blessed Mother Angela.

"Angela, not having yet fulfilled entirely her three-year term as Prioress, offered to make a foundation in Segovia, to receive the nuns from Pastrana, whom she expected any day. Thus, she made the foundation on the feast of the glorious Saint Joseph, 1574, and on that day the nuns from the other convent arrived, because, as we have said, the Princess adapted so poorly to convent life that it was necessary to order her to leave. After that she continued to be so displeased with the nuns and to bother them, that when least expected our Mother ordered them to abandon it one day altogether, leaving in the house everything the Princess had given them, even the smallest trifle. In this our holy Mother and her Daughters showed how much more they esteemed living in perfection than all the riches and favors there are on earth; for they scorned both in leaving this house of which, because it was founded with the favor of Ruy Gómez[240] and with his riches and gifts (in which it had advantage over the other houses), it seemed that anyone would grow fond. But above all the saint desired that her nuns follow Christ unencumbered. What was most astonishing about this was that it was done against the will of the Princess herself, who put guards on the roads to keep the nuns from passing, and they rode roughshod over everything.

"The convent in Segovia was the ninth, or let us say the eighth, subtracting the Pastrana convent, as if it had never been founded; the ninth was Beas; Seville was the tenth; and the eleventh was Caravaca, where she could

240. Ruy Gómez de Silva was the husband of the princess of Eboli and a grandee of the realm. He and his wife were patrons of a Discalced monastery and convent. After Ruy Gómez died in 1573, his wife took the Discalced habit, but she caused so much turmoil that, as María explains, Teresa decided to dismantle the foundation in 1574. See Alison Weber, "Saint Teresa's Problematic Patrons," *Journal of Medieval and Early Modern Studies* 29, no. 2 (1999): 357–79.

not go in person as she had gone to the others, because it was so far. She sent nuns in her stead while she was in the Seville convent and made the foundation from there, relying on her letters and instructions.

"Between the Caravaca foundation and that of Villanueva de la Jara, which was the twelfth, lay a stormy sea of persecution which our Mother herself had prophesied four years earlier, as I saw written in a paper in her own hand that she sent to Father Eliseus. In it she said that she had seen a great sea of persecutions and that just as the Egyptians had drowned in the sea while pursuing the children of Israel, and the people of God had passed over safely, so too our enemies would drown and the army of the Virgin would pass through to freedom. And thus it was that the Devil began to spread abominations with his usual weapons, which are lies and false testimony, first of all about those two purest of souls, Mother Angela and Father Eliseus, and then about the congregation of nuns and friars. And since there is always someone willing to believe such things (and perhaps more willing than to believe the good), the persecution began, just as the Devil had planned for her and God had permitted, so that the foundations of this edifice might be made strong. And thus it was that when the Devil thought to destroy us and drown us, the Lord gave us by this means a dry and firm path, because our invincible and Catholic King and Lord Don Philip II, 'with his heart in the hands of the Lord,'[241] as the Sage says, was not deceived. Rather, taking on the protection of this little flock of the sovereign Virgin, he asked for and obtained from the sovereign pontiff that very favorable brief with which the separation of the province was accomplished. This was in 1581 on the sixth of March, the feast of the glorious Saint Cyril. Our most fortunate Angela rejoiced greatly in this, and asked, like the saintly Simon in his old age, 'that the Lord take her in peace,'[242] since many years before His Divine Majesty had promised her that He would not take her from this life until He saw all matters of her Order in great prosperity, as with this she left us.

"All that was lacking for our complete contentment was for our pious Mother to live with us a few years, but that was not the Lord's wish, moved as He was by the pious prayers with which, like the Apostle,[243] she constantly implored Him, desiring to be unchained; or else He took her because of our unworthiness, for after that she lived less than two full years.

"Before the separation, which was in 1581, as we have said, she founded the convent of Villanueva, early in 1580. After the separation she founded Palencia and Soria in the same year that the province was divided, and in the

241. Proverbs 21:1.

242. Luke 29:2.

243. The reference is to the Apostle Paul. See Philippians 1:23.

last year of her life, Burgos. From there she also sent her nuns to found the convent in Granada.

"And on her return from the foundation of Burgos, where she said she had suffered many trials like those of the first foundation, she became ill while passing by Alba. And there she died at sixty-seven years of age, on the eve of the feast of the glorious Saint Francis, to whom she was very devoted, in the year 1582, the day on which the calendar was shortened by ten days. She died between nine and ten o'clock at night, on a Wednesday, having lived in the habit and observance of the Primitive Rule for twenty years. During that time she founded seventeen monasteries, counting Pastrana, fifteen of them herself, and only two, Caravaca and Granada, by sending her nuns.

"Our saint was of medium height, more on the tall side than short. In her youth she was known as a great beauty and to the end of her days this was evident; her face was far from ordinary but rather quite extraordinary, of a sort that could not be called either round or narrow. It was evenly proportioned, the forehead wide and smooth and very beautiful; her eyebrows, broad and slightly arched, were a dark blond color that bore little resemblance to black. Her eyes were black, round, and lively, not very large but very well placed. Her nose was round and went straight down between the corners of her eyes; at the top it was small and lay flat with her eyebrows, forming a gentle space between the brows, while the point was round and slightly tilted down, the little nostrils arched and small and overall not very prominent.

"Scarcely can the pen portray what perfection was hers in all things: her mouth, which was of a very good size, had a thin, straight upper lip and a thicker lower lip with a slight pout, which had a very lovely grace and color. And her face looked thus to the day she was of great age and had many illnesses, so that it was a great pleasure to look at her and listen to her, for she was very gentle and witty in all her words and actions.

"She was more robust than thin and well proportioned in all ways; she had very lovely hands, though they were small. On the left side of her face, she had three moles raised like little warts, all in a straight line, beginning with the largest one below her mouth, and the next between her mouth and nose, and the last on her nose, closer to the bottom than the top of it.

"She was perfect in all ways, as can be seen in a portrait painted from life by Fray Juan de la Miseria, one of our friars and a saint as far as we understand. I hope to make a record of it and of several others that have been done by him, so that the Sisters who are still to come may know the clothing and wimples that their Mother wore, and that are worn in all our convents.

"And although our Constitutions declare how these should be, I wish to note for our Sisters to come (so they won't be taken in by paintings that have been poorly done), that in some portraits and engravings, to disguise a few torn pieces that she had in the sleeves of her habit when her portrait was done, they have made something like lace cuffs; and on her veil, to cover up how threadbare it was, it looks as though they have put on some pleats and things that could be thought to be fine work.

"Her manner of dress was, as it is of all of us nuns alive today, a wool tunic, with an outer skirt of sackcloth woven with the black and white goatshair. And to avoid the fastidiousness and special care that white always requires, it is not used for anything except the capes, which must be white; they are made of sackcloth or kersey, which is thick too, as is the habit. The wimples are of thick linen, and let it be noted that although the Constitution says that they should be made of flax—and some nuns have tried to say that this meant that the wimples should be made of fine flax or fine linen, it should be known that the saint never wore such wimples, nor have they ever been worn for one single day in any of her monasteries. But rather, by flax she meant tow, not the very thickest kind, and that was her intention when she had it put in the Constitution. The veils are made of thick linen, the sandals of hemp. In short, the entire dress and wimple kept to the spirit of poverty.

"Overcome by the tears of the Sisters in Seville, she consented to have that friar paint her portrait as we have mentioned, for she thought it cruel to leave them disconsolate for her—because she was returning to Castile—when she herself was going off with great emotion and tenderness for them.

"Because this is a brief summary, we shall leave it here, and go on to our purpose, by setting forth many other revelations and travails that our Mother went through.

"In particular, I wish to record all her virtues together—since in this tale of her life they are scattered and mixed in with other things—returning to the basis we took, of that strong and worthy woman whom Solomon portrays for us [in Proverbs]. Although my going on longer with such a delightful subject as this, of speaking of the life of our holy Mother—which, like nectar and ambrosia, not only nourishes the senses but elevates and absorbs them entirely—might be a most righteous excuse for not hearing the bell that reminds us of our obligations, we should not fail to carry them out, leaving the rest of this story for another occasion."

She got up before Justa and Atanasia could respond; they went off, agreeing to return to the spot as soon as custom should allow.

NINTH RECREATION

Together they returned to the spot the following day. When they had seated themselves as before and Gracia was beginning to speak, Justa cut her off, saying, "Just because you got up and left yesterday without letting us say a word, Sister, do not think that your quickness and our lack of concern are now going to help you avoid giving us satisfactory answers on any points that might serve as recreation to our spirits. You remember quite well that when you referred to the founding of the convent in Seville you started to mention the trials that were endured in it, and then without speaking of them you went right on—which I pretended not to notice so as not to interrupt you and lead you off the track. And so I kept the topic for this occasion, for to speak of trials suffered for Our Lord Christ is our true recreation."

"Justa has gotten there ahead of me, and indeed stolen the wish that was in my thoughts," said Atanasia, "but that does not leave me out. For my part, I want you to tell about the convents of friars that our Mother founded and all you know about them."

"It is my pleasure to give you what you ask," answered Gracia, "and since I have to open such a weighty and lengthy parenthesis, I would rather not waste time on anything else.

"The house of the glorious Saint Joseph in the city of Seville was founded in 1575, on the Feast of the Holy Trinity, which that year was celebrated on the twenty-ninth of May. But to understand thoroughly how that foundation began, it is necessary to go somewhat further back. While our holy Mother Teresa of Jesus was in the Convent of Saint Joseph in the town of Beas, which she had founded that same year, Father Fray Jerónimo Gracián came from Seville to see her on the Feast of Saint Matthew, because they had never seen one another, though each of them had greatly desired to do so. It was then that our holy Mother had the vision of Our Lord Christ, who took each of them by the right hand and commanded our Mother that, for as long as she lived, she should consider this man to stand in place of Our Lord and should submit to him in everything, for this was right in the service of Our Lord and was best for the Order; and the saint fulfilled this so perfectly that she bound herself by vow [of obedience], as we shall see later.[244]

"There she was, on the point of going to found a convent in Caravaca, where she was taking me with five other nuns, when Father Gracián's arrival brought all that to a stop. He obliged our Mother to leave off that foundation and instead, with the nuns she had named for that purpose, to make a foundation in Seville, for he was Apostolic Visitator of the Calced and Discalced Carmelites in Andalusia, and the house in question fell within his district. Both he and Father Mariano,[245] who had come with him, promised her that

244. On this vow, see below in "Ninth Recreation," 141–42. Teresa's account is given in "Spiritual Testimonies," nos. 35, 36.

245. Father Mariano: Ambrosio Mariano de Benito (c. 1510–94). A brilliant mathematician and engineer, he also studied law and theology. He attended the Council of Trent as a theologian

the Archbishop of Seville, Don Cristóbal de Rojas y Sandoval, greatly desired this foundation and asked for it to be made, and that in addition to the archbishop's help and favor she would find many very wealthy nuns and a thousand kinds of comfort and assistance. Our Mother was persuaded—or, more accurately, was forced by obedience, because, as we have said, that place falls within the province of Andalusia, which was a very new matter for her. Had she known it was Andalusia, she would not have gone, because she knew quite well that it was not to the liking of the most Reverend Prior General of the Order, who was then Fray Juan Bautista Rubeo of Ravenna,[246] as he was somewhat upset with his Andalusian friars; thus, she found herself perplexed. But in the end, as Father Gracián commanded apostolic obedience, she obeyed, although she feared or perhaps indeed knew what the Devil was to provoke there, and this was that the Prior General grew very angry with her, so that from regarding her with great friendship he came to withdraw all favor from her and speak against her. Thinking that she had angered him was the trial that hurt her most deeply in those times, for she loved and respected him like a true daughter.

"When the day came that we were to leave, which was Wednesday the eighteenth of May in the year we have already mentioned, we set out with our holy Mother, quite happy to be in her company and to know, from the accounts that certain servants of God had given us, that we were going to suffer many trials in founding that convent. Indeed, our holy Mother said the very same thing to a Sister who went to tell her what she had understood while in prayer, for she answered: 'They are so many trials, my beloved Daughter, that there will be no lack of them; I too have seen this.'

"We were six nuns who went with Her Reverence: Sister Ana de San Alberto, who later was Prioress in Caravaca and a Daughter of the house in Malagón; Sister María del Espíritu Santo and Sister Leonor de San Gabriel, also professed nuns from Malagón; Sister Isabel de San Jerónimo, who made her profession in Medina del Campo and was one of the nuns who founded the house in Pastrana; Sister Isabel de San Francisco, a professed nun from the house in Toledo—all very good nuns and, as our holy Mother says in the

---

and later served as an adviser on engineering projects to Phillip II. In 1569 he took the Discalced habit and in 1570 was ordained a priest. He accompanied Gracián on his visitation to Andalusia from 1573 to 1575. See Peers, *Handbook*, 112.

246. Juan Bautista Rubeo (Giovanni Battista Rossi, 1507–78), as general of the Carmelites, made an extensive visitation in Spain in order to extirpate abuses of the order. He met Teresa in 1567, approved her reform, and gave her permission to found further convents in Castile only. Hence Teresa's dilemma when she discovered that the foundation that Gracián had ordered her to make was in Andalusia.

Book of Her Foundations,[247] all quite determined to suffer for Christ and very happy to go wherever necessary. Sinner that I am and unworthy to go in this company, I set off no less happy, though not with the spirit and perfection of the other Sisters.

"That first day at the hour of the siesta we came to a lovely grove from which we could scarcely pull our holy Mother away, for at the abundance of flowers and the songs of a thousand little birds she entirely dissolved in praises of God. We went to pass the night in the hermitage of San Andrés, which is below the village of Santisteban. There, sometimes praying and sometimes resting on the cold, hard flagstones of the church, we spent the night very happily though with little enough ease, because we traveled quite unequipped and unencumbered—that is to say, utterly destitute of the most essential things; and our Sisters at Beas did not have anything to give us, since the house there had just been founded. Indeed, they took from us what little they might have given, because of the reports of the greatness and riches that Father Mariano had led us to think we would find in Seville; with this expectation, we even tried to assist them. And so with the certainty we felt, they were frugal while we gave lavishly, though we had little enough to lavish upon them. The Sisters at Malagón lent us all the money we spent for the cost of the journey, and as that house was the first that did well by us it is right to say so here, especially because that holy house was my Mother convent and that of the other Sisters who made this trip, and has helped so many nuns.

"We set forth again on our journey, which was quite wearisome because this was early summer there in Andalusia, where the heat is so severe, and with few provisions for a great many people. As I have said, there were six of us nuns, and our Mother made seven; and Father Julián of Avila,[248] whom we might call the companion of our holy Mother, because he accompanied her in founding so many convents; Antonio Gaitán, a gentleman from Alba; and Father Fray Gregorio Nacianceno,[249] who had just received the Carmelite habit in Beas from Father Gracián, at the petition of our Mother, on which occasion Her Reverence and all of us nuns helped to give him blessings. He

247. Teresa of Avila, *Book of Her Foundations*, 24, sec. 6.

248. Julián de Avila (1527–1605) was a lay priest who accompanied Teresa on many of the journeys necessitated by her foundations. He is the author of one of the first biographies of Teresa (1605). See Peers, *Handbook*, 124.

249. Gregorio Nacianceno Martínez y López (1548–99), given the Discalced habit by Gracián at Beas in 1575, played an active role in the foundation of various Discalced monasteries and convents. See Peers, *Handbook*, 163–64.

was a priest whom we knew well and who was very devoted to us in Malagón, where he frequently heard our confessions and said Mass, and he had accompanied our Mother and those of us nuns who went from there to Beas—a long way from the resolution he later made never to return to his homeland—and so strong was his fervor that, as I said, there in our house in Beas he took the habit. Our Mother loved him dearly and called him her son, and that is how he turned out, like the son of just such a mother; this priest accompanied us and later he helped us through many trials. There were also mule boys and cart drivers along. As we were traveling during a time of vigils and Ember days,[250] nothing could be found to eat—not that we nuns would have wanted meat even if it happened to be a day when it could be eaten, nor could we ever make our Mother eat it, even when she was ill[251]—but there were many days when we ate nothing but beans or bread and cherries and things like that, and if we found an egg for our Mother, it was a great thing.

"We passed the whole journey laughing and composing ballads and verses on all the events that befell us, and these pleased our Mother no end. She thanked us a thousand times for undergoing so many trials with such great pleasure and satisfaction, because there were more trials than I shall tell here so as not to be tedious. I will only tell of a few that caused us the most distress, such as the time we found ourselves in great difficulty while crossing the Guadalquivir River. For when all the people had crossed to the other side and tried to bring the carts across, then—either because it was necessary, on account of the carts, to shift the boat, or because the boatman did not have the skill to manage—the great force of the current swept the boat away and carried it downstream with one or two carts aboard, so that it seemed we would be left there helpless, with nothing to be done and night coming on. We were sorely distressed, for one thing because we badly needed the carts, since without them we could not travel on; and for another because we were a league and a half distant from any dwelling place; and for a third, you can imagine how drivers and boatmen would respond to what had happened— they started the sort of lengthy recital that is their custom, and no one could quiet them down. As soon as she saw this, our Mother began to take charge of her convent and set it to rights[252] and went under a bluff at the river's edge.

---

250. Ember days [cuatro témporas]: "These days, sometimes called the Quarter Tenses, occur at intervals of about three months. They are the Wednesday, Friday and Saturday which follow December 13, the first Sunday in Lent, Pentecost, and September 14" (John F. Sullivan, *The Externals of the Catholic Church* [New York: Kennedy, 1917], 293).

251. The Discalced Carmelites abstained from meat except during illness.

252. Teresa had been severely criticized for her failure to observe enclosure during the years of foundation—a papal nuncio had referred to her as a "restless gadabout." María makes clear that

Thinking that we were to spend the night there, we began to unpack our bedding and our gear, which consisted of a sacred image and holy water and books. We sang Compline and in that way passed the time while the men, poor things, were working to stop the boat with a cable—although they needed our help as well, and we set to pulling on the rope, which very nearly dragged all of us nuns away. In the end, because our holy Mother was there with her powerful way of prayer, the Lord willed that the boat should come to a stop where it was possible to bring it back. And that is how we no sooner escaped from this peril than we found ourselves in another, well into the night, for we lost our way and did not know what road to take. From a long way off, a gentleman had witnessed our trials that evening, and he sent us a man who helped us with everything, though at first he stood there uttering a thousand abominations against monks and nuns without making a move to set to the task for which he had been sent. I don't know whether it was seeing us pray that moved him, but as it was he did assist us most mercifully; and when at last he went his own way, it was not before we had once more mistaken the road and he pointed it out, walking half a league with us and begging our pardon for what he had said.

"When we arrived at an inn outside of Córdoba, on Pentecost Sunday, our Mother came down with such a high fever that she became delirious. For that terrible fever and fierce sun, the only shelter and relief from the heat that we had to give her—which she needed a great deal—was a little room that I think previously held pigs. The roof was so low that we could scarcely walk upright in it, and by hanging up blankets and veils we repaired the way the sun came through the roof in a thousand places—our Mother describes this bed in the *Book of Her Foundations*.[253] That was all she noticed, rather than the crowd of spider's webs and crawling bugs that were there. Whatever was in our power to make better, we did. You could not believe what we went through while we were there, with the people in the inn shouting and swearing and the torment of their dances and tambourines—neither prayers nor bribes served to make them move away from a place over our Mother's very head, while she was almost unconscious with her raging fever. In the end we thought it best to take her out of there, and we left in the full fury of the heat at the siesta hour.

"That night, before reaching the entrance into Córdoba, we came to some inns that I think are near the Alcolea bridge. We stayed in the fields

---

Teresa and her followers made every effort to recreate cloistered life, even in the most inauspicious circumstances.

253. Teresa of Avila, *Foundations*, 24:8.

without going into the inns, for it was our custom to stay in the fields surrounded by the people who were accompanying us, and that allowed us to shun the hubbub of inns and taverns, and thus we got down out of the carts as little as we could. Our Mother underwent severe trials that night, and so did we as we watched her suffer, although it was the Lord's will that she recovered, which she attributed to the prayers and pleas of the Sisters.

"The next day we passed through Córdoba, having waited for permission to take the carts over the bridge; it was obtained after a thousand difficulties. Many more griefs and obstacles occurred here, as our Mother relates in detail.[254] We arrived at Ecija on the third day of Pentecost and were directed outside the town to a hermitage of the glorious Saint Ann, where we heard Mass, made our confession, and received communion. Our Mother wished to stay there because the place offered good conditions for being in seclusion, and she asked that the door of the hermitage be closed for us. She directed the people accompanying us to go to the inn and look for something for us to eat. We were left there until two before anyone came back, and then when they returned they brought us lettuce, radishes, and bread, from which we very happily made our dinner. Our Mother assured us that in none of her other travels or foundations did she go through what she went through in this one, passing so many days without finding anything to supply her nuns; I don't know if this was through the lack of ability of the people who were supposed to supply us, or if it was the Lord's will that the trials to be undergone in the founding of this convent should begin.

"That day, with the pretext that she was unwell, our Mother would not let us accompany her as on other days, but instead, without allowing us to speak to her, she passed the whole day alone in a little sacristy in the place. There her time was well spent in devising new services to do for the Holy Spirit, on whose feast days she clearly showed what an ardent love she held for the divine Spirit, as can be clearly seen in a paper I have that was written by her hand; and the brother-and-sisterhood and unity that the Lord created between her and our Father Gracián, along with the vision that I have said she had in Beas, also appear in that document. But as I have already written elsewhere of both these things, I will not relate them now, other than to say that in the hermitage where we were that day, she made a vow to obey Father Gracián for all the days of her life in everything that would not go against obedience to her Prelates.

"In yet another document that is in her own handwriting, the vow makes its declaration in the following way: 'While in Ecija one day during Pente-

254. Ibid., 24:12.

cost, a person who recalled a great favor she had once received from our Lord on the eve of this feast, and who desired to do something very directly for His service, thought it well to promise not to hide a single fault or sin she might commit from that point on in all her life, putting him [Gracián] in place of God, because one does not have this obligation to one's prelates. Although this person had already made a vow of obedience, she believed that the new vow was greater and that it included doing everything he might tell her to do so long as there was nothing that went against the obedience she had already pledged, that is to say, in serious matters. Although this seemed harsh to her at first, she promised it. The first thing that brought her to this decision was her belief that it would be of some service to the Holy Spirit; the second was that she considered the person she chose to be a great servant of God and very learned, so that he would give light to her soul and help her to serve our Lord. The other person knew nothing about the matter until several days after the promise had been made. That person is Father Fray Jerónimo Gracián de la Madre de Dios.'[255]

"All of this is written in our Mother's hand in a document that I have in my possession, as well as another also in her writing where she declares in greater detail how she made this vow which, as I say, I have included elsewhere.[256]

"Leaving there, we went on our way until we arrived in Seville, where no fewer trials befell us than those that had already occurred. I shall end with the final day on Wednesday of the Ember days before Trinity Sunday, when we arrived at midday at an inn where we found nothing to eat but some very salty sardines, and no one could improve this by giving us water. These sardines gave us such a terrible thirst that when we saw how it was and that there was no water, we stopped eating them. The day was extremely hot, and our Mother was in the cart, which was in a refuse yard where the sun was so severe we thought it would roast us. Those of us who were riding with her and those in another cart all asked permission to get out of the carts and join together at the door of hers, so that we could see her and be together, because we thought in that way we would feel the heat less. We improved things somewhat with a few sackcloth blankets put up against the sun, so that we could better withdraw together from the multitude of hellish people that

255. See n. 6 above. María's portrayal of Gracián is remarkably ambivalent in this chapter. Although she lets it be known that he was seriously misguided in ordering Teresa to undertake the Sevillan foundation, she takes pains to emphasize Teresa's particular devotion to him. At the time María was writing this text, Gracián was her ally in her struggles against the Discalced general Doria. See introduction, 7–8.

256. See n. 244 above; in Teresa, "Spiritual Testimonies," no. 36.

were in that inn and around it. They caused us much greater torment than all the other torments I have named—if we hadn't seen it we could not have believed that such abominable people existed among Christians. Our ears could not bear to hear the curses and blasphemy and abominations spoken by that crowd of lost souls, who when they had finished eating grew even more furious than before; perhaps the lack of water made them so. At last they took up their swords and began such a riot that it seemed everything was coming down upon us. Although our Mother had at first been sadly grieved when the people cursed and blasphemed, now when we put our heads inside her cart to take shelter with her we found her laughing soundly, which consoled us, for we were thinking that our end had come. She understood that the uproar was caused by the demons to disturb us, and just so, it stopped at once with no one wounded, though there were more than forty swords, and we also heard harquebuses fired and all in the hands of people in a fury and deprived of reason, carried away by the fury of hell. Oh, what rage the demons showed against this brave and holy woman! We saw it very clearly a great many times and it was shown in the founding of this convent, as you shall see. I don't know, dearest Sisters, what tales our enemies spread about; please God, may it be by our virtues and those of the Sisters still to come that the war against hell shall be waged.

"We entered Seville the next day, on Thursday the twenty-sixth of May, having spent nine days on the road. Father Mariano had rented a house for us, quite small and damp, on the Calle de las Armas, where two ladies who were his friends received us. That day they accompanied us there and then left, and for a very long time we saw nothing more of them, nor did they or anyone else send us so much as a jug of water. Only Father Mariano provided us with all he could, and he did a great deal to give us bread and look for funds to furnish the house, because the day we arrived we had just one *blanca*,[257] and the good Father did not find as much help for these labors as his own expectations had promised him he would. Yet this was permitted by the Lord, whose will it was that the house should be founded in the greatest poverty, so as to take from us the human expectations that one might have in that city more than any other, because of its wealth and the great alms that are given there, as we have since experienced. I give His Majesty infinite thanks for granting such a beginning to this foundation, for it assures me of its certain and prosperous end.

"Let us relate in detail the furniture and effects we found in that house. First were half a dozen old cane-stalk frames that Father Mariano had or-

257. *Blanca*: the smallest monetary unit in sixteenth-century Spain; one-half a *maravedí*.

dered brought from his own priory called Los Remedios;[258] these lay on the floor to be used as beds. There were two or three very dirty little mattresses, like those of Discalced monks, and accompanied by a crowd of such creatures as usually do accompany them;[259] these were for our Mother and one or two of the weaker nuns. There was not one sheet, blanket, or pillow, save two that we ourselves had brought. We found a palm mat, one frying pan, one or two oil lamps, a brass mortar, and a ladle or little bucket for drawing water. Just when we had begun to think that these made up at least the beginnings of a house, along with a few jugs and plates and things of that sort that we found, then the neighbors—who had lent these things for that day—began sending, this one for the frying pan, another for the oil lamp, and another for the ladle and the table, so that finally not one thing was left to us, not a frying pan or a mortar or even the rope to the well. And this, Sisters, is no exaggeration, for it happened just so, as some of you who were there saw for yourselves.

"It all went to increase our happiness and to take away the sadness that our other necessities might have caused us, when we saw this comical little farce. So that you may see clearly how all this was ordained by the Lord, as I have said, I shall relate the scheme that the Lord permitted so that no one would be left to help us; and along the way I shall make a memorial to our dearest Doña Leonor de Valera, the wife of Enrique Freile, both of whom were Portuguese and the parents of our Sisters Blanca de Jesús and María de San José.

"This lady was the first benefactress of this house after the Sisters of Malagón—because I am also telling this to relate our benefactors. This lady was certainly one of them, and very fond of us, and she helped us for as long as she could. At that time she was enjoying her prosperity, which failed her with the bank failures that took place that year.[260] And as soon as she learned that our holy Mother was coming she took our needs to heart, because she doted upon holy people and gave all she had to people in need. Wishing to help us secretly without our knowing about it, which was the way she did things, she called a *beata*,[261] a true servant of God in that city who busies her-

258. Los Remedios: The priory, located outside Seville, was called Nuestra Señora de los Remedios.

259. A crowd . . . accompany them: that is, vermin. The remark about these *gente*, or "folk," is typical of humor in Teresa's work.

260. On September 1, 1575, the crown decreed bankruptcy and suspended payments on all debts; widespread recession followed. See John Lynch, *Spain 1516–1598* (Oxford: Blackwell, 1964; reprint, 1991), 200–201.

261. *Beata:* an unmarried or widowed woman who made informal vows of chastity and poverty and dedicated herself to charitable works. As can be inferred from this passage, Teresa and her followers were sometimes skeptical of the piety of the beatas.

self with all kinds of charitable works, especially in saving fallen women. That good-hearted Doña Leonor had helped her more than a little with great funds for this work. Doña Leonor asked the woman to provide us with whatever she could see we needed, in secret and without saying that it was she who was giving it; Father Mariano too had asked the *beata* to assist our house, convinced that she alone would be enough to help us. What the woman did was this: everything that Doña Leonor gave her for us—which was a great deal, so much so that just for the day that we were to arrive she had given enough so that we could have sheets, linen tunics (for she guessed the extreme need we would have, having come such a long way and through such bad heat spells), with a thousand other details of tablecloths, porcelain, *búcaros*,[262] and funds to provide us with oil and fish—all of these things the good woman, perhaps persuaded with her merciful spirit that the lost souls were in greater necessity and danger than ours, bore off entirely to these other good works. Thus, we nuns suffered and were left entirely ignorant of the obligation we bore to this lady. And when Doña Leonor came to the house to visit our holy Mother, the latter only greeted her warmly and thanked her for her charity, without knowing that we were obliged to her.

"To return to the foundation of our convent: when our Mother learned that the license was prepared, the Archbishop[263] made the statement that he had not intended us to come to make a new foundation, but rather that our Mother and her nuns should reform the monasteries already subject to him. This caused our holy Mother deep regret, and she nearly decided to return. In the end, Father Mariano placated him and managed that we should be given permission to hear Mass the following Sunday, which was the Feast of the Holy Trinity. In the three intervening days this was granted and arranged, on the condition that we not ring any bells or make any sort of monastery. Our Mother was afflicted by this, and Father Mariano very much so; our Father Gracián was in Madrid, where he had gone from Beas to answer a call from the Nuncio. In the end, Father Mariano little by little placated the Archbishop and managed things so that he would give us permission. After some twenty days, more or less, he gave it and the convent was finished, although as the church was not in very good shape, the Most Blessed Sacrament was not placed there and we spent a year there without it. This was no little source of grief. There were many griefs for those of us who were there that year, and if we had not had the company of our Mother, I

---

262. *Búcaros*: cups of scented clay from the Indies that imparted a pleasant taste and fragrance to the water drunk from them; a luxury item.

263. Archbishop: Cristóbal Rojas y Sandoval (1502–80). An active member of the Council of Trent, he was appointed Archbishop of Seville in 1571. Although he was initially hostile to Teresa's foundation in Seville, she eventually won his support. See Peers, *Handbook*, 218.

don't know how we could have borne so much poverty and loneliness and so many persecutions.

"Our poverty was great, as I have said, and the roads very long, all that summer sleeping on those cane-stalk bedframes while we had nothing to use to cover ourselves, though the heat was so great that it kept us from needing any bedcovers. That house was well set up indeed for the heat to afflict us. Many days our dinner was nothing but apples and bread, sometimes cooked up and sometimes in salad, and there were days when there was nothing but one loaf of bread, and that one shared with great pleasure among all of us. That sufficed us, though it was quite small.

"Since they did not know our Mother in this city as they did in the cities in Castile where she had already made foundations, we could not find anyone to lend us anything. Although Father Mariano worked very hard, every bit was needed to construct the turn[264] and screens for the locutory and everything else that was necessary for us to be cloistered, and for this purpose a merchant from Medina del Campo, an acquaintance of our Mother's, sent funds for her to pay these expenses.

"The priests had already agreed that a young lady who was the daughter of honorable parents should take the habit, and because our people had given their word, our Mother received her; this was on the feast of the Holy Trinity, when the first Mass was said. And although there was little confidence that they would give us permission to make the foundation, as we have already said, our Mother must have had such great confidence that she received the first nun, and calling us to Chapter, she ordered me to take care of the Sisters, through the power she had from the Prelates to name Prioresses in the new foundations.[265] Since it seemed right to her to hold elections, this order of obedience was no small trouble to me, though I had already done my best to become used to the idea, because our Mother had made this clear ever since Beas and had brought me for this purpose. For in order that we nuns might begin to feel love and respect for each other from the time we set out to make the foundations, she would say which one she intended to name, although this was under order of obedience, and she quite deliberately did not name them until the foundation was complete.

"So that it may be more clearly seen what a prophetic spirit our saint possessed in the trials that were suffered here, and also to show my own pride

264. Turn [torno]: a revolving shelf <None>at the entrance to convents that allows objects to be passed through without the receiver's being seen.

265. The power she had . . . in the new foundations: Prioresses were elected by the nuns of their convent, although as this passage makes clear, in the early foundations Teresa exerted considerable influence over their selection.

and lack of mortification, I shall tell of an examination to which our Mother put me before we set out from Beas. As she had already picked me out for the foundation in Caravaca and then the one in Seville had to be done first, and she was concerned to find a prioress for Seville, she wanted to know from me if I would like to go there. For it was a great concern of hers that no nun should go unhappily or unwillingly to make a foundation, as it seemed to her —and this is true—that such nuns never work to the good. Thinking that I would already be somewhat taken with the idea, as the founding nuns in Caravaca had written to me and given me their obedience with great affection, and there was already a house and annual income, she asked me if I would like to go to Seville. I said, "Has Your Reverence determined to make me prioress in whichever of these two places you take me?" She answered, "Yes, my Daughter, for lack of better men . . . " "Well if it must be so," I said, "I would rather be prioress in Seville than in Caravaca." The saint answered, laughing heartily, "Well then, she has chosen, and let her take what comes to her," letting it be known that there would be great trials there and thanking me for the desire I showed to go to Seville rather than Caravaca. That same day I have mentioned, the feast of the Holy Trinity, the Lord had done me the sovereign favor of accepting me to be his slave, because that was the day on which I professed and took the veil.

"Many women came wanting to be nuns with different purposes and different natures, but not one that was good for us. We had received Sister Beatriz de la Madre de Dios, the one I have already mentioned, to be a nun of the choir; after a month and a half, two more Sisters to be outside it, Margarita de la Concepción and Ana de San Alberto; and soon after, we received a great *beata* who had already been canonized by the entire city, and through the pleadings of many important and spiritual persons she was received. The poor woman was a great deal more holy in her own opinion than in that of the townspeople, and since once she entered the convent she missed hearing herself praised, and the finger of religious life began to accomplish what it does, which is to search out the true carat-value in what had seemed to shine so brightly in her, she found herself left with nothing and grew unhappy. We were the more so with her because there was never any possible way to make her adapt to a single point of religious life. And because she was already a woman of forty, with great authority, who knew how to find a way out of everything, she sometimes excused herself by saying that she was sick, and so she did not even want to eat our meals, putting forth that each food would cause illness and swelling, as might be read in Galen. At other times, she said that the customs and great heat of that land were her excuse. It seemed to our Mother that with time she would mend her ways, and to avoid putting her under pressure, she ordered us to put up with her and gave her permission to confess and consult with priests whom she already knew. In the end, without our Mother or anyone in the house knowing of it, she arranged her departure, and when we had safely retired for the night, they came for her and for another novice whom she had persuaded to follow her.

"When some of the people who knew her had begun to reproach her and consider her less holy than before because she had left the convent, she thought to remedy this by accusing us to the Inquisition, saying that we had touches of Illuminism.[266] Among the things she presented as being bad was that, as we were poor and did not have many veils, or because at other times the Sisters were careless and did not wear them, some of the nuns would take veils from the others in order to cover themselves to go receive communion. She said we did this as a religious rite. We had our little communion window in a patio that was in the full sun, and to shade ourselves from it and to be more recollected, after receiving communion each nun would draw close to her own corner or wall and turn her face to it. She said this too was done as a rite.[267] And she said many other things of this ilk, with a thousand lies and testimonies that she brought against our holy Mother. The Inquisitors came to the house and found out the truth; there was no more to it than that. But nonetheless, as we were strangers and unknown, and this woman told whoever went to see her all these bad things —and for their part, the Carmelite Fathers said many more, on account of the visitation that our Father Gracián began at about that time[268]—and as people saw the Inquisition come from one day to the next, the harm done to us by all this was great indeed.

"So that I may shed full light on what we are discussing, and you may understand clearly the trials that our Mother underwent in this, it is necessary that we begin to tell of the basis and causes there were for the Prior General of the Order[269] to turn, as we have indicated, against our Mother and the reform that she had begun in founding these convents.

---

266. By accusing us . . . of Illuminism: The Seville foundation coincided with the persecution of a group of priests and *beatas* in the western province of Extremadura. The group's eucharistic enthusiasm and public ecstasies had attracted the attention of certain inquisitors, who alleged that they were members of a widespread heretical sect, *alumbradismo*, or Illuminism.

267. Each nun would . . . as a rite: The *beata* may have been suggesting maliciously that the nuns' practice of facing the wall following Communion was a Jewish or Moorish rite.

268. The visitation . . . at about that time: Gracián was appointed apostolic visitor to the Calced Carmelites of Andalusia in 1573, and in 1575 he was reappointed visitor to the Calced Carmelites in Andalusia and provincial superior of the Discalced Carmelites. He incurred the enmity of the Calced friars of Seville when he attempted to put an end to their practice of holding private property.

269. The Prior General of the Order: Fray Juan Bautista Rossi, or Rubeo, of Ravenna, as noted above.

"During the time that our Prior General was in Spain, which was in the year 1566, he granted our Mother the license to found two monasteries of friars, and when she had founded the first of them with all the trials and difficulties that she relates in the *Book of Her Foundations,*[270] she went to found the convent of nuns in Valladolid in the year '68, and in '69 they founded the one in Pastrana, with our Mother herself helping as can be seen in her book. In founding those two monasteries, the two licenses that the Prior General had granted our Mother were employed, and for the third, the Discalced college in Alcalá, Ruy Gómez[271] obtained the license, again from the Prior General.

"The Fathers of the Mitigated Rule were inclined to consider only these three monasteries, which had been founded with the license of the Prior General, as being well founded. They did not like to see how the Discalced were beginning to grow in number and in the esteem of others. And as it happened that Gracián, together with Father Mariano, was making the visitation to the Carmelite Order with the license of the Visitator, who was Father Pedro Fernández of the Dominican Order[272] (through our holy Father Pius V), they took themselves to Andalusia to flee from the battle that they thought would arise with the entrance of Ruy Gómez's wife in our monastery. The Dominican Visitator who was making his visitation in Andalusia received them very warmly; this was Father Fray Francisco de Vargas. He gave a license so that Discalced monasteries might be founded in Seville, and in the year '74 he made our Father Gracián Vicar of all of Andalusia—indeed, of the Fathers of the Mitigated Rule themselves. At this time the Nuncio, Ormaneto, called Father Gracián to Madrid, and on the way he went through Beas and our Mother and he met each other. The benefit of this call by the Nuncio was to make him Visitator of all the Discalced and Calced religious in Andalusia. By now there were more than the three Discalced monasteries that I have mentioned, because with license from the Apostolic Visitators they had been founded both in Castile and in Andalusia; our Mother had abundant patents from the Prior General allowing her to found houses wherever she would like, and the Visitators also granted these to her.

"Our Father the Prior General began to grow displeased with our Mother because she had gone to make foundations in Andalusia, since he was

---

270. Teresa of Avila, *Foundations*, chap. 14.

271. Ruy Gómez de Silva, prince of Eboli (1517–73), raised in the royal palace as a companion to the future Phillip II, became the king's favorite and confidante. He and his wife, Ana de Mondoza y la Cerda, were important patrons of the Discalced reform. See Peers, *Handbook*, 149–50.

272. Pedro Fernández Orellana (d. 1580), a Dominican priest and apostolic visitator to the Carmelites of Castile (1569), was sympathetic to the reform and instrumental in resolving the conflicts between the Calced and Discalced Carmelites. See Peers, *Handbook*, 154–55.

displeased with the Andalusian Fathers for I don't know what quarrel he had with them while he was in Spain. He did not like her going there to found convents, and the more so as it was by command of Father Gracián (for it was he who made her go to Seville), with whom he was angry on account of the visitation Gracián was beginning, as he was also angry with all the Discalced. The Fathers of the Mitigated Rule helped this displeasure along, because they said that our Mother had started this schism and destruction—as they called it—and they laid the blame on the Prior General, because he gave her the license for the two monasteries. And they said that since then, she and the others had risen against him and apostatized against their vow of obedience —for so they termed what she had done—because monasteries were founded with license from the Nuncio and Apostolic Visitators. So it happened that he grew very angry with our Mother, nor was it any use for our Mother to write him letters, or to take any other means to dispel his anger.

"Our holy Mother was deeply sorry at this trouble. In the end it reached such a point that when a general chapter was called at this time, all the Discalced religious were named in it as apostates and were excommunicated, and it was ordered that all the houses that had been founded without license from the Prior General should be dissolved—which is to say the houses in Seville, Granada, Almodóvar, and La Peñuela—leaving only the three that had been founded with license from the Prior General. In this chapter it was commanded that the patents and commissions that our Mother possessed to make foundations should be taken from her, and that she should be kept in solitary confinement in one monastery without being able to leave, and that the barefoot friars and nuns of the Discalced should once again wear the shoes of the Calced and sing with musical notation,[273] and other such things.

"Father Gracián had lingered for six months in the court when he went there by order of the Nuncio. There was great outcry over whether he would accept the commission that was being given him, because the friars of the Mitigated Rule were opposing it strongly, and they presented a counterbrief they had prepared so as to bring an end to this visit, and they made whatever accusations they could to free themselves from his visitation. Gracián's friends and relatives insisted that he should not accept the appointment. The one who most objected was his brother the secretary Antonio Gracián,[274] even though it was believed to be the other way around and people said that

273. Sing with musical notation [cantasen por punto]: The Discalced constitutions stipulated that the nuns should chant their liturgical prayers "in a monotone and with uniform voices" rather than with the tunefulness of the Gregorian chant.

274. Antonio Gracián was secretary to Phillip II.

he had worked to obtain the position. I saw letters of his in which he urged our Mother not to allow his brother to get involved in such a battle. Our Mother and all of the Discalced religious saw themselves lost unless we took advantage of help, having such a good opportunity as this of coming to an agreement about our affairs with the Father Visitor. But if we came under the power of the Prior General and the Fathers of the Mitigated Rule, they would dissolve us—as was later seen by what emerged from the chapter, which made our Father reach his decision and hurried everyone. And so Gracián came to Seville with broad powers from the Nuncio, which was what he desired more than anything else. He began his visit, which the other Fathers took so badly that the day he was to go to take his vow of obedience, the friars took arms to defend themselves, and there was such uproar that people came to tell our Mother, who was at prayer with all of her nuns, that they had killed Father Gracián and that the doors of the monastery were closed; and there was such shouting and noise, that the saint was greatly disturbed. That was when our Lord said to her, "Oh woman of little faith, calm yourself, for good is being done!" This was on the eve of the Feast of the Presentation of our Lady, and our Mother promised that if the Lord freed her of this and carried her through it successfully, she would celebrate that feast every year with great solemnity.

"At that time, a great *beata* who was considered very saintly had entered our house—this is the one I have already mentioned, who accused us to the Holy Office and did us so much harm, although from many harms God often brings forth many good things. In this case the good was that, as our Mother was so obedient and punctual in doing all that her Prelates ordered and desired to please the Prior General, and as he had ordered her to go to a convent in Castile and not to leave it or make any foundations or have any news from the others, she persuaded the Father Visitor to let her go to carry out the Prior General's order. First, she had this order of obedience; second, the obedience from the Visitor, which was the opposite, that she should stay where she was and finish her foundation; and yet again, the solitary and helpless state in which she would be leaving us. In the end, she grew tranquil when I told her that it was not fitting to go at the very time when the Inquisition was looking into the false rumors that woman had raised against us, because if it became necessary to take her before the Inquisition, and they came for her and did not find her, it would not look well and things would be worse. She answered me, "Daughter, I am sure you are right, and now I see that it is God's will for me to stay here"—for all her troubles lay in not knowing what would be most perfect and pleasing to God, but He permitted that doubt and ignorance so that she might be more deserving. Later this seemed very funny to her, and she said to me many times, "What a thing that was, for my Daughter to comfort me in my great affliction by saying that after all, they might have to take me before the Inquisition!" The truth is that to distract her I quite deliberately put this possibility before her, saying that she would surely have to go there, because it seemed to me there was no better remedy for calming and encouraging her than to think about an affront and trouble like that.

"The Prior General was so angry with us that he sent Tostado[275] as Vicar General to dissolve us. It was the worst possible moment that this could occur, because at that time the Nuncio who had favored us died[276] and a new one came, briefed by the Prior General and so much in favor of the Fathers of the Mitigated Rule that they found a way not only to free themselves from the visitation [of Gracián], but to make this Nuncio believe every evil thing about us and about the Visitator that they could think to tell him. He removed all powers from Father Gracián and commanded instead that the Fathers of the Cloth[277] make a visitation to us. And since they were emerging from the yoke and subjection that had weighed so heavily on them, from which they so furiously and passionately desired to free themselves, it seemed to them that right there in the visits they had to make to our convents they would be able to manage things so as to color and excuse all that they had done and show how much worse we were than they. They had let it be known that they wanted to begin making the visitation with one Visitator in Castile and another in Andalusia.

"His Majesty King Phillip II, understanding these things and desirous of avoiding the evil that could be feared from the fury and passion of these Fathers, had orders sent saying that this visitation should not be received until the Nuncio was better informed, for the latter had given ear only to the friars of the Mitigated Rule. All the convents in Castile, both of nuns and of friars, followed only the royal measure. Yet in Andalusia the only houses to obey the Nuncio's letter were the friars' convents in Seville and the convent of nuns that was ours where I was prioress. For we did not wish to take advantage of the royal measure: it did not seem to us to matter whether we were

---

275. Jerónimo Tostado: a Calced Carmelite who, as vicar general, was sent to Spain in 1576 with powers to suppress the Discalced foundations. However, Phillip II lent his support to the reform, and Tostado was unable to fulfill his mission.

276. Nicolas Ormaneto died on June 18, 1577. His successor, Felipe Sega (c. 1537–96) was initially prejudiced against Teresa's reform, but he later agreed to the creation of the separate province for the Discalced Carmelites. See Peers, *Handbook*, 222.

277. The fathers of the Cloth [los del paño]: an epithet for the Fathers of the Mitigated Rule.

visited by the one group or the other, as we had nothing to fear or anything at all that could not be seen by the entire world. It also seemed fitting to give our obedience there, as it was in Seville that the greatest rage and clamor about the visitation had been raised. Moreover, an even greater scandal could result if we refused to give our obedience, and they would post our names on the church doors as excommunicants who had been disobedient to the Pope (I believe they did just this in Granada). The populace, being ignorant of the real causes, would easily believe whatever they were told—so for these reasons we obeyed. They proceeded more tactfully with the convent of friars, since they were men; but we, being poor women, received the full brunt of their fury.

"At this time our Mother was no longer in Seville. It had been more than two years since she had gone, leaving us a confessor who, though he was a servant of God, was ignorant and confused, without learning or experience.[278] The Devil had at that time provided this priest with yet another pious woman for his own aims; this caused me to try to take him in hand in certain matters in which he was interfering and some singular practices he took up with two Sisters, finding excuses to stay with them from morning until night. Sometimes he was with both of them, at other times with each one separately in the confessional, and he said that this was necessary for some general confessions that they were making with him—and that they could each do this whenever he called them, without asking me for permission. These confessions lasted some three or four months. When I wished to put an end to such excess, he went to all the convents in Seville to ask whether they thought that the Prioress could interfere in confessions, and based on what he told them they gave him signatures, and with every signature he took more liberties. He was upsetting everything and bringing the house down about my ears, freeing the nuns from their obedience. Finding myself in this state, I informed our Mother so that she could solve the problem. She told me I should endure him and dissemble, for it was not the right time to do anything more, since God had given the Devil permission to torment and afflict us. And that is just how it was, because this priest went to all the learned persons there were in Seville whom he knew I could consult, and he told them that I was so cunning, and had such command of speech, that I would convince them of whatever I wanted. And so they were already thoroughly

278. A confessor . . . without learning or experience: This confessor has been identified as Garciálvarez, the first chaplain and generous benefactor of the Convent of Saint Joseph in Seville. If he was the priest who procured María's deposition as Prioress, her lavish praise for him later in this chapter is remarkable.

prepared not to believe me, and he had set so many traps and nets for me that I could not find anyone who would believe me. He told them to ask me certain questions, catching me unawares, and thus I could not find anyone with whom to make my confession simply and honestly.

"It so happened that it occurred to our Father, Master Fray Pedro Fernández, who had been our Visitator, to come to Seville with his [Prior] General, and our Mother gave him the responsibility of looking into this dispute. Once he had come and understood this tangle, he ordered that I should under no circumstances allow my nuns to confess with that man but instead commend him to God and send him away. Our Father Fray Nicolás[279] shared this opinion also; he helped me not only in this battle and trial but in the one waged against me by the Carmelite Fathers, for which I owe him a great deal. In the end, I dismissed the priest because these two Fathers had ordered me so strongly to do so. But at the same time there soon arrived the Carmelite Provincial Visitator, who came on the visitation I have already mentioned. The priest I am speaking of went to see him, seeing what a good help the Provincial Visitator could be to him. The Visitator gave him a patent bestowing full powers to hear the nuns' confessions even against my wishes, by doing so undoing what I had done[280] and in this way deceiving these two Sisters, if they were not already deceived. The one was a lay Sister; the other was a little simpleton[281] whom the novice who left had persuaded to leave with her and to serve as witness to what the novice had already planned to say against us. But Our Lord saw fit that she should not leave but rather make her profession for the sake of her own salvation (which I think her tears are obtaining for her, because she is blind with weeping), and that with her ignorance she should help me to purge my sins. With just these two nuns—for there was not another one who felt any discontent—the priest made further

---

279. Nicolás de Jesús María (surnamed Doria; 1539–94) was born into a wealthy Genoese banking family and took the Discalced habit in 1577. After Teresa's death, he and Gracián became bitter rivals. Although he supported María in this instance, he later turned against her. See introduction, 7.

280. Even against . . . what I had done [aunque yo no quisiese, hacer y deshacer . . .]: The meaning of the rather cryptic phrase "hacer y deshacer" is not entirely clear, but the passage suggests that the Vistitator's action here (giving the priest power to hear confessions) undoes María's action (having dismissed the priest earlier).

281. Little simpleton: Beatriz de la Madre de Dios (Chaves, 1538–1624). In chapter 26 of *The Book of Foundations*, Teresa describes her abnormal childhood and determination to join the Discalced Carmelites. The foundress believed her to suffer from mental illness ("melancholy") but always showed great pity for her. Beatriz eventually retracted her charges against María. The second nun to take part in the campaign against María was Margarita de la Concepción, a lay sister. See Peers, *Handbook*, 129, 191.

reports for the Inquisition and gave them to the Carmelite Fathers. This was all the latter could have desired. They brought false charges against us and against our Mother from the time she was in Seville, and against our Father Gracián, and against me, just as they desired. And this priest was so assiduous that never once did he leave the confessional all day long or for days on end while the visitation lasted. He would call first these nuns and then those, forcing them with threats and filling them with fear so that they would go tell the Provincial what he, the confessor, was ordering them—the nuns did not even know to what end or purpose. And since the web was already woven, they knew that whatever the next nun might say foolishly was likely to matter to them, without their knowing what good or evil it might hold. For they were all novices and simple women, and it had never occurred to any of us that they could come to such a pass. And even though I was the most suspicious and had already seen the way that priest acted, I could never have convinced myself that they would scheme such things. Everything they did seemed to me somewhat lacking in intelligence, because his was quite limited and cloudy; but he seemed so excessively scrupulous that I believed in such weighty matters he would go too far.

"This was the first time, in a visitation by the Inquisition, that we saw excommunications, oaths before Christ, and threats in our house, and thus foolishly all the nuns helped the Inquisitors and said what the latter needed in order to give credit to the lies that had already been spread. This resulted in my office being taken away and in the accumulation of lies that they themselves had invented about Father Gracián and the rest of the Discalced nuns, and especially about our holy Mother, in a suit these Fathers had brought against her with the most abominable and filthy words that can be imagined. Of the best of them, all that can be said is that they are unmentionable. But so that you may see the Devil's malice, I shall mention one or two. They said: 'They had to put that old woman into the hands of white men and black men so that she could have her fill of wickedness; and she would carry young women from place to place, under the pretense of founding convents, so that they could be just as wicked.' They said these things and even worse in that suit, with each man declaring what he felt about our holy Mother. Let our own priests see now whether they ought to hold this opinion of our Mother, because those men said things like these about her—since it seems to them that some of us should be considered vile, for such tongues once spoke infamy of us with abominations that they now want to revive.[282]

---

282. Such tongues . . . want to revive: María is referring to the fact that in 1585, she and Gracián again found themselves the victims of malicious slander.

"Great was the tribulation the Sisters underwent in those days, because when that priest took from me the office of Prioress, they appointed as Vicaress[283] the Sister I already mentioned who had been deceived by the priest. What I most regretted was that they wanted to send me to Castile, and the priest was helping toward this end and would have done so if a great many important persons had not hindered him, moved only by Our Lord, because neither I nor any of our nuns spoke a single word except to God; we saved our only complaints for Him. And although we were strangers and out of favor with almost everyone, it was something to see how the town council sent an important officer directly to me to offer me their favor, saying that if I wished to complain to the Nuncio or to the King of the offenses that this Carmelite priest was committing against us, they would send someone to give my report. I answered that he was our Prelate and was not doing us any offense, nor did we Discalced nuns consider it an injury against us to take away our offices but rather a benefit to us. They were not contented with this but went through the streets to dishonor him, saying he was a corrupt friar and spelling out particular defects they said he possessed. If he went to certain private houses to carry out business, they told him that he was persecuting the holy women who had come to found a convent and was putting the house into the hands of a novice—and so it was, for she had only made her profession a short time before. Indeed, she had not been ready to profess at the end of one year because of her lack of ability. There were three other nuns, our companions, whom His Majesty placed there—great servants of God, who could have governed much better than I—and the confessor refused to let a single one of them be in charge of the house. I tell all this so that you can see what affliction the poor nuns were cast into. Almost all novices, they showed such faith and fortitude that not one grew lukewarm; instead, they were determined to leave with us if we should be cast out, as we expected from one day to the next. When our enemies were unable to accomplish this they went to the Inquisition with the reports I have mentioned, and traveling capes were already waiting inside the house, because they believed that as soon as their papers got there, we would be ordered to leave at once. They were so ignorant, and they wanted to be seen as being so good, that they assiduously provided capes, and we knew that they were waiting from one moment to the next for the Inquisition to come for us—at least for me, the only evildoer. Our Lord granted me such courage that I desired that hour to come once and for all.

"In the end, as things were thought to be just as the other nun had said,

---

283. Beatriz de la Madre de Dios was appointed vicaress or interim prioress.

which they had already verified, they paid no attention to our nuns. All of the favors that had been done to me I had to repay, because the Provincial said I was stirring up all the trouble, and he complained knowing full well that however I might wish to complain, I could not, because they had me so strictly guarded that I could not speak or converse with anyone. They did not even let me speak to the other nuns; they imposed the command that the nuns could not call me Mother, but only Sister, and other impertinences like that. When throughout the city they told the Provincial the things that I have told here, he came at once to strike at me with incredible fury. When he ordered that I should be brought before him, the Sisters started weeping as if I were being carried before a judge who was going to pass sentence on me. I went with such good spirits, which the Lord gave me, that none of this troubled me—I knew that they were only words, though very harsh ones, for he called me Judas among the apostles, wolf in sheep's clothing, seditious rebel, and other things worse than that. He shouted these things so loudly that it made us tremble, and people came to our church, where several times he positioned himself to make these allegations with the doors wide open. All this must have been a scheme to make people think that in our house there was something that had to be reprimanded and set right. When this was over he ordered me to return to my cell, where he ordered that nobody should speak to me, depriving me of voice and vote.[284] He knew that he was doing this with Discalced nuns, who suffer and keep quiet and tremble before a single word that is given as an order of obedience. He carried out butchery with a thousand excommunications and commands that were all aimed at the destruction of our house and at the fortune of a lady who had died and left us (in the midst of all this uproar) upwards of six thousand *ducados;* and as the poor nuns could not speak with me and had no one they could ask for advice, this caused much more suffering than can be described.

"Father Gracián began his visit at the end of the year 1575, and it lasted until '78 during all this uproar I have described. At that time, the Nuncio in Madrid was holding not only our Father Gracián, but also Father Fray Antonio de Jesús and Father Mariano in seclusion in three different monasteries, where each one suffered a great many false accusations from the Calced Fathers. But as all was principally leveled against Father Gracián, it afflicted him deeply, and the Nuncio imposed a punishment on him.[285] Our Mother was

---

284. Depriving me of voice and vote: María was forbidden to express opinions or vote in convent matters.

285. The Nuncio imposed a punishment on him: Gracián, sentenced to reclusion in the monastery at Alcalá de Henares, was ordered to fast three days a week and was prohibited from communicating with anyone other than his parents and the nuncio himself. See Peers, *Handbook,* 59.

very worried about the effect on the larger work of the Discalced reform, which was well on the way to being overthrown if left in the power of the Calced Fathers—as indeed it was left while they were our Prelates. And while we were not allowed to write or to have any news of each other, she also worried about the afflictions of those who were suffering.

"It was our Lord's will that Father Fray Nicolás de Jesús María should be free while things were in this state, because he had played no part in the visit, and therefore they were not persecuting him like the others. He was ordered to go to court under the pretext of going to do business for a relative of his, and at the petition of this relative the Nuncio gave him permission to go. There he communicated with the three Fathers who were being held like prisoners. All of them discussed it with our Mother, who always asked that someone should go to Rome and ask, with the favor of His Majesty the King,[286] for the provincial authority to be made separate. In keeping with her opinion and the plan she devised—as I know from many letters of hers that I had, in which she always advised the Fathers not to think themselves safe until they had reached the Pope himself—and because she learned that the Prior General and the Fathers of the Cloth were misinforming His Holiness and the cardinals about the Discalced nuns—in the end, she ordered that some of the Prelates and persons who dealt with us and knew us, where there were monasteries, should report what they felt about us. This was done in such a way that, as she wrote to me later, after these reports had been made, 'I am greatly embarrassed and ashamed, Daughter, to see what these gentlemen have said about us, and they have placed us in great obligation to be as they have described, so that we do not expose them as liars.'

"These statements of good credit were sent to Rome, and the good Bishop of Palencia[287] stepped ahead of all the rest, as he always would do in our favor. He asked the Nuncio's opinion of this separation, and the Nuncio replied that it was very favorable because now he was better informed—or possibly seeing that His Majesty wished to favor us made him change his opinion. And with both the nuncio's and His Majesty's favor, the papal brief decreeing the separation was obtained from His Holiness. There is no mention made in it of our Mother, or that she first founded the [Discalced] convents of nuns or began the friars, because this grace was requested in tumultuous times. And because a woman had begun and continued this work,

---

286. With the favor of His Majesty the King: In 1579 Philip II endorsed a petition to Rome in favor of a separate Discalced Carmelite province.

287. Bishop of Palencia: Alvaro de Mendoza. A member of a powerful aristocratic family and bishop successively of Avila and Palencia, he was always well disposed toward the Discalced Carmelites.

many disdained it and spoke badly of it—it was for this reason that our holy Mother did not want herself or her nuns to be recorded any more than had already been done.

"This recommendation [for separation] was made on behalf of the King,[288] and although he charged his ambassador with responsibility for the negotiations, it still seemed to our Mother and all the rest that two Discalced friars should be present in Rome. And so Father Fray Juan de Jesús (who is now the Provincial in Barcelona and was originally from there) and Father Fray Diego de la Trinidad (who has since died) went there. When these two Fathers went to Rome they were there, I believe, for more than a year, in the habits of lay Brothers, petitioning the ambassador and the cardinals as relatives of friars in the Order. In order to obtain audiences it was necessary for them to present themselves in fine attire, and the greater part of all their expenses during this time came from all the convents of nuns, where our Mother ordered a collection to be taken up; and the house of nuns in Seville made a deposit of seven hundred *ducados* all told, from a legacy that had been sent to us from the Indies. With this legacy, it was possible for them to get by until the separation was complete, and in the end our contribution was three hundred, which was more than from any other house. I say this so that you may see how our holy Mother helped and was the all-in-all to her monasteries, and how much the friars owe to the nuns, and what is owed to the convent in Seville, the one that was most afflicted—but clearly this has been through my sins, and the house in Lisbon is now beginning to be the same, because I am in it.

"With the King restraining the Nuncio who had begun with such fury, the Nuncio gave us Father Fray Angel del Salazar[289] to be Vicar General, who restored me to my office with great honor. Father Gracián was reinstated by the Nuncio himself, and the Vicar General sent him as his representative to the entire province of Andalusia, where he stayed until the papal brief arrived, at the beginning of 1581. With this, once the division and separation from the Mitigated Rule had been established, it pleased God that things should begin to improve.

"We had made arrangements to buy a house, and in this we encountered a thousand difficulties , because it was . . .

[Here two sheets, folios 125 and 126, are missing from the manuscript;

---

288. This recommendation . . . on behalf of the King: The nuncio, Felipe Sega, forwarded the king's recommendation to Rome on November 11, 1579.

289. Angel de Salazar (c. 1519–c. 1600), a Calced friar, was alternately antagonistic and sympathetic toward the reform. He was appointed first vicar general of the Discalced Carmelites after the formation of a separate province in 1579. See Peers, *Handbook*, 219.

these relate the purchase of the new house for the foundation in Seville and the community's move into it on June 3, 1576, done with all due ceremony, as Teresa describes in *Book of Her Foundations*, chapter 25. The following day, at two in the morning, Teresa left Seville.]

. . . all mixed together on a marble stone, next to which the man was standing, and there were marks of the fireworks[290] that are still there to this day. We see them daily on the marble itself, which had been like alabaster and was left all pitted by the gunpowder. All this could not have been anything less than a miracle. Many witnesses saw this and how the marble was entirely covered, especially good Father Garciálvarez, to whom we are greatly indebted for many benefits. He worked very hard on this feast day and arranged everything that was brought to it, for he sought it out. We are obliged to him for many other things as shall be told further on, and with good reason our Mother remembers him in her book about the foundations. He is the cousin of our Sister Jerónima de la Madre de Dios and of Doña Costanza del Río, whom I am obliged to mention for many good works. It was not our Lord's will for us to enjoy for long the great happiness and contentment we had in having him there and being at last in our own house, because that very night, at two in the morning, our Mother set out. This was because she was greatly needed in the monasteries in Castile and had been waiting only to see us in our own house before she set out; and her brother was waiting to take her while in the meantime his own business required his attention. She took with her our own dear Teresa.[291] You can imagine the great sadness and loneliness we felt.

"The next day they came to collect the taxes on the sale of the house, for they had ruled against us and we had to pay three hundred *ducados*—which was an immense sum given the need in which we had been left—without our having any way to remedy the situation. This trial was all the more painful as it came to us just when our Mother had left the house. Yet Our Lord gave us spirit and confidence in Him in spite of it all. His Majesty provided for us so that Father Garciálvarez and others stepped in to help to do us a good turn, and He managed things so that the others would wait for a period of time for their money. This was no little thing, because we had been left feeling great

290. Marks of the fireworks: On 5 April 1576 the nuns celebrated their move to a permanent location with a display of fireworks. One of the rockets exploded and nearly set fire to the new house. The marks on marble that are described here were likely from this fire.

291. Our own dear Teresa: Teresa (or Teresita de Jesús, 1566–1610), daughter of Teresa's brother Lorenzo Cepeda. Born in Quito, she first met her aunt upon her father's return to Seville in 1575. As a girl she lived in the convents of Seville and Saint Joseph's in Avila. She made her profession in 1582, shortly after Teresa's death. See Peers, *Handbook*, 224.

abandonment and loneliness. For we had no one to turn to save this good Father, who was our confessor. He served in that capacity, and said Mass, for the love of God; and the Archbishop too gave us some alms—but a certain Majordomo of his carried this out so lukewarmly that it was difficult to get by. The Reverend Prior of the Carthusians began to feel concern for us and gave whatever he could, which we used to maintain ourselves; but with the house so early in its beginnings and with so many things lacking, all that they gave us was little enough to keep these needs from being sorely felt.

"From the time our Mother set out, we were left until October with the trials and loneliness that I have mentioned. At that time our Father Gracián —wishing to reform the convent of nuns of Paterna of the Mitigated Rule, and to remove the bad reputation their own friars had falsely spread about these nuns, and wishing to know the truth of the case—decided to send my two good companions, for he chose as president Madre Isabel de San Francisco together with Isabel de San Gerónimo. Their departure proved no less a trial, or to be more accurate, it was the greatest yet, because it left only three of us who had come to make that foundation.

"No matter how much I told you, I would never finish describing how lonely we felt being left behind. Nor could I tell in full of the trials the two nuns who went there suffered in one year—as you will understand, given that the Visitator had sent them there to reform the house. It is enough to say one thing only, which is that the others did not even want to give them food to eat, and so they had to receive help from elsewhere. The bad words they heard at every turn need not even be repeated; it is enough that there came a night when those two together with Sister Margarita de la Concepción, a lay Sister who went along to help them, grew so perturbed that these three poor nuns shut themselves up in a little chamber. They passed the entire night without sleeping or leaving the room, sitting on a piece of rush matting on which they scarcely fit, because all night long the others were outside threatening to kill them and trying their best to get in.

"They spent a whole year with these obstacles, and although they had heavy work of it, their labor did not fail to bear fruit—so much so that the other nuns themselves admitted it, and said they were saints, leaving them confused and embarrassed. And although the others abhorred their practices, after the three had returned, the nuns carried out many of the reforms. At the very least they established some sort of convent and began the formation of a community in the choir and refectory, for previously they had known nothing of this and not anything at all of the church; while they had other unsuitable practices of which our three removed quite a few.

"With matters related to the visitation proceeding as we have already said, and with the visitation that Father Gracián was making coming to an end, the three Sisters returned to Seville, having left Paterna on the Feast of Saint Barbara. We suffered so greatly with loneliness the year that our Sisters were there—as if there had been grave illnesses or deaths—that it seemed, given how few nuns we were, that those three were a great many.

"We had a good old woman in the Portress's cell [at the entrance to the convent] who helped with our necessities, the sister of our dear Juana de la Cruz; I give her name because she was our benefactor, and later I shall tell what we inherited from her. She was a great servant of God, and for this reason, since she could not be a nun along with her sister and her niece, she decided to make her retreat in our Portress's cell. There she made it her concern to close the door, giving the Portress the key to close the door to the street. [Once] when she had finished shutting the lock, she had an attack of apoplexy and fell down senseless and unable to speak. The Portress saw that it was taking her a very long time and that she didn't respond even when the little bell was rung, and then she heard some loud snores; and so the Portress came to tell me that the other woman was ill in bed. I arose and was obliged to open the door and go out. We found her stretched out on the ground, speechless and senseless, and, making a bed there, we laid her in it. It pleased our Lord to have a boy who served in the sacristy and assisted with Mass do us a good turn by staying there that very night. This offered us a solution we would otherwise have lacked, being strangers and almost unknown in the neighborhood. The woman was in such a state that she didn't respond to us. At once we notified the priest from the Cathedral chapel, and they brought her extreme unction; the doctor and the barber came, and that night was spent in treating her with various remedies, though to no avail, for she never spoke again and in the morning she died. This was a great disturbance and trial, and the beginning of others in which Our Lord strengthened and assisted us, as is His way with the sad and afflicted.

"Soon after, on the eve of Saint Andrew, our Mother Subprioress María del Espíritu Santo fell so ill and had such fits, falling unconscious, that we thought her end had come. She passed many hours like that, and then it pleased the Lord to make her well. Shortly after that Sister Blanca and Sister Jerónima entered the convent on the eve of the Feast of our Father Saint Joseph. That was the day we had worked to celebrate the feast, receiving help for this and in all that he could do from good Father Garciálvarez—for as I have already said, he was the only one we had; and also from Father Don Fernando de Pantoja, Prior of the Carthusians, because of his respect for and devotion to our glorious Saint Joseph, to whom he was greatly devoted. On this occasion Sister Bernarda de San José fell ill with the sickness of which she died, a year from the very day when she had taken the habit. This Sister had a lovely disposition and was very pretty, with such a look and color that her face and every one of her actions showed the purity of her soul, of which I saw many indications. I write this, as I said before, to tell the virtues of our Sisters, so that their memory and example may remain for the nuns who are still to come.

"This Sister was the daughter of an honorable man of Corsican nationality. His name was Pablo Matías, and her mother's was Mariana Ramírez, both good Christians who showed great charity and mercy toward the poor. This was especially true of her father, who was greatly devoted to our Lady; he was a very rich man, and because of this and the way he was greatly beloved by all for his good nature, he was very deserving. He had many sons and three very beautiful daughters, who were praised by all for being very chaste and virtuous, and our Sister Bernarda de San José exceeded them all in every way, because she persevered always in refusing to marry. She was given the name "de San José" because she took our habit on the feast of Saint Joseph, which was the first we celebrated in this house. She came to see the festivities and to hear our Father Gracián preach—after which there was no possibility of her wanting to return to her home. And so she was given the habit at once, because we had already heard of her and of her desires and of her parents' great resistance to them. She was given the habit without their consent, which she greatly lamented. She was there six months with the greatest happiness and health, and then for the next six things went on in such a way that she went through intolerable torments and afflictions with demons, with every type of temptation that the Devil can bring. She never moved one jot in her intent to persevere; but she suffered so, especially whenever she was alone, that as a remedy I took to bringing her about with me always, by day and by night, because she said that the Devil did not torment her with horrendous visions when she was holding on to the Prioress's belt. These six months were a great trial to me, although knowing the purity of her soul and her firm determination not to offend God, I expected a good end.

"There were many times when the Devil visibly brought her ropes with which to hang herself. The times that I was alone with her in our cell, although I did not see the demons, I saw how they tormented her and left her lifeless; at least once she remained that way in my presence. She said to us many times, and many Sisters are witnesses to this: 'I will never put on the black veil.' The others would say to her, 'Why? Are you thinking of leaving us?' She would say, 'That, never; but I shall die before we complete the feast of our glorious Saint Joseph.' And she caught such a severe fever that it left her senseless, and she remained almost senseless through the sermon and the

Mass. Then she began to be delirious until the eve of Saint Benedict, when she was restored to her perfect senses and asked to make her profession. She was examined there in her bed, and made her confession, and while the priest held the Most Blessed Sacrament she made her vows with the greatest fervor and spirit. As soon as she had made them, she received the Most Blessed Sacrament and remained in a heavenly stillness, saying to me many times: 'Mother, I am no longer myself; now the battle has ended and my soul is at peace.' And that is how she stayed until she died, and we all witnessed how during those days she seemed to be in the age of innocence. She died on Saturday, and as she had said so many times, it was fulfilled that she would die having professed but not wearing the veil. Her body and face in death were so beautiful that we could not kiss her hands and feet enough. The Mother Subprioress was going about consoling and encouraging the novices—for almost all the nuns in the house were novices, because our Sisters from Paterna had still not come back—on the very day that we buried this servant of God. And that holy nun, the Subprioress, placed her hands in prayer and said with great spirit: 'May it please God, my Sisters, that the Lord may take me first if any one of you should come to die without receiving the good that I have received.' When the burial was done, she caught such a great chill that it was necessary to cut short the procession.

"But so that I do not forget the foundation of the convent in Lisbon, which was begun in the midst of these trials (and though I began to tell of it earlier, I have gotten off the track), you must know, my Sisters . . . "

[Six lines before the end of this page of the manuscript comes this interruption in the copy of the *Book for the Hour of Recreation* by María de San José, which deprives us of the end of this fourth section, dealing with the monasteries founded by Saint Teresa, and of the whole of part five, which was to contain "a brief summation of the effects created by the love of God in those souls where it is found."]

SUGGESTIONS FOR
FURTHER READING

The following bibliography, suggestive rather than exhaustive, emphasizes studies in English and Spanish on women's monastic traditions in Spain.

WORKS BY MARÍA DE SAN JOSÉ SALAZAR

Avisos para el gobierno de las religiosas. Edited by Juan Luis Astigarraga. Rome: Instituto Histórico Teresiano, 1977.

Escritos espirituales. Edited by Simeón de la Sagrada Familia. Rome: Postulación General O.C.D., 1979.

EDITIONS AND ANTHOLOGIES OF MONASTIC WOMEN'S WRITING IN EARLY MODERN SPAIN

Ana de San Bartolomé. *Obras completas*. Critical edition with introduction by Julián Urkiza. 2 vols. Rome: Teresianum, 1981, 1985.

Arenal, Electa, and Stacey Schlau, eds. *Untold Sisters: Hispanic Nuns in Their Own Works*. A bilingual anthology with translations by Amanda Powell. Albuquerque: University of New Mexico Press, 1989.

García de la Concha, Victor, and Ana María Alvarez Pellitero, eds. *Libro de romances y coplas del Carmelo de Valladolid*. Salamanca: Consejo de Castilla y León, 1982.

Marcela de San Felix, Sor. *Literatura Conventual Femenina: Sor Marcela de San Felix, hija de Lope de Vega: Obra Completa*. Edited by Electa Arenal and Georgina Sabat-Rivers. Madrid: PPU, 1988.

María de San Alberto. *Viva al siglo, muerta al mundo: Selected Works/Obras Escogidas*. A bilingual anthology edited with introduction by Stacey Schlau. New Orleans: University Press of the South, 1998.

Simeón de la Sagrada Familia et al., eds. *Humor y espiritualidad en la escuela teresiana*. Burgos: Monte Carmelo, 1966. An anthology of humorous writings by Teresa de Jesús, Jerónimo Gracián, Ana de Jesús, and María de San José.

Teresa de Jesús. *Obras completas*. Edited by Efrén de la Madre de Dios and Otger Steggink. Madrid: Católica, 1962.

————. *The Collected Works of St. Teresa of Avila.* Translated by Kieran Kavanaugh and Otilio Rodríguez. 3 vols. Washington, D.C.: Institute of Carmelite Studies, 1976–85.

————. *The Letters of Saint Teresa of Jesus.* Translated by Edgar Allison Peers. 2 vols. London: Burns and Oates, 1951. Reprint, Sheed and Ward, 1981.

HISTORICAL AND LITERARY STUDIES ON MARÍA DE SAN JOSÉ SALAZAR

Herpoël, Sonja. "Sainte Thérèse et le *Libro de recreaciones* (1585)." In *Écrire sur soi en Espagne: Modèles et Écarts: Actes du IIIème Colloque International d'Aix-en-Provence,* 45–56. Aix-en-Provence: Publications Université de Provence, 1988.

Manero Sorolla, María Pilar. "La Biblia en el carmelo femenino: La obra de María de San José (Salazar)." In *Actas del XII Congreso de la Asociación Internacional de Hispanistas, 21–26 de agosto de 1995, Birmingham,* edited by Jules Whicker. 7 vols., 3:52–58. Birmingham, England: University of Birmingham, 1998.

————. "Diálogos de Carmelitas: *Libro de recreaciones* de María de San José." In *Actas del X Congreso de la Asociación Internacional de Hispanistas,* edited by Antonio Vilanova. 4 vols., 1:501–15. Barcelona: PPU, 1992.

————. "Exilios y destierros en la vida y en la obra de María de Salazar." In *Actas del VII Simposio de la Sociedad Española de Literatura General y Comparada,* 51–59. Madrid: Castalia, 1988.

————."La poesía de María de san José (Salazar)." In *Estudios sobre escritoras hispánicas en honor de Georgina Sabat-Rivers,* edited by Lou Charnon-Deutsch, 188–222. Madrid: Castalia, 1992.

Schlau, Stacey. "María de San José." In *Spanish Women Writers: A Bio-Bibliographical Source Book.* Edited by Linda Gould Levine et al., 279–85. Westport, Conn.: Greenwood, 1993.

Weber, Alison. "On the Margins of Ecstasy: María de San José as (Auto)biographer." *Journal of the Institute of Romances Studies* 4 (1996): 251–68.

STUDIES OF TERESA OF AVILA AND THE DISCALCED CARMELITE REFORM

Bilinkoff, Jodi. *The Avila of Saint Teresa: Religious Reform in a Sixteenth-Century City.* Ithaca, N.Y.: Cornell University Press, 1989.

————. "Teresa of Jesus and Carmelite Reform." In *Religious Orders of the Catholic Reformation: Studies in Honor of John C. Olin on His Seventy-fifth Birthday,* edited by Richard L. De Molen, 165–86. New York: Fordham University Press, 1994.

Llamas Martínez, Enrique. *Santa Teresa de Jesús y la Inquisición Española.* Madrid: CSIC, 1972.

Moriones de la Visitación, Ildefonso. *Ana de Jesús y la herencia teresiana.* Rome: Edizioni del Teresianum, 1968.

Peers, E. Allison. *Studies of the Spanish Mystics.* 3 vols. 1930. Reprint, London: Society for Promoting Christian Knowledge, 1960.

Weber, Alison. "Saint Teresa's Problematic Patrons." *Journal of Medieval and Early Modern Studies* 29 (1999): 357–79.

————. "Spiritual Administration: Gender and Discernment in the Carmelite Reform." *Sixteenth Century Journal* 31, no. 1 (2000): 123–46.

STUDIES ON FEMALE LITERACY AND EDUCATION IN EARLY MODERN SPAIN

Cacho, María Teresa. "Los moldes de Pygmalión (sobre los tratados de educación femenina en el siglo de oro)." In *La mujer en la literatura española,* edited by Emilie Bergman et al. Vol. 2 of *Breve historia feminista de la literatura española (en lengua castellana),* edited by Iris Zavala. 5 vols., 2:177–213. Madrid: Comunidad de Madrid, 1995.

Cátedra, Pedro. "Lectura femenina en el claustro (España, siglos XIV–XVI)." In *Des femmes et des livres: France et Espagnes, XIVe–XVIIe siècle: Actes de la journée d'étude organisée par l'École nationale des chartes et l'École normale supérieure de Fontenay/Saint-Cloud (Paris, 30 avril 1998),* edited by Dominique de Courcelles and Carmen Val Julián, 7–53. Paris: École des Chartes, 1999.

Graña Cid, María del Mar. "Mujeres perfectas, mujeres sabias: Educación, identidad y memoria (Castilla, siglos XV–XVI). In *De leer a escribir I: La educación de las mujeres: ¿Libertad o subordinación?* edited by Cristina Segura Graíño, 123–54. Madrid: Al-Mudayna, 1996.

————, ed. *Las sabias mujeres: Educación, saber y autoría (siglos III–XVII).* Madrid: Al-Mudayna, 1994.

Herpoël, Sonja. "El lector femenino en el siglo de oro español." In *La mujer en la literatura hispánica de la edad media y el siglo de oro,* edited by Rina Walthaus, 91–100. Amsterdam-Atlanta, GA: Rodopi, 1993.

Nalle, Sara T. "Literacy and Culture in Early Modern Castile." *Past and Present* 125 (1989): 65–96.

Saugnieux, Joël. "Culture féminine en Castille au XVIe siècle: Thérèse d'Avila et les livres." In *Cultures populaires et cultures savantes en Espagne du Moyen Age aux Lumières,* edited by Joël Saugnieux, 45–77. Paris: Editions du Centre National de la Recherche Scientifique, 1982.

STUDIES OF MONASTIC WOMEN'S WRITING IN EARLY MODERN SPAIN

Amelang, James S. "Los usos de la autobiografía: Monjas y beatas en la Cataluña modern." In *Historia y género: Las mujeres en la Europa moderna y contemporánea,* edited by James S. Amelang and Mary Nash, 191–212. Valencia: Ediciones Alfons el Magnànim, 1990.

Arenal, Electa, and Stacey Schlau. "Strategems of the Strong, Strategems of the Weak: Autobiographical Prose of the Seventeenth-Century Hispanic Convent." *Tulsa Studies in Women's Literature* 9 (1990): 25–42.

Donahue, Darcy. "Writing Lives: Nuns and Confessors as Auto/Biographers in Early Modern Spain." *Journal of Hispanic Philology* 13 (1989): 23–39.

Poutrin, Isabelle. *Le voile et la plume: Autobiographie et sainteté féminine dans l'Espagne moderne.* Madrid: Casa de Velázquez, 1995.

Powell, Amanda. "Women's Reasons: Feminism and Spirituality in Old and New Spain." *Studia Mystica* 15 (1992): 58–69.

Slade, Carole. *St. Teresa of Avila: Author of a Heroic Life.* Berkeley: University of California Press, 1995.

Smith, Susan M. "The Female Trinity of Sor Marcela de San Félix." In *Engendering the Early Modern Stage: Women Playwrights in the Spanish Empire,* edited by Valerie Hegstrom and Amy R. Williamsen, 239–56. New Orleans: University Press of the South, 1999.

Surtz, Ronald E. *Writing Women in Late Medieval and Early Modern Spain: The Mothers of Saint Teresa of Avila.* Philadelphia: University of Pennsylvania Press, 1995.

Velasco, Sherry. *Demons, Nausea, and Resistance in the Autobiography of Isabel de Jesús, 1611–1682.* Albuquerque: University of New Mexico Press, 1996.

Weber, Alison. "The Partial Feminism of Ana de San Bartolomé." In *Recovering Spain's Feminist Tradition,* edited by Lisa Vollendorf, 69–87. New York: Modern Language Association, 2001.

———. *Teresa of Avila and the Rhetoric of Femininity.* Princeton, N.J.: Princeton University Press, 1990.

STUDIES OF COUNTER-REFORMATION MONASTICISM IN HISTORICAL CONTEXT

Arenal, Electa. "The Convent as Catalyst for Autonomy: Two Hispanic Nuns of the Seventeenth Century." In *Women in Hispanic Literature,* edited by Beth Milller, 147–83. Los Angeles: University of California Press, 1983.

Bilinkoff, Jodi. "Confessors, Penitents, and the Construction of Identities in Early Modern Avila." In *Culture and Identity in Early Modern Europe (1500–1800): Essays in Honor of Natalie Zemon Davis,* edited by Barbara B. Diefendorf and Carla Hesse, 83–100. Ann Arbor: University of Michigan Press, 1993.

Marshall, Sherrin, ed. *Women in Reformation and Counter-Reformation Europe: Public and Private Worlds.* Bloomington: Indiana University Press, 1989.

McNamara, Jo Ann Kay. "The Early Modern Era." In *Sisters in Arms: Catholic Nuns through Two Millennia,* 385–562. Cambridge, Mass.: Harvard University Press, 1996.

Norberg, Kathryn. "The Counter-Reformation and Women: Religious and Lay." In *Catholicism in Early Modern History: A Guide to Research,* edited by John W. O'Malley, 133–46. St. Louis: Center for Reformation Research, 1988.

Perry, Mary Elizabeth. *Gender and Disorder in Early Modern Seville.* Princeton, N.J.: Princeton University Press, 1990.

Sánchez Lora, José L. *Mujeres, conventos y formas de la religiosidad barroca.* Madrid: Fundación Universitaria Española, 1988.

INDEX